AAT

Qualifications and Credit Framework (QCF)
AQ2013
LEVEL 4 DIPLOMA IN ACCOUNTING

TEXT

Financial Performance

2015 Edition

For assessments from September 2015

Third edition June 2015
ISBN 9781 4727 2170 9

Previous edition
ISBN 9781 4727 0904 2

British Library Cataloguing-in-Publication Data
A catalogue record for this book is available from the British
Library

Published by
BPP Learning Media Ltd
BPP House
Aldine Place
London
W12 8AA

www.bpp.com/learningmedia

Printed in the United Kingdom by Martins of Berwick
Sea View Works
Spittal
Berwick-Upon-Tweed
TD15 1RS

CONTENTS

A NOTE ABOUT COPYRIGHT

BPP LEARNING MEDIA'S AAT MATERIALS

The AAT's assessments fall within the **Qualifications and Credit Framework** and most papers are assessed by way of an on demand **computer based assessment**. BPP Learning Media has invested heavily to ensure our materials are as relevant as possible for this method of assessment. In particular, our **suite of online resources** ensures that you are prepared for online testing by allowing you to practise numerous online tasks that are similar to the tasks you will encounter in the AAT's assessments.

Resources

The BPP range of resources comprises:

- **Texts**, covering all the knowledge and understanding needed by students, with numerous illustrations of 'how it works', practical examples and tasks for you to use to consolidate your learning. The majority of tasks within the texts have been written in an interactive style that reflects the style of the online tasks we anticipate the AAT will set. When you purchase a Text you are also granted free access to your Text content online.

- **Question Banks**, including additional learning questions plus the AAT's sample assessment(s) and a number of BPP full practice assessments. Full answers to all questions and assessments, prepared by BPP Learning Media Ltd, are included. Our question banks are provided free of charge online.

- **Passcards**, which are handy pocket-sized revision tools designed to fit in a handbag or briefcase to enable you to revise anywhere at anytime. All major points are covered in the Passcards which have been designed to assist you in consolidating knowledge.

- **Workbooks**, which have been designed to cover the units that are assessed by way of computer based project/case study. The workbooks contain many practical tasks to assist in the learning process and also a sample assessment or project to work through.

- **Lecturers' resources**, for units assessed by computer based assessments. These provide a further bank of tasks, answers and full practice assessments for classroom use, available separately only to lecturers whose colleges adopt BPP Learning Media material.

This Text for Financial Performance has been written specifically to ensure comprehensive yet concise coverage of the AAT's **AQ2013** learning outcomes and assessment criteria.

Each chapter contains:

- Clear, step by step explanation of the topic

- Logical progression and linking from one chapter to the next

- Numerous illustrations of 'how it works'

- Interactive tasks within the text of the chapter itself, with answers at the back of the book. The majority of these tasks have been written in the interactive form that students can expect to see in their real assessments

- Test your learning questions of varying complexity, again with answers supplied at the back of the book. The majority of these questions have been written in the interactive form that students can expect to see in their real assessments

The emphasis in all tasks and test questions is on the practical application of the skills acquired.

Supplements

From time to time we may need to publish supplementary materials to one of our titles. This can be for a variety of reasons, from a small change in the AAT unit guidance to new legislation coming into effect between editions.

You should check our supplements page regularly for anything that may affect your learning materials. All supplements are available free of charge on our supplements page on our website at:

http://www.bpp.com/about-bpp/aboutBPP/StudentInfo#q4

Customer feedback

If you have any comments about this book, please email nisarahmed@bpp.com or write to Nisar Ahmed, AAT Head of programme, BPP Learning Media Ltd, BPP House, Aldine Place, London W12 8AA.

Any feedback we receive is taken into consideration when we periodically update our materials, including comments on style, depth and coverage of AAT standards.

In addition, although our products pass through strict technical checking and quality control processes, unfortunately errors may occasionally slip through when producing material to tight deadlines.

When we learn of an error in a batch of our printed materials, either from internal review processes or from customers using our materials, we want to make sure customers are made aware of this as soon as possible and the appropriate action is taken to minimise the impact on student learning.

As a result, when we become aware of any such errors we will:

1) Include details of the error and, if necessary, PDF prints of any revised pages under the related subject heading on our 'supplements' page at: www.bpp.com/about-bpp/aboutBPP/StudentInfo#q4

2) Update the source files ahead of any further printing of the materials

3) Investigate the reason for the error and take appropriate action to minimise the risk of reoccurrence.

A NOTE ON TERMINOLOGY

The AAT AQ2013 standards and assessments use international terminology based on International Financial Reporting Standards (IFRSs). Although you may be familiar with UK terminology, you need to now know the equivalent international terminology for your assessments.

The following information is taken from an article on the AAT's website and compares IFRS terminology with UK GAAP terminology. It then goes on to describe the impact of IFRS terminology on students studying for each level of the AAT QCF qualification.

Note that since the article containing the information below was published, there have been changes made to some IFRSs. Therefore BPP Learning Media have updated the table and other information below to reflect these changes.

In particular, the primary performance statement under IFRSs which was formerly known as the 'income statement' or the 'statement of comprehensive income' is now called the 'statement of profit or loss' or the 'statement of profit or loss and other comprehensive income'.

What is the impact of IFRS terms on AAT assessments?

The list shown in the table that follows gives the 'translation' between UK GAAP and IFRS.

UK GAAP	IFRS
Final accounts	Financial statements
Trading and profit and loss account	**Statement of profit or loss (or statement of profit or loss and other comprehensive income)**
Turnover or Sales	Revenue or Sales Revenue
Sundry income	Other operating income
Interest payable	Finance costs
Sundry expenses	Other operating costs
Operating profit	Profit from operations
Net profit/loss	Profit/Loss for the year/period
Balance sheet	**Statement of financial position**
Fixed assets	Non-current assets
Net book value	Carrying amount
Tangible assets	Property, plant and equipment

UK GAAP	IFRS
Reducing balance depreciation	Diminishing balance depreciation
Depreciation/Depreciation expense(s)	Depreciation charge(s)
Stocks	Inventories
Trade debtors or Debtors	Trade receivables
Prepayments	Other receivables
Debtors and prepayments	Trade and other receivables
Cash at bank and in hand	Cash and cash equivalents
Trade creditors or Creditors	Trade payables
Accruals	Other payables
Creditors and accruals	Trade and other payables
Long-term liabilities	Non-current liabilities
Capital and reserves	Equity (limited companies)
Profit and loss balance	Retained earnings
Minority interest	Non-controlling interest
Cash flow statement	**Statement of cash flows**

This is certainly not a comprehensive list, which would run to several pages, but it does cover the main terms that you will come across in your studies and assessments. However, you won't need to know all of these in the early stages of your studies – some of the terms will not be used until you reach Level 4. For each level of the AAT qualification, the points to bear in mind are as follows:

Level 2 Certificate in Accounting

The IFRS terms do not impact greatly at this level. Make sure you are familiar with 'receivables' (also referred to as 'trade receivables'), 'payables' (also referred to as 'trade payables'), and 'inventories'. The terms sales ledger and purchases ledger – together with their control accounts – will continue to be used. Sometimes the control accounts might be called 'trade receivables control account' and 'trade payables control account'. The other term to be aware of is 'non-current asset' – this may be used in some assessments.

Level 3 Diploma in Accounting

At this level you need to be familiar with the term 'financial statements'. The financial statements comprise a 'statement of profit or loss' (previously known as an income statement), and a 'statement of financial position'. In the statement of profit or loss the term 'revenue' or 'sales revenue' takes the place of 'sales', and 'profit for the year' replaces 'net profit'. Other terms may be used in the

statement of financial position – eg 'non-current assets' and 'carrying amount'. However, specialist limited company terms are not required at this level.

Level 4 Diploma in Accounting

At Level 4 a wider range of IFRS terms is needed, and in the case of Financial statements, are already in use – particularly those relating to limited companies. Note especially that a statement of profit or loss becomes a 'statement of profit or loss and other comprehensive income'.

Note: The information above was taken from an AAT article from the 'assessment news' area of the AAT website (www.aat.org.uk). However, it has been adapted by BPP Learning Media for changes in international terminology since the article was published.

ASSESSMENT STRATEGY

Duration

The assessment will consist of 10 tasks and 2.5 hours of time. 8 tasks will be computer marked and 2 tasks will be human marked.

Competency

Competency	For the purpose of assessment the competency level for AAT assessment is set at 70 per cent. The level descriptor below describes the ability and skills students at this level must successfully demonstrate to achieve competence.

QCF Level descriptor	**Summary** Achievement at level 4 reflects the ability to identify and use relevant understanding, methods and skills to address problems that are well defined but complex and non-routine. It includes taking responsibility for overall courses of action as well as exercising autonomy and judgement within fairly broad parameters. It also reflects understanding of different perspectives or approaches within an area of study or work. **Knowledge and understanding** ■ Practical, theoretical or technical understanding to address problems that are well defined but complex and non-routine ■ Analyse, interpret and evaluate relevant information and ideas ■ Be aware of the nature and approximate scope of the area of study or work ■ Have an informed awareness of different perspectives or approaches within the area of study or work **Application and action** ■ Address problems that are complex and non-routine while normally fairly well defined ■ Identify, adapt and use appropriate methods and skills ■ Initiate and use appropriate investigation to inform actions ■ Review the effectiveness and appropriateness of methods, actions and results **Autonomy and accountability** ■ Take responsibility for courses of action, including where relevant, responsibility for the work of others ■ Exercise autonomy and judgement within broad but generally well-defined parameters

AAT UNIT GUIDE

Financial Performance (FPFM)

Introduction

The assessment for this Level 4 unit covers the learning outcomes and assessment criteria of the revised QCF unit for Financial Performance covering both knowledge and skills. Financial Performance is a compulsory unit, forming part of the Level 4 Diploma in Accounting. The purpose of this document is to describe what is assessable for each of the assessment criteria which make up the learning outcomes.

Purpose of the Unit

The creation of the Financial Performance unit at Level 4 is recognition of the importance of calculating and measuring financial performance in every organisation. This unit builds on the basic costing concepts and techniques required at Level 3. However, an understanding and application of performance indicators and cost management extends costing into management accounting.

Learning Objectives

The Financial Performance unit is about understanding the principles of managing financial performance. Students will have the knowledge to be able to use a range of techniques to analyse information on expenditure. They will be able to make judgements to support decision making, planning and control by managers. Students will also be required to demonstrate skill in measuring financial performance. Students will have the skills to collect and analyse information, monitor performance, and present reports to management.

In order for students to be successful they will need to be able to explain, define, describe, calculate and analyse a range of fundamental concepts and techniques. Many of the concepts and techniques are interrelated and students will need to understand how the concepts and techniques interrelate. They may also be required to explain and describe these relationships.

Students will need to have a detailed understanding of the fundamental management accounting concepts and techniques in order to demonstrate competence in the learning outcomes. Students will also need to be able to define and explain the fundamental concepts and apply their knowledge to questions which may require the calculation or application of one or more of these fundamental concepts or techniques. The fundamental management accounting concepts and techniques which students need to be able to explain, describe, identify, calculate and apply will be covered in the delivery guidance below.

Learning Outcomes

The unit consists of five learning outcomes. The learner will:

1. Collate and analyse cost information from various sources

2. Be able to use standard costing to analyse performance

3. Be able to use appropriate techniques to measure performance and manage costs

4. Make suggestions for improving financial performance by monitoring and analysing information

5. Prepare performance reports for management.

There are a number of assessment criteria linked to each learning outcome and these have been incorporated into the delivery guidance under the appropriate topics. Those referenced K relate to knowledge and those referenced S relate to skills.

Learning Outcome	Assessment Criteria	Covered in Chapter
1 Collate and analyse cost information from various sources	1.1K Explain the purpose and structure of reporting systems within the organisation	1, 2
	1.2K Explain the impact of the external environment and related costs on an organisation	1, 2
	1.3S Obtain income and expenditure information from different departments within an organisation and consolidate in an appropriate form	Throughout
	1.4S Identify other valid information from internal and external sources	Throughout
	1.5K Explain types of cost centre, profit centre and investment centre	1
	1.6S Identify costs of materials, labour and expenses and the sources of information about these costs	1, 5 ,6
	1.7K Identify fixed, variable, semi-variable and stepped costs and explain their use in cost recording, cost reporting and cost analysis	1
	1.8S Reconcile income and expenditure information	Throughout
	1.9S Account for transactions between departments of an organisation	Throughout
2 Be able to use standard costing to analyse performance	2.1K Describe the use of standard units of inputs and outputs	5
	2.2K Recognise the differences between standard, marginal and absorption costing in terms of cost recording, cost reporting and cost behaviour	2, 5
	2.3S Calculate materials, labour and overhead variances	5, 6
	2.4S Analyse routine cost reports and compare with budget and standard costs to identify any differences and their implications	5, 6

Learning Outcome	Assessment Criteria	Covered in Chapter
3 Be able to use appropriate techniques to measure performance and manage costs	3.1K Identify relevant performance and quality measures for monitoring financial performance	7
	3.2K Identify appropriate key business indicators to use for: – Efficiency – Productivity – Cost per unit – Balanced scorecard – Benchmarking – Control ratios (efficiency, capacity and activity) – Scenario planning ('what-if' analysis)	7
	3.3S Calculate ratios, performance indicators and measures of value added in accordance with the organisation's procedures	7
	3.4S Use these cost management techniques: – Life cycle costing – Target costing – Activity based costing	2, 8
	3.5S Prepare estimates of capital investment projects using discounted cash flow techniques	3

Learning Outcome	Assessment Criteria	Covered in Chapter
4 Make suggestions for improving financial performance by monitoring and analysing information	4.1K Explain the use and purpose of these techniques: – Indexing – Sampling – Time series	4
	4.2S Compare results over time using methods that allow for changing price levels	4
	4.3S Analyse trends in prices and market conditions on a regular basis	4
	4.4S Compare trends with previous data and identify potential implications	4
	4.5S Consult relevant staff in the organisation about the analysis of trends and variances	4, 5
	4.6S Interpret the results of performance indicators, identifying potential improvements and estimating the value of such improvements	6, 7, 8
	4.7S Identify ways to reduce costs and enhance values	8
5 Prepare performance reports for management	5.1S Prepare reports in an appropriate format and within the required timescales	**Throughout**
	5.2S Prepare exception reports to identify matters which require further investigation	
	5.3S Make specific recommendations to management in a clear and appropriate format	

Delivery guidance

This section provides detailed delivery guidance covering assessable topics and the depth and breadth to which these topics will be assessed. The examples given are to provide guidance on the sort of tasks that students may be required to undertake but should not be considered an exhaustive list. Task types include multiple choice, drag and drop, linked boxes, drop-down list and gap fill. Clear instructions are provided for each task and students should ensure that they read the full question (RTFQ) and follow the requirements carefully.

1   Cost classification, cost recording, cost reporting and cost behaviour

Learning outcomes 1, 3 and 5 and assessment criteria 1.2K, 1.3S, 1.4S, 1.5K, 1.6S, 1.7K, 1.8S, 1.9S, 3.1K, 3.3S, 5.1S, 5.2S, 5.3S

(a) Production costing and the elements of direct and indirect costs, cost classification into materials, labour, and overhead

(b) Cost classification by behaviour (fixed, variable, stepped fixed and semi variable) and the relevant range for fixed costs

(c) Prime cost, full production cost, marginal product cost

(d) Explain cost centres, profit centres and investment centres

(e) The high-low method of cost estimation

A fundamental cost technique is the high-low method which can be used to estimate the fixed and variable elements of any cost. The technique could be assessed as a simple split of fixed and variable costs or where the fixed costs step up above a certain level activity.

Example 1 – costs are either fixed or variable

Volume of production	12,000 units	15,000 units
Total cost	£510,000	£525,000

In the above example total costs have been provided for two activity levels, 12,000 and 15,000. The total costs include a fixed element and a variable element and the variable element can be calculated by taking the difference between the two cost levels and dividing this by the difference between the two activity levels. This is because the only difference in the two cost levels must be the variable costs.

Therefore the variable cost per unit must be 15,000/3,000 = £5 per unit ((£525,000 less £510,000)/(15,000 less 12,000))

Example 2 – costs are fixed with a step up at an activity level of 27,000 units. The variable cost per unit is constant.

Volume of production	25,000 units	29,000 units
Total cost	£418,750	£458,750

In the above example fixed costs step up at 27,000 units. In order to calculate the fixed and variable elements, further information is required. Tasks will either state the fixed cost at the lower or higher level of output, the variable cost per unit or the stepped fixed cost increase. Then the other elements can be calculated.

For example, in this case the fixed costs step up by £25,000 at an output level of 27,000 units. Therefore the difference in cost between the £458,750 and the £418,750 consists of the fixed cost of £25,000 and the variable cost per unit multiplied by 4,000 units. So £40,000 = fixed costs of £25,000 plus 4,000 units × VC/unit. Therefore the variable cost per unit is £3.75.

2 Marginal costing and absorption costing

Learning outcomes 1, 2, 3, 4 and 5 and assessment criteria 1.1K, 1.2K, 1.3S, 1.4S, 1.6S, 1.7K, 1.8S, 1.9S, 2.2K, 3.1K, 3.2K, 3.3S, 3.4S, 4.6S, 4.7S, 5.1S, 5.2S, 5.3S

(a) Absorption costing – definition, explanation and calculation of an overhead absorption rate, calculation of under and over absorption, explanation of the advantages and disadvantages of absorption costing – link with financial accounting requirements of inventory valuation and price setting models.

(b) Marginal costing – definition, explanation and calculation of the marginal cost, explanation of the advantages and disadvantages of marginal costing, marginal costing and decision making, see link with contribution theory below.

(c) Marginal costing v Absorption costing – explain the differences between the treatment of costs, calculation of profit and effects of changing inventory levels. Preparation of an absorption costing income statement, a marginal costing income statement, calculation of the changes in profit when inventory levels change and a reconciliation between the marginal costing profit and the absorption costing profit.

(d) Absorption costing v Marginal costing in decision making. Students need to understand how absorption costing and marginal costing can be used in tasks which measure performance and which consider ways of enhancing value. Absorption costing may be relevant for measuring the performance of a business and it may also be appropriate to use absorption costing principles in enhancing value. A product may be re-

engineered in order to reduce production costs and it would be perfectly appropriate to consider the full absorption cost of the redesigned product.

Lifecycle costing needs to consider both fixed and variable costs. However, it may be inappropriate to use absorption costing in certain circumstances. For example, if the business is considering contracting out the manufacture of a product, selling surplus capacity or other limiting factor decisions, then marginal costing is the appropriate method as fixed costs will not change as a result of the decision.

However, students need to understand that certain fixed costs may well change when a decision is made and the marginal (incremental) cost may in these circumstances include both variable and fixed components.

(e) Practical limitations of cost classification, non-linear behaviour. Students need to recognise that in practice costs may not fit neatly into linear relationships with output and may behave in a non-linear fashion.

(f) Absorption costing v marginal costing could feature in standard costing questions and decision making and 'what if' scenario questions.

(g) Contribution analysis. Students must be able to deal with tasks requiring the analysis of a situation by considering the contribution of a product or business. This is an area where many students struggle. Often the fundamental concept of contribution is not understood and students include fixed cost in their calculations.

(h) Break even analysis and margin of safety. Students must be able to deal with calculations of breakeven analysis and the margin of safety. The information may be given so that calculations can be undertaken by calculating contribution per unit, or by calculating the contribution-to-sales ratio.

3   Standard costing and variance analysis

Learning outcomes 1, 2, 3, 4 and 5 and assessment criteria 1.1K, 1.2K, 1.3S, 1.4S, 1.6S, 2.1K, 2.2K, 2.3S, 2.4S, 4.7S, 5.1S, 5.2S, 5.3S

(a) Explain how standard costs can be established, the different types of standard (ideal, target, normal, basic) and how the type of standard can affect the behaviour of the budget holder and workforce.

(b) Explain the role of standard costing in the planning, decision making and control process. Standard costing variances aid budgetary control by breaking down the simple variance identified in a budgetary control system into components based upon an expected outcome (the standard). Standard costing is a method of analysing a variance from a budget when standard costs are used in creating the budget.

(c) Extract relevant data from the question in order to calculate various requirements. Students may be required to calculate any of the following:

   (i) Standard quantity of inputs (materials, labour, overheads)
   (ii) Standard cost for given production volumes
   (iii) Actual quantity of inputs (materials, labour, overheads)
   (iv) Actual costs for given production volumes

(d) Explain and calculate the following variances or elements of the calculation

   (i) Raw materials total, price, usage
   (ii) Labour total, rate, efficiency
   (iii) Labour idle time variance
   (iv) Variable overhead and efficiency variances
   (v) Fixed overhead expenditure variance
   (vi) Fixed overhead volume, capacity and efficiency

Information can be presented in a variety of ways, in standard costing tasks, including a standard cost card, budgetary control report, a schedule of information or a mixture of all three. Students therefore need to be able to identify and extract information to calculate the variances.

Students may be given information including the variance and be required to manipulate the variance calculation in order to calculate one unknown, required, piece of information.

For example, the raw material price variance is £300 adverse and the company paid £9,000 for 1,200 kilograms of material. What is the standard price of materials per kilogram? The answer is £7.25.

This can be calculated in several ways, two of which are shown below.

   (i) Actual quantity purchased × (Standard price per kilogram – Actual price per kilogram) = variance (if adverse then the actual price per kilogram is greater than the standard price per kilogram).

   Therefore 1,200 × (SP – 7.50) = £300 A, therefore rearrange to give SP = £7.25

   (ii) SP = Actual price per unit less Adverse variance/actual Q purchased, or £7.50 less £300/1,200 = £7.25

(e) Prepare an operating statement under both absorption costing principles and marginal costing principles.

Operating statement under absorption costing

Budgeted/Standard cost for actual production			
Variances	Favourable	Adverse	
Direct materials price			
Direct materials usage			
Direct labour rate			
Direct labour efficiency			
Fixed overhead expenditure			
Fixed overhead volume			
Total variance			
Actual cost of actual production			

(f)   Prepare journal entries for the posting of variances.

(g)   Explain the difference between controllable and non-controllable variances, apply index numbers to variances in order to explain how general rising prices can cause variances, and adjust variances for changes in prices.

(h)   Break down variances using index numbers to isolate controllable and non-controllable parts. Further subdivision of variances using index numbers may be assessed as a small part of a larger task and will not feature as a substantial proportion of a question. Students will not be required to use changes in exchange rates to subdivide variances.

(i)   Prepare reports giving possible reasons for the variances, showing an understanding of the interrelationship between the variances. This will normally feature in one of the longer written tasks. Often students will be provided with a schedule of variances, additional narrative and the following requirement.

'Using this information, prepare a report to the Managing Director to cover an analysis of each variance by:

- Identifying the sign of those variances where the sign has not been shown

- Explaining what the variance means

- Providing one possible reason for each variance

- Explaining any links between the variances

- Providing an action which could have been taken'

(j) Comment on additional information provided by the budget holder as to reasons for the variance. For example, the production manager may say that the quality of raw materials or the old, poorly maintained machines or unskilled staff have caused the adverse raw material usage variance, when the raw materials price variance was adverse, implying that the material was of better than expected quality. This may not be the case – it could be that the buyer bought an inferior material but still paid more than the standard. It may be that an independent assessment of the quality of the material needs to be made.

(k) Explain how standards are developed and appreciate the concepts of ideal standard, attainable (expected) standard and basic standard. Explain how the chosen standard may affect the behaviour of managers and staff.

4 Performance indicators and 'what if' analysis

Learning outcomes 1, 3, 4 and 5 and assessment criteria 1.1K, 1.2K, 1.3S, 1.4S, 1.5K, 1.6S, 1.7K, 1.8S, 1.9S, 3.1K, 3.2K, 3.3S, 3.5S, 4.2S, 4.6S, 4.7S, 5.1S, 5.2S, 5.3S

(a) **Calculate performance indicators**

Students will be asked to calculate a range of performance indicators. Some, such as the return on capital employed or the gearing ratio, are applicable to many organisations, whilst others might be unique to a particular type of organisation. For example, if the task relates to a hotel, students might be given data and asked to calculate the cost per room night, the percentage occupancy and the average discount given to customers.

The following is a list of the type of performance indicators students might be asked to calculate.

(1) Financial (Profitability, Liquidity, Efficiency and Gearing)

(a) Gross profit margin = Gross Profit/Sales Revenue × 100%

(b) Profit margin = Profit/Sales Revenue × 100%

(c) Administration costs as a percentage of revenue, any cost as a percentage of revenue = Cost/Sales Revenue × 100%

(d) Current ratio = Current assets/Current liabilities

This can be expressed as a number only or as a number : 1, for example if current assets are £10,000 and current liabilities are £8,000 the ratio is 1.25 or 1.25:1. In questions students should just use 1.25 as their answer.

(e) Quick ratio = (Current assets less inventory)/Current liabilities and again should be expressed as a single number in assessments.

(f) Trade cycles (Receivable days = Receivables/Revenue × 365, inventory days = Inventory/Cost of sales × 365, payable days = Payables/Cost of sales × 365)

(g) Gearing ratio

The gearing ratio can be calculated as either Total debt/(Total debt plus Equity) × 100% or Total debt/Total equity × 100%. Total debt must include both long term and short term debt. Both computer marked and human marked tasks will allow both calculations.

(h) Value added = Revenue less the cost of materials used and bought in services

(2) Efficiency, Capacity and Activity ratios **(the formula for these ratios will be provided in assessment questions)**

(a) Labour efficiency ratio = Standard hours for actual production/Actual hours worked expressed as a percentage

(b) Capacity ratio = Actual hours worked/Budgeted hours expressed as a percentage

(c) Labour activity ratio = Standard hours for actual production/ Budgeted hours, or Actual output/Budgeted output. Expressed as a percentage

(3) Indicators to measure efficiency and productivity

(a) Measures of efficiency include ROCE or RONA, profit margin and efficiency ratio for labour. ROCE = Return/Capital employed, in tasks return will be equal to the profit in the statement of profit or loss (income statement). This ratio is always expressed as a percentage.

RONA = Return/Net assets, return will be equal to the profit in the statement of profit or loss (income statement). This ratio is always expressed as a percentage.

(b) Productivity measures are likely to be measured in units of output, or related to output in some way. Examples include number of, say, vehicles manufactured per week, operations undertaken per day, passengers transported per month, units produced per worker per day, rooms cleaned per hour or meals served per sitting.

(4) Indicators to measure quality of service and cost of quality

    (a) The number of defects/units returned/warranty claims/customer complaints, the cost of inspection/repairs/ re-working

    (b) Prevention costs, appraisal costs, internal failure costs, external failure costs

(5) Students may be asked to compare given indicators with performance indicators that they have calculated. They may have to undertake a benchmarking exercise and need to understand the purpose of benchmarking.

(6) Students need to recognise that a business has to select key performance indicators and monitor these in order to manage the business. The balanced scorecard is an approach often used and students need to understand the concept of a balanced scorecard and may be asked to prepare one from given performance indicators.

(7) Tasks may require the calculation of specific performance indicators. If this is the case the calculation of the indicator will either be obvious or the formula for the indicator will be provided. For example, if the task is based on a hotel the occupancy rate calculation should be obvious given the number of rooms sold in the month divided by the total number of room nights available in the month. If the indicator is more complicated the formula will be given.

(b) **Comment on the information generated from the calculation of the performance indicators**

Students need to be able to explain what the ratios are designed to show and analyse given ratios.

(c) **Understand the interrelationships and limitations of performance indicators**

Students need to be able to explain and describe the limitations of the ratios and the interrelationships. Students may also be required to apply their understanding of the interrelationship in order to make recommendations to management.

(d) **Prepare estimates of capital investment projects using discounted cash flow techniques**

Students need to be able to explain, describe and calculate discounted cash flow calculations of net present value, net present cost and net terminal cost and make recommendations to management.

(e) 'What if' analysis

After having prepared performance indicators, students may be faced with taking or recommending action. They may be asked to do one or more of the following:

- Show what the results would have been if benchmark data had been achieved.

- Forecast the performance indicators for the next period based upon a set of assumptions.

- Re-calculate the performance indicators, taking account of given changes to the business, or perhaps select changes which will maximise given indicators.

- Work backwards through a ratio. For example, they may be asked, 'What would the revenue need to have been for the asset turnover to be 3 times if the total assets are £950,000?' The answer is £2,850,000 or 3 × £950,000. Or 'What would the profit need to have been for the ROCE to be 25% if the net assets are £450,000? The answer is £112,500'. This is simple equation manipulation.

- Given several options, students may be asked to evaluate and recommend a course of action. This could be to improve a key performance indicator like ROCE. They might also be asked to comment on options which cause an improvement in one indicator with a deterioration of another.

- Calculate indicators for two years and explain changes in performance.

- Compare two businesses and comment on their relative performance.

- Identify potential improvements and estimate the value of them.

- Suggest ways of improving the performance of a poorly performing business.

- Make recommendations.

- Make calculations and recommendations to management for any of the following scenarios

    - Make or buy decision – students may be required to prepare workings and key ratios to aid the assessment of outsourcing manufacture

- Limiting factor decision making – students may have to adjust figures and recalculate ratios if a resource constraint limits production.

- Break-even analysis and margin of safety – students need to be able to calculate and comment on measures of risk, particularly where a business changes or proposes to change the fixed cost and variable costs of production.

- Closure of a business segment, transferring production overseas – students may have to prepare calculations and make recommendations to management regarding the closure of a business segment.

- Mechanisation – students may be required to provide calculations and make recommendations to management regarding changing the production process from a labour intensive one to a machine intensive one. They may also be required to bring in break-even analysis in order to demonstrate the changing risk in the business.

With scenario planning or 'what if' analysis, students have to understand how elements of the income statement and statement of financial position are linked. For example, a 10% increase in sales volume will lead to a 10% increase in variable costs as more units are produced but no increase in fixed costs, assuming that capacity exists (fixed costs are fixed over the relevant range). A 10% increase in sales price, however, will not lead to any changes in costs. The increase in sales will change the profit and, if no dividends are paid, this will increase the net assets of the business. The change in sales will therefore affect several ratios.

(f) **Key performance indicators and the behaviour of managers**

Students need to understand that the way in which business unit managers are assessed can have a great influence on the decisions they make. The use of key performance indicators such as ROCE can lead to a lack of goal congruence where managers make decisions which improve performance in certain indicators but which may not be best for the organisation as a whole.

For example, a manager may not be prepared to invest in new machinery if the increase in the net asset position will reduce the ROCE, even though the investment may reduce other costs, lead to zero defects or increase customer satisfaction.

5 **Cost management**

Learning outcomes 1, 3, 4 and 5 and assessment criteria 1.1K, 1.2K, 1.3S, 1.4S, 1.6S, 1.7K, 1.8S, 1.9S, 3.1S, 3.4S, 4.7S, 5.1S, 5.2S and 5.3S

(a) Life cycle costing and how it can be used to aid cost management. Students may be required to calculate life cycle costs for different options. Life cycle cost calculations may require the use of discounted cash flow techniques.

(b) The concepts behind target costing (including value analysis/engineering). Students may be required to explain target costing and prepare a target cost from information in the task. Students may also have to analyse information provided from functional specialists like designers, engineers and marketing professionals.

(c) Activity based costing and how it can be applied to an organisation. Students may be given information and asked to calculate the absorption rates under activity based costing and comment on its applicability.

(d) The principles of total quality management. Students may be provided with information about the various costs incurred to prevent faulty production and costs incurred to rectify faulty production and settle warranty claims. Students may then be asked to calculate the cost of quality. Whilst the general theory is that organisations should plan to have zero defects, students should be aware that there may be commercial justifications for allowing some defects, perhaps because of expensive quality assurance systems.

(e) Product life cycle and how costs change throughout the life of a product. Concepts of economies of scale, mechanisation, a switch from variable to fixed costs may be assessed.

(f) Understanding of the planning, decision making and control stages in management accounting and how cost management techniques can aid management at each stage.

6 **Basic statistical methods**

Learning outcomes 1, 3, 4 and 5 and assessment criteria 1.2K, 1.3S, 1.4S, 3.1K, 4.1K, 4.2S, 4.3S, 4.4S, 4.5S, 5.1S, 5.2S, 5.3S

Students must be able to explain the use and purpose of indexing, sampling and time series (eg moving averages, linear regression and seasonal trends).

Index numbers – students must be able to calculate index numbers and use them to forecast costs and prices and also to subdivide variances. Students must also be able to interpret indices and compare them with methods of securing contracts to reduce the risk of rising prices.

Moving averages – students must be able to calculate moving averages and seasonal variations and use calculations to extrapolate a forecast of sales or costs.

Seasonal variations – students need to understand types of variation from the trend and may be required to identify the seasonal variation or use the seasonal variation and a given trend to forecast sales volume, prices or cost information.

Regression analysis – students will **not** be required to derive the regression equation $y = a + bx$ but they may be given the equation and asked to use it to calculate a and b, given y and x, for several points, or to calculate y and x, given a and b. The equation could then be used to predict prices, demand and costs.

The assessment

Task	Learning outcome	Assessment criteria	Max marks	Title for topics within task range
1	1,2,3	1.5K 1.6S 1.7K 1.9S 2.1K	12	Identification of cost information
2	2	2.1K 2.2K 2.3S 2.4S	16	Direct materials, labour and variable overhead variances
3	2	2.1K 2.2K 2.3S 2.4S	16	Fixed overhead variances
4	1,2	1.8S 2.1K 2.2K 2.3S 2.4S	12	Operating statement
5	4	4.1K 4.2S 4.3S 4.4S 4.5S	12	Statistical information
6	2,5	2.1K 2.2K 2.3S 2.4S 5.1S 5.2S	22	Variance analysis (written report)
7	3,5	3.1K 3.2K 3.3S 5.1S 5.2S	20	Calculation of performance indicators

Task	Learning outcome	Assessment criteria	Max marks	Title for topics within task range
8	3,4,5	1.6S 1.7K 1.8S 3.2K 5.1S 5.2S	12	Decision making
9	3	3.4S 3.5S	12	Cost management techniques
10	1,3,5	1.7K 1.8S 3.1K 3.2K 4.2S 4.3S 4.4S 4.5S 4.6S 4.7S 5.1S 5.2S 5.3S	22	Report on performance indicators and scenario planning ('what if' analysis) (written report)

chapter 1:
COSTS

chapter coverage 📖

In this initial chapter we will introduce the concept of cost accounting by looking at the various ways that costs can be classified, recorded and reported.

The topics covered are:

✍ Overview of a costing system

✍ Classification of costs by behaviour

✍ High low method of cost estimation

OVERVIEW OF A COSTING SYSTEM

One of the key concerns for the management of a commercial organisation is to know how much the products that it makes, or the services that it provides, cost. This information is needed for many purposes including the following:

- Setting the selling price
- Determining the quantities of production and sales
- Continuing or discontinuing a product
- Controlling costs
- Controlling production processes
- Appraising the performance of individual managers

Types of cost

Costs in both manufacturing and service industries are traditionally split between:

- Material costs
- Labour costs
- Expenses

These costs in turn can be described as direct costs or indirect costs. Indirect costs are normally called OVERHEAD COSTS or 'overheads'. This analysis depends on whether the cost in question can be directly attributed to a unit of production or unit of service, or whether the cost is shared between production units or service units.

A COST UNIT is an item of product or service for which a cost is measured. In a manufacturing business the cost unit may be each unit of finished product or each batch of production output. In a service business the identification of the cost unit may not be quite so straightforward. For example in a transport business the cost unit might be each lorry mile travelled; in a restaurant it might be each meal served; in a hospital it might be the cost of each in-patient day.

The full cost of a cost unit may therefore be shown as the sum of direct costs and overheads, as follows.

	£
Direct materials	6.00
Direct labour	3.00
Direct expenses (if any)	–
Total direct cost	9.00
Share of overheads	
(share of indirect materials, indirect labour and	
indirect expenses costs)	6.00
Full cost	15.00

Cost centres

Any material cost or labour cost or expense that can be directly related to the cost unit is a DIRECT COST of that cost unit. However many costs of the business cannot be directly attributed to a cost unit and these costs are initially taken to a cost centre.

A COST CENTRE is an area of the business, which may be a department such as the factory engineering maintenance department or the inspection team, for which costs are incurred that cannot be directly attributed to individual cost units. These costs are INDIRECT COSTS or overheads and include, for example, the rent of the factory and the wages of a departmental supervisor.

There are two types of cost centre in a manufacturing operation. Some departments or work sections are directly involved in the production or provision of the cost units, such as a machining department and an assembly and finishing department. These are known as PRODUCTION COST CENTRES. There are also cost centres that, while not actually producing the cost unit, do provide a service to the production cost centres, such as the engineering maintenance department or inspection team, or even the factory canteen. These are known as SERVICE COST CENTRES.

All the costs that are charged to these cost centres are overhead costs. So costs can be recorded as:

- Direct costs of cost units, and
- Overhead costs of cost centres.

To calculate a full cost for each cost unit, we add overhead costs from the cost centres to the direct costs for the cost units. The process of adding a share of overhead costs to direct costs in order to calculate a full cost can be fairly complex, and involves APPORTIONMENT and then ABSORPTION or OVERHEAD RECOVERY of overheads. This is explained in the next chapter.

Profit centres and investment centres

We have seen that a cost centre is an area or department of a business which incurs costs involved in the business operations.

A PROFIT CENTRE is an area of the business which not only incurs costs but also earns revenue. It is therefore possible to measure the profit or loss of the profit centre. For example, a business might have two divisions, one making washing machines and the other making fridge-freezers. Each division could be a profit centre, earning revenue from the sales of their products and incurring costs.

An INVESTMENT CENTRE is similar to a profit centre, but may be bigger. The difference between an investment centre and a profit centre is that an investment centre has its own capital investment, such as land and buildings, machinery and equipment, which is measured by the costing system. This means that for an investment centre, we can measure not only the profit but also the return on capital invested. For example, a large business might have a production centre in Wales making washing machines and a production centre in Scotland making fridge-freezers. If the capital investment of each centre is measured, the centres could be treated as investment centres, rather than profit centres.

CLASSIFICATION OF COSTS BY BEHAVIOUR

It probably seems fairly obvious that the total cost of operations will increase as the volume of business activity rises. For example, it will cost more to make 1,000 units of a product than it costs to make 100 units. However, different items of cost 'behave' in different ways with changes in the level of activity in the organisation. Items of cost can be classified according to their behaviour, and the main classifications of cost by behaviour are:

- Variable costs
- Fixed costs
- Stepped costs
- Semi-variable costs

Each of these types of cost behaviour will be explained in this chapter and the concepts of cost behaviour will be used in later chapters to produce relevant management information about costs.

Variable costs

VARIABLE COSTS are costs that vary directly in total with changes in the level of activity. The cost per unit is constant, but total variable costs increase at a constant rate as the level of activity increases. Direct materials and direct labour are often viewed as variable costs. For example, if 1 kg of a material is needed for each cost unit and each kilogram costs £2, then 100,000 kg will be required for 100,000 units of production at a cost of £200,000 and 500,000 kg will be needed for 500,000 units of production at a cost of £1,000,000.

The total variable cost can be expressed as:

Total variable cost = Variable cost per unit × Number of units

A graph can be used to illustrate the total variable cost as activity levels change.

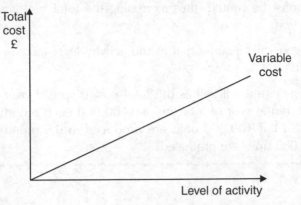

Direct costs such as materials costs may not always be 'true' variable costs. For example, if a supplier offers a bulk purchasing discount for purchases above a certain quantity, then the cost per unit purchased will fall if orders are placed for more than this quantity.

Fixed costs

A FIXED COST is one which does not change as activity levels alter. An example often used is the cost of the rent for a factory. This cost will remain the same in each time period whether 100,000 units are produced or 200,000 units.

The behaviour of fixed costs can be shown graphically:

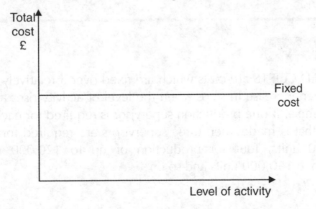

In practical terms, fixed costs are only 'truly' fixed over a RELEVANT RANGE of activity levels. For example the rent of the factory will only remain constant provided that the level of activity is within the production capacity of the factory. If production levels increase above the capacity of the current factory then more factory space must be rented, thus increasing the total rent cost for this higher level of production.

However, we generally assume that as the activity level increases, the fixed cost remains fixed in total.

The fixed cost per unit will fall as the total cost is spread over more units. For example, if the rental cost of a factory is £100,000 each month, the rental cost per unit will be £1 if 100,000 units are produced in the month but only £0.50 per unit if 200,000 units are produced.

Task 1

A business incurs fixed costs of £100,000. Complete the table below showing the budgeted fixed cost per unit at each production level.

Production level	Budgeted fixed cost per unit £
20,000 units	
40,000 units	
80,000 units	

Stepped fixed costs

STEPPED FIXED COSTS are costs which are fixed over a relatively small range of activity but then increase in steps when the level of activity rises above a certain level. For example, if one production supervisor is required for each 30,000 units of a product that is made, then three supervisors are required for production of up to 90,000 units, four for production of up to 120,000 units, five for production up to 150,000 units and so on.

Stepped fixed costs can be illustrated on a graph:

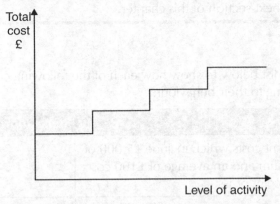

A stepped fixed cost is really a fixed cost with a relatively short relevant range.

Task 2

Insert the missing term:

The [   ] is the span of activity over which certain cost behaviour holds true.

Semi-variable costs

SEMI-VARIABLE COSTS are costs which have a fixed element and also a variable element. For example, a quarterly telephone bill includes a fixed element, which is the fixed line rental for the period, and a variable element which increases as the number or length of calls increase.

The total of a semi-variable cost can be expressed as:

Total cost = Fixed element + (Variable cost per unit × Number of units)

A semi-variable cost can be illustrated on a graph as follows:

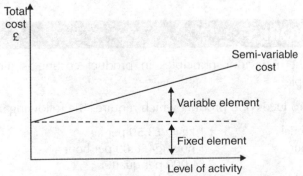

The calculation of the fixed and variable elements of a semi-variable cost will be explained in the next section of this chapter.

Task 3

Choose from the list below to show how each of the following costs would be classified according to their behaviour.

Cost	Behaviour
Stores department costs which include £5,000 of insurance premium and an average of £100 cost per materials receipt or issue	
Machinery depreciation based upon machine hours used	
Salary costs of lecturers in a training college, where one lecturer is required for every 200 students enrolled	
Buildings insurance for a building housing the stores, the factory and the canteen	
Wages of production workers who are paid per unit produced, with a guaranteed weekly minimum wage of £250	

Picklist:

Variable
Fixed
Semi-variable
Fixed, then semi-variable
Stepped

HOW IT WORKS

The use of cost behaviour principles in product costing is illustrated in the following example.

Cameron Ltd produces one product which requires the following inputs:

Direct materials	1 kg @ £3.50 per kg
Direct labour	1 hour @ £6.00 per hour
Rent	£4,000 per quarter
Leased machines	£1,500 for every 4,000 units of production
Maintenance costs	£1,000 per quarter plus £1.00 per unit produced

Calculate the total cost of production and the cost per unit for each of the following production levels for the coming quarter:

(a)   4,000 units
(b)   10,000 units
(c)   16,000 units

Direct materials – These are a variable cost with a constant amount per unit (1 kg × £3.50 = £3.50) therefore the total materials cost is found by multiplying the number of units by the unit cost:

£3.50 × 4,000 units   =   £14,000
£3.50 × 10,000 units   =   £35,000
£3.50 × 16,000 units   =   £56,000

Direct labour – This is another variable cost, with a unit cost of 1hr × £6 = £6:

£6.00 × 4,000 units   =   £24,000
£6.00 × 10,000 units   =   £60,000
£6.00 × 16,000 units   =   £96,000

Rent – This is a fixed cost. Provided we are still operating within the relevant range, it will remain at £4,000 whatever the production level.

Leased machines – This is a stepped cost and the number of machines leased will depend upon the quantity of production.

4,000 units   =   1 machine   =   £1,500
10,000 units   =   3 machines   =   £4,500
16,000 units   =   4 machines   =   £6,000

Maintenance costs – This is a semi-variable cost with a fixed element of £1,000 and a variable cost of £1 per unit. The total cost for each activity level is:

4,000 units   =   £1,000 + (4,000 × £1.00)   =   £5,000
10,000 units   =   £1,000 + (10,000 × £1.00)   =   £11,000
16,000 units   =   £1,000 + (16,000 × £1.00)   =   £17,000

Thus the total costs of production are:

	Production level – units		
	4,000	*10,000*	*16,000*
	£	£	£
Direct materials (variable)	14,000	35,000	56,000
Direct labour (variable)	24,000	60,000	96,000
Rent (fixed)	4,000	4,000	4,000
Leased machines (stepped)	1,500	4,500	6,000
Maintenance costs	5,000	11,000	17,000
Total cost	48,500	114,500	179,000
Number of units	4,000	10,000	16,000
Cost per unit	£12.13	£11.45	£11.19

The cost per unit is decreasing as the production quantity increases. This is because the fixed cost and the fixed element of the semi-variable cost are being spread over a larger number of units.

Variable costs with a discount

Suppose now that the supplier of the materials offers a bulk purchasing discount of 6% for all purchases if an order is placed for more than 8,000 kgs.

What is the direct materials cost in total and per unit at each level of production?

4,000 units

Total cost	4,000 × £3.50	=	£14,000
Cost per unit	£14,000/4,000	=	£3.50

10,000 units

Total cost	10,000 × (£3.50 × 94%)	=	£32,900
Cost per unit	£32,900/10,000	=	£3.29

16,000 units

Total cost	16,000 × (£3.50 × 94%)	=	£52,640
Cost per unit	£52,640/16,000	=	£3.29

The direct materials are now not a 'true' variable cost, since the cost per unit falls once production is in excess of 8,000 units.

Task 4

A salesperson receives a fixed salary of £800 per month plus commission of £20 for each sale confirmed in the month.

Complete the table to show the salesperson's monthly salary for the month, if confirmed sales are at each of the following levels.

Sales	Monthly salary £
4 sales	
8 sales	
15 sales	

Practical limitations of cost classifications

As we have seen in this chapter so far, it can be useful to classify costs according to their behaviour. However, in order to make these classifications of cost behaviour, we assume that the cost behaviour is linear, and they are shown as a straight line when drawn on a graph. This may not always be the case in practice. For example, we have seen that if a discount is given for

purchases of materials above a certain level, then the materials purchases cost will not be a true variable cost. Thus unit variable costs may fall as economies of scale are achieved. Similarly, although the direct labour cost is often viewed as a variable cost, if activity exceeds a certain level then overtime might be incurred. This would mean that the cost is no longer a straightforward variable cost, because the rate of pay per hour is higher in overtime than in normal time.

The normal assumption is that variable costs (or the variable element of a semi-fixed cost) increase or decrease with changes in the number of units of output. However, the relevant activity may not always be units of output. For example an organisation's telephone bill is normally assumed to have a fixed element, the line rental, and a variable element, call costs, which increase as activity levels increase. In this case the relevant activity causing the call cost to vary is the number of calls made (or the length of call time). But in some organisations, if we look at telephone call costs in relation to the number of units of output, total call costs may increase when the number of units of output falls, because the sales team spend more time on the phone trying to boost sales when sales demand and production volume is falling.

Prime cost and full production cost

In the example 'How it works' above (Cameron Ltd) the different items of cost were simply added together to calculate the total cost. However, for management accounting purposes it is sometimes useful to categorise the costs, and to show some sub-totals within the grand total cost.

The PRIME COST of a product is the total of all the direct costs of producing the product.

The MARGINAL COST of a product is the total of all the variable costs of producing the product (both direct variable costs such as direct materials and direct labour and indirect variable overheads).

The FULL PRODUCTION COST is the total of all the costs of making the product, both fixed and variable. This includes all the overheads costs, both fixed and variable.

HOW IT WORKS

Using the figures for the 4,000 units level of production from the previous example, we can now classify the costs as prime cost, marginal cost and full production cost.

	£
Direct materials	14,000
Direct labour	24,000
Prime cost	**38,000**
Variable element of maintenance costs	4,000
Marginal cost	**42,000**
Rent	4,000
Leased machines	1,500
Fixed element of maintenance costs	1,000
Full production cost	**48,500**

The marginal cost is the total variable cost.

HIGH LOW METHOD OF COST ESTIMATION

Semi-variable costs are more complex than variable costs and fixed costs, because they have a fixed element which is not related to the level of activity, and a variable element which is related to the level of activity. For a semi-variable cost we need to be able to estimate, at any given level of activity, both the fixed cost element and the variable cost element.

One method of estimating the fixed and variable elements of a semi-variable cost is the HIGH LOW METHOD. With this method historical data is collected about the total amount of the semi-variable cost at various activity levels. A comparison is then made between the cost at the highest level of activity and the cost at the lowest level of activity, in order to identify the variable rate of increase in the cost between the two activity levels. Having identified and calculated the variable cost, we can then calculate the fixed element of the cost. The high-low method assumes that there is a linear relationship between the total cost at the highest and lowest activity levels.

HOW IT WORKS

The costs of the factory maintenance department for Kilman Ltd appear to be partially dependent on the number of machine hours operated each month. The machine hours and the maintenance department costs for the last six months are given below:

	Machine hours	Maintenance cost
		£
June	4,000	104,000
July	4,800	127,000
August	4,200	111,000
September	4,500	119,000
October	3,800	107,000
November	4,100	107,500

Step 1 Find the highest and lowest levels of activity. (Note that this is the highest and lowest activity level, which is not necessarily the highest and lowest cost.)

In this case the highest level is 4,800 hours in July and the lowest level is 3,800 hours in October.

Step 2 Compare the total costs for each of these activity levels and measure the differences in the cost and the differences in the activity levels:

	Machine hours	Cost £
Highest	4,800	127,000
Lowest	3,800	107,000
Increase	1,000	20,000

This shows that for an increase in 1,000 machine hours there has been an increase of £20,000 of costs. The increase in total cost must consist entirely of variable costs, because fixed costs are the same at both activity levels. Therefore the variable cost per machine hour can be estimated as:

Variable rate of increase	=	£20,000/1,000 hours
	=	£20 per machine hour

Step 3 We can now find the fixed element of the cost, by substituting the variable rate into either the highest or lowest activity level, with the fixed element appearing as the balancing figure. This will provide you with the same answer whether you use the highest or lowest level of activity.

Highest level

	£
Variable element 4,800 hours × £20	96,000
Fixed element (balancing figure)	31,000
Total cost	127,000

Lowest level

Variable element 3,800 hours × £20	76,000
Fixed element (balancing figure)	31,000
Total cost	107,000

Therefore the fixed element of the maintenance department costs is £31,000 and the variable rate is £20 per machine hour.

Step 4   We can now use this analysis of the semi-variable cost to forecast figures for the maintenance department. Suppose that the expected number of machine hours per month for the next three-month period are as follows:

	Dec	Jan	Feb
Machine hours	4,000	4,500	5,000

The forecast maintenance department costs for these three months can be calculated:

	Forecast maintenance department costs
	£
Dec (4,000 × £20) + £31,000	111,000
Jan (4,500 × £20) + £31,000	121,000
Feb (5,000 × £20) + £31,000	131,000

Interpolation and extrapolation

In the previous example we applied the high low method to historical costs in order to estimate the future costs of the maintenance department. To find the variable and fixed elements of the cost we looked at an activity range from 3,800 hours to 4,800 hours and estimated how the costs moved within that range.

For December and January the expected number of machine hours is within this activity range, and it may therefore seem likely that our estimates of cost will be fairly accurate. (Estimates of cost using the high low method do not coincide with the historical costs that may have been recorded for those levels – the high-low model is not totally accurate as it is based on the assumption of a linear relationship between output and total costs, which is unlikely to apply perfectly in practice). When costs are predicted for activity levels within the historical range, this is known as INTERPOLATION.

However for February the estimated machine hours are 5,000. This is outside the high-low range that we considered. We can still use the high low method to predict what costs will be, but our estimate of future cost is known as EXTRAPOLATION. Extrapolation may not be as accurate as interpolation, as the activity level is outside our historical data range. We cannot be sure that costs will behave in the same way outside this range, and extrapolation of costs is more likely to be inaccurate than interpolation.

Task 5

The production costs at various levels of production for a business are given below:

Production level units	Production costs £
24,000	169,000
20,000	143,000
28,000	191,000

The variable rate of production costs is

The fixed amount of production costs is

The high low method is a very important technique that you will need for your assessment. It could be assessed as a simple split of fixed and variable costs as we have seen in the example above. Alternatively you may be required to use the high low method where fixed costs increase by a step between the lowest and highest levels of output.

HOW IT WORKS

The costs of the factory maintenance department for Freer Ltd include a variable element that varies with the number of units produced. The fixed element of the costs steps up by £30,000 when 32,000 or more units are produced. The variable cost per unit is constant at all levels of output. Historical data has been obtained for total costs at 28,000 units and 34,000 units of output.

Volume of production Units	£
28,000	160,000
34,000	208,000

Step 1   Find the highest and lowest levels of activity (note that this is the activity level and is not necessarily the highest and lowest cost).

In this case we only have two levels of activity so we use those.

Step 2   Compare the costs for each of these levels of activity, but deduct the extra step-up fixed cost from the total costs of 34,000 units. This is to make the fixed costs comparable at each level of output.

	Number of units	Cost £
Highest	34,000	208,000 – 30,000 = 178,000
Lowest	28,000	160,000
Increase	6,000	18,000

This shows that for an increase in 6,000 units there has been an increase in total variable costs of £18,000. Therefore the variable cost per unit can be estimated as:

Variable rate of increase   =   £18,000/6,000 units

                                =   £3 per unit

Step 3   We can now find the fixed element of the cost at each activity level, by substituting the variable rate into the activity levels, with the fixed element appearing as the balancing figure.

Fixed cost at 28,000 units = £160,000 – (28,000 × £3) = £76,000

Fixed cost at 34,000 units = £208,000 – (34,000 × £3) = £106,000

Notice that the fixed cost at 34,000 units is £30,000 higher than at 28,000 units. This is reassuring as we were told this originally. Alternatively to find the fixed cost at 34,000 units we could have just calculated the fixed cost at 28,000 units and then added on the extra £30,000.

In a different type of assessment, you may be given the fixed element for one level of activity and asked to calculate the variable element and the fixed element for the other activity level.

HOW IT WORKS

The costs of the factory maintenance department for C Ltd include a variable element that varies with the number of units produced. The fixed element of the costs steps up when 20,000 or more units are produced. At an activity level of 22,000 units, the fixed element of the cost is £25,000. The variable cost per unit is constant. The following historical cost data is available.

Volume of production Units	£
18,000	200,000
22,000	245,000

What would be the total cost for 19,000 units?

What would be the total cost for 21,000 units?

Step 1   We have been told what the fixed cost element is for 22,000 units so we can break the total cost into its fixed and variable elements and then find the variable cost per unit from this.

Variable cost of 22,000 units = £245,000 – £25,000

$$\text{Variable cost per unit} = \frac{£245,000 - £25,000}{22,000} = £10$$

Step 2 Now that we have the variable cost per unit, we can substitute this into the lower level activity (18,000 units in this example) to find the fixed cost element for an activity level below 20,000.

Fixed element for lower activity level = £200,000 – (18,000 × £10) = £20,000.

Step 3 We can now find the cost at activity levels of 19,000 and 21,000 units. Remember the fixed element will be different in each case because of the step.

Cost at 19,000 units = £20,000 + (19,000 × £10) = £210,000
Cost at 21,000 units = £25,000 + (21,000 × £10) = £235,000

In the assessment, you may be given the variable element of cost and asked to calculate the fixed cost elements for different activity levels when there is a step-up in cost between the two levels.

HOW IT WORKS

The costs of the factory maintenance department for H Ltd include a variable cost element that varies with the number of units produced. The fixed cost element steps up when 20,000 or more units are produced. The variable cost per unit is constant at £15.

Volume of production	
Units	£
18,000	287,000
22,000	249,000

What would be the total cost for 19,000 units?

What would be the total cost for 21,000 units?

Step 1 We have been told that the variable element is £15 per unit so we can find the fixed element from this at each activity level.

Fixed element at 18,000 units = £287,000 – (18,000 × £15) = £17,000
Fixed element at 22,000 units = £349,000 – (22,000 × £15) = £19,000

Step 2 We can now find the cost at activity levels of 19,000 and 21,000 units.

Cost at 19,000 units = £17,000 + (19,000 × £15) = £302,000

Cost at 21,000 units = £19,000 + (21,000 × £15) = £334,000

CHAPTER OVERVIEW

- Direct costs are costs that can be related directly to a cost unit whereas indirect costs are initially allocated or apportioned to a cost centre, before being charged to cost units

- Costs are often classified according to their behaviour as activity levels change – the main classifications are variable costs, fixed costs, stepped fixed costs and semi-variable costs

- Semi-variable costs include both a fixed element and a variable rate element – a method of calculating these two elements is the high low method

Keywords

Cost unit – the individual product or service for which costs are to be gathered

Direct costs – costs that can be directly attributed to cost units

Cost centre – an area of the business for which costs are to be gathered

Production cost centre – directly involved in the production of the cost unit

Service cost centre – provides a service to the production cost centres

Indirect costs – costs that cannot be attributed directly to a cost unit but are initially attributed to a cost centre

Allocation – overheads that relate to just one cost centre are charged directly to that cost centre

Apportionment – overheads that relate to a number of cost centres are shared between each relevant cost centre on some fair basis

Re-apportionment – sharing total service cost centre costs among the production cost centres to ensure that all overheads are now included within the production cost centre costs

Absorption – process of allocating overheads of each production cost centre into the cost of cost units on some fair basis

Profit centre – an area of the business which incurs costs and earns revenues

Investment centre – an area of the business which incurs costs, earns revenues and is also responsible for its own capital investment

Variable costs – costs that increase/decrease directly in line with any changes in activity level

Fixed costs – costs that remain constant as activity levels change

Relevant range – the range of activity levels within which certain cost behaviour holds true

Stepped fixed costs – costs which are fixed over a relatively small range and then increase in steps

Semi-variable costs – costs which have both a fixed element and variable element

Prime cost – all the direct costs of producing a product

Marginal cost – all the variable costs of producing a product (both direct eg materials and labour, and indirect eg variable overheads)

Full production cost – all the costs of producing a product, including the overheads or indirect costs of production

High low method – a method of estimating the fixed and variable elements of a semi-variable cost using historic data

Interpolation – estimation of a forecast figure within the historical range of activity levels

Extrapolation – estimation of a forecast figure outside the historical range of activity levels

TEST YOUR LEARNING

Test 1

The direct materials cost for 10,000 units is estimated to be £43,600 and for 12,000 it is estimated to be £52,320. This is a variable cost.

True or False? Tick the correct answer.

True ☐

False ☐

Test 2

A business expects to incur fixed costs of £64,000 in the following month.

Complete the table below to show the total fixed cost and the fixed cost per unit at each of the following activity levels.

Activity level	Total fixed cost £	Fixed cost per unit £
3,000 units		
10,000 units		
16,000 units		

Test 3

A business makes 3,500 units per month with the following costs:

Direct materials	£5 per unit
Direct labour	£10 per unit
Rent	£10,000 per month
Supervisor costs	£7,500 per month for every 5,000 units of production

The marginal cost per month is

☐

The full production cost per month is

☐

Test 4

Given below are the activity levels and production costs for the latest six months for a factory:

	Activity level Units	Production cost £
July	103,000	469,000
August	110,000	502,000
September	126,000	547,000
October	113,000	517,000
November	101,000	472,000
December	118,000	533,000

(a) The variable element of the production cost is

The fixed element of the production cost is

(b) Complete the following table to show the estimated production costs at each of the following levels of production.

Level of production	Production cost £
120,000 units	
150,000 units	

(c) Comment on which of the two estimates of production costs calculated in (b) is likely to be more accurate and why.

chapter 2:
METHODS OF COSTING

chapter coverage 📖

In this chapter we will consider a variety of different methods of costing – absorption costing, marginal costing and activity based costing.

The topics that are to be covered are:

- ✍ Methods of costing
- ✍ Absorption costing
- ✍ Marginal costing
- ✍ Marginal versus absorption costing: profit and inventory
- ✍ Under- and over-absorption of overheads
- ✍ Fixed overheads: reasons for under- or over-absorption
- ✍ Marginal costing and absorption costing compared
- ✍ Activity based costing (ABC)

METHODS OF COSTING

There are different ways of measuring costs and calculating a cost for cost units. This chapter describes three methods of costing for the production of goods (rather than services). The three methods are:

- **Absorption costing**. This is a method of costing that adds a share of overhead costs on to direct costs to calculate a full cost for cost units. Traditional absorption costing may be used in traditional manufacturing businesses, which rely heavily on production line workers or production machinery to produce the output.

- **Variable costing, also known as marginal costing**. This method of costing makes a distinction between variable costs and fixed costs. Only the variable cost of output is measured. The fixed overheads are treated as a 'period charge' and are not added to the cost of cost units. The fixed overheads are simply charged to the statement of profit or loss (income statement) as an expense for the period.

- **Activity based costing** (ABC). This is an alternative method of absorption costing, which might be used in businesses where a large proportion of total costs are overhead costs, and direct labour and machining are comparatively insignificant as a part of the total activity and cost of the business. The methods used to apportion and absorb overhead costs are different from 'traditional' absorption costing.

Each of these three costing measures is explained in this chapter, and traditional absorption costing and variable costing (marginal costing) will be compared.

ABSORPTION COSTING

ABSORPTION COSTING is a method of costing in which the full cost of cost units is measured by adding a share of the overhead costs of production cost centres and service cost centres to direct costs. The process of adding overhead costs into the costs of cost units consists of several stages:

- Stage 1: Allocation of overheads to cost centres.

- Stage 2: Apportionment phase 1: Apportion shared costs between production cost centres and service cost centres.

- Stage 3: Apportionment phase 2: Apportion costs of the service cost centres between the production cost centres.

- Stage 4: Absorption or overhead recovery: Charge overheads from the production cost centres to the cost of cost units that are produced in the production cost centres.

These four stages will now be described in some further detail.

Allocation of overheads

The first stage in costing for overheads is to charge items of indirect cost directly to a specific production cost centre or service cost centre, where the cost of the item can be attributable in full to the cost centre. This is known as ALLOCATION of overhead costs. For example, the salary of a foreman in the finishing department can be allocated to the finishing department, and the cost of depreciation of the machines in the machining department can be allocated in full to the machining department.

Apportionment of overheads: the first phase

Some items of overhead cost cannot be allocated in full to a cost centre because they are shared by more than one cost centre. These items of cost are shared on a fair basis between the cost centres. For example, the rental cost of a factory cannot be allocated to a single cost centre, because the factory is used by all the cost centres. The rental cost is therefore shared between the cost centres on a fair basis, such as the floor area used by each cost centre. APPORTIONMENT simply means sharing out a joint cost on a fair basis.

Another example is the cost of the factory canteen. This is shared by employees from all the cost centres. A fair way of sharing this joint cost between the cost centres might be on the basis of the number of employees in each cost centre.

Apportionment of overheads: the second phase

After the first phase of apportionment, all indirect costs have been allocated or apportioned to the production cost centres and service cost centres.

The next phase in the apportionment process is to share the costs of the service cost centres between the production cost centres. The objective is to make sure that all the overhead costs are either allocated or apportioned to a production cost centre.

There are different ways of sharing the overhead costs of service cost centres between the production cost centres, and there are no 'rules'. The only requirement is that the apportionment should be on a fair basis. If you are given a task in which you are required to apportion the costs of one or more service cost centres, you will be told what basis of apportionment to use.

Absorption of overheads

When apportionment has been completed, all indirect costs are allocated or apportioned to a cost centre. We can now work out how to charge these overhead costs as indirect costs of the cost units that are made in each production cost centre. This is known as ABSORPTION and sometimes as OVERHEAD RECOVERY.

Overhead costs are added to the cost of cost units using an overhead ABSORPTION RATE. For each production cost centre, an absorption rate can be calculated as follows:

Absorption rate $=$ $\dfrac{\text{Total overhead costs of the production cost centre}}{\text{Total activity in the production cost centre}}$

The total activity in the production cost centre can be measured in different ways, but commonly-used measures of activity are:

- The total number of direct labour hours, or
- The total number of machine hours.

A direct labour hour absorption rate is likely to be used in a department that is not machine-intensive. A machine hour absorption rate is more likely in a cost centre with extensive machining work.

There is no 'rule' about which activity to use for an absorption rate. It is all a matter of common sense and judgement.

The process of measuring a full cost for cost units in a system of absorption costing is illustrated in the following diagram.

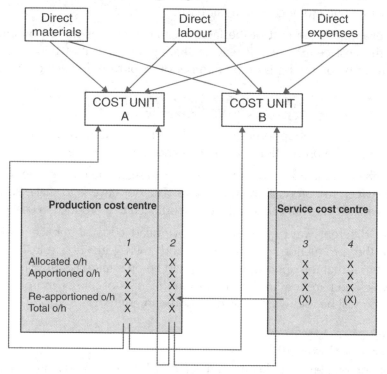

HOW IT WORKS

Calculating an absorption rate is illustrated in the following example. In this example, a single absorption rate is used for the entire production department, instead of a separate absorption rate for each production cost centre.

The total annual overhead costs for the production department of a company that makes double glazing products is £3,600,000. The number of direct labour hours worked during the year is 180,000 hours.

The overhead absorption rate using a direct labour hour rate would be £3,600,000/180,000 = £20 per direct labour hour.

Overhead costs would be added to the cost of cost units by measuring the direct labour time needed to make the unit, and adding an overhead cost at the rate of £20 per hour.

MARGINAL COSTING

MARGINAL COSTING, also known as VARIABLE COSTING, is very different from absorption costing. The costing system measures only the variable cost or marginal cost of cost units.

Sometimes, marginal costs may consist of direct materials costs and direct labour costs only. In other cases, there may also be some variable overhead costs. These may be estimated, for example, using the high-low method described in the previous chapter. If there are semi-variable costs, these are analysed into a variable cost per unit and a fixed cost amount. The variable part of semi-variable costs is then included in marginal cost.

All costs that are not marginal costs (variable costs) are fixed costs. In marginal costing, fixed costs are treated as a charge against profit in each time period.

A marginal costing analysis is illustrated in the following example. In this example.

	Per unit £	£	Total: 10,000 units £	£
Sales revenue		20		200,000
Variable costs:				
Direct materials	5		50,000	
Direct labour	3		30,000	
Variable overhead	1		10,000	
Total marginal cost		9		90,000
Contribution		11		110,000
Fixed cost				80,000
Profit				30,000

Notice the term CONTRIBUTION in this table. Total contribution is the difference between sales revenue and total variable costs. The contribution per unit is the difference between the sales price and the variable cost per unit.

Contribution can be thought of as standing for 'contribution towards covering fixed costs and making a profit'.

Contribution is an important concept, and we will look at the use of contribution for decision making in Chapter 3.

HOW IT WORKS

Fenton Partners produce one product, the Fenton. The factory has two production departments, assembly and packing, and there is one service department, maintenance. 75% of the maintenance department's time is spent in the assembly department and the remainder in the packing department.

The expected costs of producing 100,000 units in the next quarter are as follows:

Direct materials	£24.00 per unit
Direct labour	2 hours assembly @ £7.00 per hour
	1 hour packing @ £6.00 per hour
Assembly overheads	£320,000
Packing overheads	£240,000
Maintenance overheads	£200,000

In each of the production and service departments it is estimated that 40% of the overheads are variable and the remainder are fixed. Overheads are absorbed on the basis of direct labour hours.

Calculate the cost per unit using the following costing methods:

    (a)   Absorption costing

    (b)   Marginal costing

Absorption costing

Production overheads

	Assembly (Production) £	Packing (Production) £	Maintenance (Service) £
Allocated and apportioned	320,000	240,000	200,000
Apportion Maintenance (75%/25%)	150,000	50,000	(200,000)
Total overhead	470,000	290,000	–
Total hours 2 × 100,000	200,000		
1 × 100,000		100,000	
Absorption rate per hour =	$\dfrac{470,000}{200,000}$	$\dfrac{290,000}{100,000}$	
$\dfrac{\text{Budgeted overheads}}{\text{Budgeted activity level}}$			
=	£2.35 per labour hour	£2.90 per labour hour	

Interpretation:

For every one hour that the product is worked on in the assembly department, it is charged with a £2.35 share of the overheads incurred.

For every one hour that the product is worked on in the packing department, it is charged with a £2.90 share of the overheads incurred.

Unit cost

	£
Direct materials	24.00
Direct labour – assembly 2 hours × £7.00	14.00
Direct labour – packing 1 hour × £6.00	6.00
Prime cost	44.00
Overheads – assembly 2 hours × £2.35	4.70
– packing 1 hour × £2.90	2.90
Absorption cost per unit	51.60

Marginal costing

With this method only variable overheads are included in marginal cost and the marginal cost per unit, so these must be ascertained:

	Assembly	Packing
Total overhead (as before)	£470,000	£290,000
Variable element (40%)	£188,000	£116,000
Labour hours (as before)	200,000	100,000
Variable cost per labour hr	$\dfrac{£188,000}{200,000}$	$\dfrac{£116,000}{100,000}$
=	£0.94 per labour hour	£1.16 per labour hour

Unit cost, marginal costing

	£
Direct materials	24.00
Direct labour – assembly 2 hours × £7.00	14.00
Direct labour – packing 1 hour × £6.00	6.00
Prime cost	44.00
Variable overhead – assembly (2 hours × £0.94)	1.88
– packing (1 hour × £1.16)	1.16
Marginal cost per unit	47.04

Task 1

A business expects to produce 5,000 units of its single product in the next month, with the following costs being incurred:

	£
Direct materials	12,000
Direct labour	15,000
Variable overheads	23,000
Fixed overheads	25,000

Complete the following table to show the cost per unit under both absorption costing and marginal costing methods.

Costing method	Cost per unit £
Absorption costing	
Marginal costing	

MARGINAL VERSUS ABSORPTION COSTING: PROFIT AND INVENTORY

As we have just seen, unit costs are very different between marginal costing and absorption costing.

Under absorption costing the fixed overhead is absorbed into the cost of units produced in the period, and the full production cost of the units sold in the period is charged to the statement of profit or loss (income statement) as part of cost of sales.

However, under marginal costing a lower value (the marginal cost) is treated as the cost of sales, and the fixed costs are charged as a period expense in the statement of profit or loss.

The difference between the two costing methods is also seen in the valuation of inventory. With absorption costing, inventory is valued at full production cost, which includes the absorbed fixed overhead. However under marginal costing the value of inventory is lower, because it only includes variable production costs.

If the opening inventory and closing inventory levels and values are the same (so that sales = production) then the profit for a period shown under both absorption costing and marginal costing will be the same. However if opening and closing inventory levels are different, in other words if there has been an

increase or decrease in inventory levels between the beginning and end of the period, then absorption costing and marginal costing will not produce the same profit figure. This is because of the differences in the treatment of fixed production overheads and the valuation of inventory.

HOW IT WORKS

Spa Ltd makes a single product and produces management accounts, including a statement of profit or loss (income statement) each month. In both May and June 100,000 units of the product were produced.

The production costs in both May and June were:

	£
Direct materials	200,000
Direct labour	300,000
Fixed overheads	300,000
Total costs	800,000

There were no opening inventories at the start of May and all the production for May was sold. However in June only 75,000 units of production were sold, leaving 25,000 units in inventory at the end of the month.

Each unit is sold for £10.

(a) Calculate the cost per unit using:

   (i)   Absorption costing

   (ii) Marginal costing.

(b) Calculate the profit for each month using:

   (i)   Absorption costing

   (ii) Marginal costing.

(a) **Unit costs**

   (i)   Absorption costing:

        Full cost per unit = £800,000/100,000 = £8 per unit

   (ii) Marginal costing (ignore fixed overheads):

        Marginal cost per unit = £500,000/100,000 = £5 per unit.

   (There are no variable overhead costs in this example.)

(b) **Statements of profit or loss** (Income statements)

(i) Absorption costing:

	May £	May £	June £	June £
Sales		1,000,000		750,000
Less cost of sales				
Opening inventory	0		0	
Cost of production				
100,000 units × £8	800,000		800,000	
	800,000		800,000	
Less closing inventory				
25,000 units × £8	0		(200,000)	
Cost of sales		800,000		600,000
Profit (absorption costing)		200,000		150,000

(ii) Marginal costing:

	May £	May £	June £	June £
Sales		1,000,000		750,000
Less cost of sales				
Opening inventory	0		0	
Cost of production				
100,000 units × £5	500,000		500,000	
	500,000		500,000	
Less closing inventory				
25,000 units × £5	0		(125,000)	
Marginal cost of sales		500,000		375,000
Contribution		500,000		375,000
Less fixed costs		300,000		300,000
Profit (marginal costing)		200,000		75,000

In May the profit is the same with both costing methods, £200,000. This is because there is no movement in inventory during the period, since all the production is sold.

In June however profit with absorption costing is £150,000, whereas it is only £75,000 with marginal costing. The reason for the £75,000 difference in profit is that:

- The closing inventory with absorption costing includes fixed costs of £75,000 (£300,000/100,000 × 25,000 units) and these are carried forward in the inventory value to the next accounting period, whereas

- Under marginal costing all of the fixed costs are written off in June and no fixed costs are carried forward in inventory value.

The rules: absorption versus marginal costing – inventory and profit

The rules are as follows:

(1) **If inventory levels are rising** between the beginning and end of the accounting period, **then absorption costing will give a higher profit** as the fixed overheads are being carried forward into the next accounting period.

(2) **If inventory levels are falling** between the beginning and end of the accounting period, **then absorption costing will give a lower profit figure.** This is because more fixed overheads from the previous period are charged to the statement of profit or loss (income statement) in this period.

(3) **Where inventory levels are constant** between the beginning and end of the period (provided that unit costs are constant), **then absorption costing and marginal costing will give the same amount of profit** for the period.

For the example above, a reconciliation of the profit figures can be prepared:

	May £	June £
Absorption cost profit	200,000	150,000
Change in inventory (sales = production)	0	
Increase in inventory (25,000 units – 0) × fixed cost per unit £3		(75,000)
Marginal cost profit	200,000	75,000

Task 2

A business operates an absorption costing system. At the start of last month the business had 2,500 units in inventory. During the month it produced another 23,000 units and sold 24,000. The cost per unit of the product is as follows:

	£
Direct materials	10.00
Direct labour	14.00
Prime cost	24.00
Variable overheads	3.00
Fixed overheads (£46,000/23,000)	2.00
Absorption cost per unit	29.00

The business reported a profit of £504,000.

The profit if the business used marginal costing would have been

£ [   ]

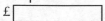

Task 3

A business operates a marginal costing system. At the start of last month opening inventory was £40,000 and closing inventory was £16,000. The reported profit for the month was £14,000.

It has been calculated that if the business had used a system of absorption costing, opening inventory would have been £60,000 and closing inventory £24,000.

The profit if the business used absorption costing would have been

£ ⬚

UNDER- AND OVER-ABSORPTION OF OVERHEADS

Overhead absorption rates are obtained from budgeted figures. The method explained in this chapter is applied to budgeted overhead costs and budgeted levels of activity in order to calculate a budgeted absorption rates.

The budgeted absorption rates are then used in practice to calculate actual costs.

This may seem an odd thing to do, but the alternative would be even worse – having to wait until the end of each month or the end of the year before calculating overhead rates on actual costs and actual activity levels. This would make the costing process administratively difficult and slow.

So overhead absorption rates are decided in advance from:

Budgeted overhead cost/Budgeted level of activity.

You may see that a **problem with this method** is that actual overhead costs may be different from the overhead costs in the budget. Similarly the actual level of activity may be difference from the level of activity in the budget. In fact, they almost certainly will be.

Consequently, overhead costs absorbed into the cost of production will differ from actual overhead costs incurred. Unless this difference is corrected, the profit measured in absorption costing will be 'wrong'.

(1) If more overheads are absorbed than have actually been incurred, this is known as OVER-ABSORPTION.

(2) If fewer overheads are absorbed than have actually been incurred, this is known as UNDER-ABSORPTION.

The profit for the period must be adjusted for the amount of under-absorption or over-absorption, in order to offset the difference between the actual overhead costs and the overhead costs absorbed into the cost of production.

(1) If there is over-absorption, too many overhead costs have been added to the cost of production, and **profit must be adjusted by adding the over-absorbed overhead to profit**.

(2) If there is under-absorption, not enough overhead costs have been added to the cost of production, and **profit must be adjusted by subtracting the under-absorbed overhead from profit**.

If fewer overheads are absorbed than have actually been incurred, this is known as UNDER-ABSORPTION.

Note that over- or under-absorption is not a problem in marginal costing, as the fixed overhead is treated as a period cost and is not absorbed into the cost of units.

HOW IT WORKS

Cowslip Limited budgeted to make and sell 120,000 units of their product during the year. The units are sold for £20 each and direct costs per unit are £6. Budgeted overheads for the year were £1,800,000, and overheads are recovered using a rate per machine hour basis. Each unit requires 3 hours of machine time. The budgeted absorption rate for the year is therefore £1,800,000/(120,000 × 3 hours) = £5 per machine hour.

The actual overheads and machine hours worked in the first three months of the year were:

	Units made	Machine hours	£
January	10,000	30,000	150,000
February	10,000	30,000	140,000
March	9,000	28,000	160,000

All other actual costs, revenues and quantities were as budgeted. (Only the overheads incurred differ from budget.)

In **January** a comparison of actual overheads and absorbed overheads will show that the two are the same:

	£
Actual overheads	150,000
Absorbed overheads	
(30,000 hrs × £5)	150,000
Under-/over-absorption	0

In **February**, the actual overheads are £140,000, but 30,000 machine hours were worked, so we have a difference between actual overhead expenditure and the amount of overhead costs absorbed into the cost of production. Absorbed overheads are more than actual overhead costs, so we have over-absorption.

	£
Actual overheads	140,000
Absorbed overheads (30,000 hours × £5)	150,000
Over-absorption	10,000

This over-absorption of £10,000 is credited to the statement of profit or loss (income statement), ie it is added back to profit as an adjustment.

In **March** actual overheads are £160,000 and machine hours are only 28,000. This time, there is under-absorbed overhead.

	£
Actual overheads	160,000
Absorbed overheads (28,000 hours × £5)	140,000
Under-absorption	20,000

Under-absorption means that not enough overheads have been charged against the cost of production and profits, so we deduct the under-absorption from profit to make up for this. Profit should therefore be adjusted down by £20,000.

Note be very careful to calculate the under- or over-absorption based on actual versus absorbed costs. Budgeted overhead costs are not brought into the calculation.

Now let's say that in **April**, the number of units produced and sold by Cowslip Limited is 12,000, the actual machine hours in the month were 38,000 and overheads actually incurred amounted to £165,000. Once again both overheads and activity level are different from budget.

The overhead under- or over-absorbed is calculated as before.

	£
Actual overheads	165,000
Absorbed overheads (38,000 hours × £5)	190,000
Over-absorption	25,000

The profit calculation will take account of the over-absorption by adding £25,000 back to the profit for the period.

In summary, the under-/over-absorption is found by comparing:

	£
Actual overheads incurred for the period	X
Absorbed overheads:	
(actual hours at absorption rate per hour)*	X
Under-/over-absorption	X

* Alternatively, if we are only given an absorption rate per unit then this may be 'actual **units produced** at absorption rate per unit'. It depends on the basis that the business uses – here we are told that Cowslip Limited uses a rate per **machine hour** basis.

Task 4

Tulip Limited planned to make 30,000 units, each of which was expected to require two hours of direct labour. Budgeted overheads were £54,000. Actual production was 28,000 units, requiring a total of 55,000 direct labour hours. Actual overheads were £47,000.

(a) The overhead absorption rate based on direct labour hours is

      [   ]

(b) Complete the following sentence using the words from the list beneath:

The [   ] absorption of [   ] should be

[   ] profit.

Picklist:
under-
over-
£2,500
£4,500
added to
deducted from

Task 5

A business uses an absorption costing system and absorbs overhead costs on a direct labour hour basis. Before making an adjustment for under- or over-absorbed overhead, it recorded a profit for the year of £270,000.

	£
Sales	940,000
Cost of sales	670,000
Profit	270,000

Budgeted and actual data relating to overheads are as follows:

	Budget	Actual
Overhead expenditure	£2,000,000	£2,150,000
Direct labour hours	200,000	190,000

The actual profit for the year, after making an adjustment for under- or over-absorbed overheads, was:

£ [   ]

FIXED OVERHEADS: REASONS FOR UNDER- OR OVER-ABSORPTION

The fixed overhead absorption rate is based on budgeted figures for fixed overhead expenditure and the level of activity (such as budgeted direct labour hours or budgeted machine hours). Under- or over-absorption of fixed overheads happens for two reasons:

- The actual fixed overhead expenditure is different from budgeted expenditure.

- The actual volume or level of activity is different from the budgeted volume.

Management may want to see the reasons for under- or over-absorbed overhead, and they can be explained as:

- Under- or over-absorption due to the difference between budgeted and actual fixed overhead expenditure (a fixed overhead 'expenditure variance').

- Under- or over-absorption due to the difference between budgeted and actual level of activity (a fixed overhead 'level of activity variance' or 'volume variance'). This can be given a money value by applying the fixed overhead absorption rate per hour to the difference between the budgeted and actual levels of activity.

Expenditure variance: fixed overheads	Level of activity variance ('volume variance'): fixed overheads
= Difference between budgeted and actual fixed overhead expenditure	= Difference between budgeted and actual hours × fixed overhead absorption rate per hour
If actual expenditure is more than budgeted expenditure, this will cause under-absorption (an 'adverse variance')	If the level of activity is less than the budgeted level of activity, this will cause under-absorption (an 'adverse variance')
If actual expenditure is less than budgeted expenditure, this will cause over-absorption (a 'favourable variance')	If the level of activity is more than the budgeted level of activity, this will cause over-absorption (an 'favourable variance')

HOW IT WORKS

Flatter Limited uses a system of absorption costing. Its budgeted fixed overhead expenditure for 20X1 was £1,800,000. It uses a direct labour hour basis for absorbing fixed overheads, and there were 300,000 budgeted direct labour hours for 20X1.

Actual fixed overhead spending in 20X1 was £1,720,000 and 325,000 direct labour hours were worked.

Required:

Calculate:

(a) The under- or over-absorbed fixed overhead in 20X1

(b) The amount of under- or over-absorption attributable to a fixed overhead expenditure variance

(c) The amount of under- or over-absorption attributable to a volume variance

Total under- or over-absorbed fixed overhead

The absorption rate is £1,800,000/300,000 hours = £6 per direct labour hour.

	£
Fixed overhead incurred	1,720,000
Fixed overhead absorbed (325,000 hours × £6.00)	1,950,000
Overhead over-absorbed	230,000

Fixed overhead expenditure variance

	£
Budgeted fixed overhead	1,800,000
Actual fixed overhead	1,720,000
Fixed overhead expenditure variance: causing over-absorption	80,000
	Favourable

As the actual fixed overhead is less than the budgeted figure, this is a 'favourable variance' that contributes to over-absorption of fixed overheads.

Fixed overhead level of activity variance

Actual level of activity (direct labour hours)	325,000 hrs
Budgeted level of activity	300,000 hrs
Difference: actual hours more than budgeted hours	25,000 hrs
× Absorption rate per direct labour hour	× £6
Fixed overhead level of activity variance in £	£150,000
	Favourable

The variance is 'favourable' because more hours were worked than budgeted, and this has the effect of causing over-absorption of fixed overheads.

	£	
Fixed overhead expenditure variance	80,000	Favourable
Fixed overhead level of activity variance ('volume' variance)	150,000	Favourable
Over-absorbed fixed overhead	230,000	

You will find when you study standard costing that in a standard costing system (in Chapter 5) there are variances to explain under- or over-absorbed fixed overheads.

Task 6

A business uses a system of absorption costing and fixed overheads are absorbed using a direct labour hour rate. The budgeted fixed overheads for 20X2 were £3,000,000 and there were 250,000 budgeted direct labour hours. Actual fixed overhead expenditure in 20X2 was £2,930,000 and 220,000 direct labour hours were worked in the year.

Calculate the following figures:

(a) The total over- or under-absorbed fixed overhead

Total fixed overhead variance £ ☐

(b) The under- or over-absorption caused by an expenditure variance

Fixed overhead expenditure variance £ ☐

(c) The under- or over-absorption caused by a difference in the level of activity

Fixed overhead volume variance £ ☐

MARGINAL COSTING AND ABSORPTION COSTING COMPARED

Advantages of absorption costing:

- Fixed overheads have to be incurred to produce output so it is fair to charge each unit of product with a share of the fixed costs.

- Using full absorption cost to value inventory is consistent with the closing inventory value that is required by accounting standards (IAS 2) for the external financial statements.

- In the long run a business needs to cover its fixed costs to be profitable so when setting selling prices, an organisation needs to be aware of the full cost of the product.

Advantages of marginal costing:

- Fixed costs are the same regardless of output and therefore it makes sense to charge them in full as a period cost.

- Marginal costing does not require apportionment of fixed costs which can be arbitrary methods of apportionment and choice of activity for absorption.

- By charging fixed costs as a period cost there is no under- or over-absorption of fixed overheads.

41

- Marginal costing focuses on variable costs and contribution which can be more useful for decision making (see Chapter 3).

ACTIVITY BASED COSTING (ABC)

The third costing method in this chapter is activity based costing or ABC. This is a method of absorption costing which was developed in the 1970s and 1980s as an alternative to traditional absorption costing.

Under basic absorption costing, the production overheads of a cost centre are all absorbed into the cost of cost units on the same basis, usually labour hours or machine hours, no matter what the cause of the overhead. This could be viewed as quite an arbitrary approach to absorbing overheads, particularly as overheads now tend to form a very large part of product costs – far more than in the past – and direct labour is much less significant in the manufacturing environment than it used to be.

A principle of activity based costing (ABC) is that overhead costs should be charged to cost units in a more realistic way, and that it is not appropriate to absorb overheads on the basis of direct labour hours or machine hours in production. Instead, it is more appropriate to identify major ACTIVITIES outside direct production that incur significant overhead costs, and then find a way of charging overhead costs to cost units on the basis of these activities.

The activities selected will vary according to the nature of the business, but they might be receiving materials into store, issuing material to production, repairs and maintenance work, production planning and control work, setting up machines for a production run (production setups), quality control activities, and so on.

The concept is that overhead costs are charged to products and cost units on the basis of the benefit that each product obtains from each activity.

Cost pools

The costs associated with each activity are gathered together into COST POOLS. Overhead costs are allocated to cost pools (and any overhead costs that are shared between cost pools may be apportioned between them on a fair basis).

Then, for each cost pool, we identify a factor that causes or drives these costs to change. This is known as the COST DRIVER. (The cost driver for a cost pool is similar to the basis of activity used for absorption of overheads in traditional absorption costing. In traditional costing, the 'cost driver' is direct labour hours or machine hours. In activity based costing, it is often something different.)

The total budgeted costs of the cost pool is then divided by the budgeted number of times that the cost driver will take place. This gives an overhead rate per cost

driver. The overheads from the cost pool are then allocated to different products depending upon their particular usage of the cost driver for the activity.

For example, suppose that there is an activity and cost pool for the setting up work for new production runs. A product that is made in small batches and needs a lot of separate batch production runs should be charged with a bigger share of set-up costs than a product with long batch production runs, and which needs only a small number of production runs.

The diagram below illustrates in outline how ABC works:

Identify activities causing overheads	Activity 1	Activity 2
Gather all costs for each activity	Cost pool 1	Cost pool 2
Identify what causes the cost	Cost driver 1	Cost driver 2
Calculate cost driver rate	$\dfrac{\text{Cost pool 1 total}}{\text{No. of cost drivers}}$	$\dfrac{\text{Cost pool 2 total}}{\text{No. of cost drivers}}$
Apply to individual cost units	Use of cost driver 1 × cost driver 1 rate	Use of cost driver 2 × cost driver 2 rate

HOW IT WORKS

Copper Ltd produces two products, the C and the P. The direct costs of the two products are given below:

	C	P
Direct materials	£3.50	£4.80
Direct labour	£2.00	£1.20

The budgeted production is for 120,000 units of C and 50,000 units of P.

The two main overhead activities identified for the fairly simple production process are materials handling and production set-ups.

C requires only large production runs and large transfers of materials from stores. However P is a more complex product with a number of different types of materials required and shorter and more frequent production runs.

The budgeted overheads for Copper are £800,000 and they are made up as follows:

	£
Materials handling cost pool	300,000
Production set-up cost pool	500,000
	800,000

The use of these activities for each product is:

	C	P	Total
Number of materials requisitions	200	800	1,000
Number of production set-ups	100	400	500

Calculate the total costs incurred and the unit cost of each product, using activity based costing. Also calculate the direct (prime) cost and the overhead cost per unit.

Cost driver rate

Materials handling $\dfrac{£300,000}{1,000}$ = £300 per material requisition

Production set-ups $\dfrac{£500,000}{500}$ = £1,000 per production set-up

Total production costs and cost per unit

	C £	P £
Direct materials		
120,000 × £3.50	420,000	
50,000 × £4.80		240,000
Direct labour		
120,000 × £2.00	240,000	
50,000 × £1.20		60,000
Materials handling overhead		
200 × £300	60,000	
800 × £300		240,000
Production set-up overhead		
100 × £1,000	100,000	
400 × £1,000		400,000
	820,000	940,000
Cost per unit	£820,000	£940,000
	120,000 units	50,000 units
	£6.83 per unit	£18.80 per unit

Analysis of cost per unit

		C £	P £
Direct (or prime) costs	(3.50 + 2.00)	5.50	
	(4.80 + 1.20)		6.00
Materials handling overhead			
60,000/120,000		0.50	
240,000/50,000			4.80
Production set-up overhead			
100,000/120,000		0.83	
400,000/50,000			8.00
Unit cost		6.83	18.80

In this instance product C is charged with £1.33 of overhead, whereas the more activity-intensive product P is charged with £12.80 of production overhead. Notice that the direct labour cost of product P is only £1.20 compared to the £2.00 labour cost of product C. If the overheads had been apportioned according to labour hours, as with traditional absorption costing, then the costs per unit for each product would have been very different indeed.

Task 7

A manufacturing company uses activity-based costing and treats quality control inspections as an activity for overhead costs.

The budgeted costs of quality control activities are £74,000 for the year. The cost driver is 'inspections' and the budgeted number of quality inspections for the year is 370, for all the company's different products. Of these, Product A is expected to require 25 inspections during the year and Product B 130 inspections.

(a) Complete the table below using activity based costing to show how much overhead activity cost of the quality control cost pool will be absorbed into the cost of Product A and Product B.

Overhead absorbed in Product A	£
Overhead absorbed in Product B	£

(b) It has also been budgeted that 10,000 units of Product A and 13,000 units of Product B will be produced in the year.

Complete the table below to show the budgeted quality control overhead cost per unit for Products A and B.

Product A quality control cost per unit	£
Product B quality control cost per unit	£

CHAPTER OVERVIEW

- With absorption costing, all production overheads are allocated and apportioned to production cost centres and then absorbed into the cost of the products on a suitable basis

- With marginal costing, the cost of the products is just the variable cost of production. All fixed production costs are charged as a period cost in the statement of profit or loss (income statement)

- If inventory levels are constant then both absorption costing and marginal costing will report the same profit figure

- If inventory levels are increasing, absorption costing profit will be higher as **more** fixed overheads are carried forward to the following period in closing inventory than those brought forward in opening inventory

- If inventory levels are falling, marginal costing profit will be higher as **fewer** fixed overheads are carried forward under absorption costing in the closing inventory figure than those brought forward in opening inventory

- The difference in profit between absorption costing and marginal costing is explained by the amount of fixed production overhead included in the increase/decrease in inventory levels with absorption costing

- Overhead absorption rates are based on budgeted overhead costs and budgeted activity levels. These will differ from actual overhead expenditure and actual activity levels. Consequently there will be under- or over-absorbed overheads in each period

- An adjustment to profit must be made for the amount of under- or over-absorbed overheads

  - Under-absorption is deducted from profit in the statement of profit or loss (income statement)

  - Over-absorption is added to profit in the statement of profit or loss (income statement)

- The under-/over-absorption is found by comparing the actual overhead incurred with the overhead absorbed in the period

- The under- or over-absorption of fixed overheads can be explained by an expenditure difference between budgeted and actual fixed overheads and a volume of activity difference between the budget and actual performance

- The adjustment for under- or over-absorption should be ignored in comparing profit with absorption costing and profit with marginal costing

- Activity based costing (ABC) considers the activities that cause overheads to be incurred and the factors that give rise to these activity costs (cost drivers). It is a method of absorbing overheads into products on the basis of the amount of each activity that the particular product is expected to use in the period. It may be more suitable than traditional absorption costing in manufacturing businesses where overhead costs are much larger than direct production costs

Keywords

Absorption (full) costing – both variable and fixed production overheads are included in unit cost

Marginal (variable) costing – unit cost includes only variable production costs

Activity based costing (ABC) – a more complex approach to absorption of overheads, based upon an analysis of the detailed causes of the overheads

Contribution – sales value less variable cost of the goods sold

Overhead absorption rate – the rate at which overheads are charged to cost units, calculated by dividing budgeted overhead costs by the budgeted level of activity

Over-absorption – more overheads are absorbed into production than have actually been incurred: add back to profit

Under-absorption – fewer overheads are absorbed into production than were actually incurred: deduct from profit

Activities – the elements of the overhead cost which cause costs to be incurred

Cost pools – costs that can be attributed to each activity

Cost driver – the factor that causes the costs for each cost pool

TEST YOUR LEARNING

Test 1

A manufacturing business has two production departments P1 and P2. P1 is a labour intensive department, while P2 is highly mechanised with relatively few machine operatives. Budgeted figures are as follows:

	P1	P2
Overheads apportioned	£50,000	£60,000
Machine hours	800	4,000
Labour hours	2,500	600

(a) The overhead absorption rate for department P1 is:

£62.50 ☐

£20.00 ☐

£15.00 ☐

£100.00 ☐

(b) The overhead absorption rate for department P2 is:

£62.50 ☐

£20.00 ☐

£15.00 ☐

£100.00 ☐

Test 2

Complete the following table to show the amount of under- or over-absorption of overheads in each of the three cases below. State in each case whether there is an under- or over-absorption and indicate what adjustment is required in the statement of profit or loss (income statement).

	Amount of under-/over-absorption £	Under- or over-absorption	Add or subtract in statement of profit or loss (income statement)
An overhead absorption rate of £3 per unit, based on expected production levels of 500 units. Actual overheads turn out to be £1,600, and actual production is 650 units.			
The budget is set at 1,000 units, with £9,000 overheads recovered on the basis of 600 direct labour hours. At the end of the period, overheads amounted to £8,600, production achieved was only 950 units and 590 direct labour hours had been worked.			

Test 3

The budgeted overheads apportioned to two production cost centres, X and Y, together with the budgeted labour hours and machine hours, are given below:

	X	Y
Overheads	£260,000	£380,000
Direct labour hours	20,000	120,000
Machine hours	100,000	10,000

Production cost centre X involves a highly mechanised process, with only a few machine workers. Production Y involves a highly labour intensive process.

(a) Complete the table to calculate separate departmental overhead absorption rates for each production cost centre using an appropriate basis.

Department	Overhead absorption rate
X	
Y	

(b) Each unit of Product A utilises the following hours in each production department.

	X	Y
Direct labour hours	1	4
Machine hours	5	2

The overhead to be included in the cost of each unit of product A is
£ [　　　　　]

Test 4

Explain how fixed production overheads are treated in an absorption costing system and in a marginal costing system.

Test 5

Given below is the budgeted information about the production of 60,000 units of a single product in a factory for the next quarter:

Direct materials		£12.50 per unit
Direct labour	– assembly	4 hours @ £8.40 per hour
	– finishing	1 hour @ £6.60 per hour
Assembly production overheads		£336,000
Finishing production overheads		£84,000

It is estimated that 60% of the assembly overhead is variable cost and that 75% of the finishing overhead is variable cost.

Complete the table below to show the budgeted cost of the product using each method of costing.

Method of costing	Budgeted cost £
Absorption costing	
Marginal costing	

Test 6

Given below are the budgeted figures for production and sales of a factory's single product for the months of November and December:

	November	December
Production	15,000 units	15,000 units
Sales	12,500 units	18,000 units
Direct materials	£12.00 per unit	£12.00 per unit
Direct labour	£8.00 per unit	£8.00 per unit
Variable production cost	£237,000	£237,000
Fixed production cost	£390,000	£390,000

Overheads are absorbed on the basis of budgeted production and the selling price of the product is £75.

There were 2,000 units of the product in inventory at the start of November.

(a) Prepare the budgeted statements of profit of loss (income statements) for each of the two months using:

(i) Absorption costing

Absorption costing – statement of profit or loss (income statement)

	November		December	
	£	£	£	£
Sales				
Less cost of sales				
Opening inventory				
Production costs				
	────		────	
Less closing inventory				
	────		────	
		────		────
Profit		────		────

(ii) Marginal costing

Marginal costing – statement of profit or loss (income statement)

	November		December	
	£	£	£	£
Sales				
Less cost of sales				
Opening inventory				
Production costs				
	_____		_____	
Less closing inventory				
	_____		_____	
		_____		_____
Contribution		_____		_____
Less fixed overheads		_____		_____
Profit		_____		_____

(b) Complete the table below to reconcile the absorption costing profit and the marginal costing profit for each of the two months.

	November £	December £
Absorption costing profit		
Inventory changes		
Marginal costing profit		

Test 7

A business produces two products, the LM and the NP. The direct costs of the two products are:

	LM	NP
Direct materials	£2.60	£3.90
Direct labour	£3.50	£2.70

The total overhead cost is made up as follows:

	£
Stores costs	140,000
Production set-up costs	280,000
Quality control inspection costs	180,000
	600,000

The budgeted production is for 50,000 units of LM and 20,000 units of NP.

Each product is expected to make the following use of the service activities:

	LM	NP	Total
Materials requisitions from stores	100	220	320
Production set-ups	80	200	280
Quality control inspections	30	60	90

Complete the following table to show the budgeted cost per unit for each product using activity based costing and how much total budgeted overhead is included in the unit cost for each product. Assume that materials requisitioning, set-ups and quality control are the three activities for which there are cost pools

Product	Budgeted cost per unit £	Budgeted overhead per unit £
LM		
NP		

chapter 3:
DECISION MAKING

---

chapter coverage

In this chapter we will look at a variety of ways in which costing information can be used for decision making purposes.

The topics that are to be covered are:

- ✐ Use of marginal costing and contribution for decision making
- ✐ Cost-volume-profit analysis
- ✐ Limiting factor analysis
- ✐ Make or buy decisions
- ✐ Closure of a business segment
- ✐ Discounted cash flows

USE OF MARGINAL COSTING AND CONTRIBUTION FOR DECISION MAKING

In the chapter on methods of costing we defined CONTRIBUTION as sales revenue less variable costs. We can look at contribution in total, as we did in marginal costing, or at contribution per unit.

Provided that the selling price and variable costs remain constant at different levels of activity, then:

(a)   contribution per unit is a constant figure at each level of activity, but

(b)   total contribution increases directly with increases in output and sales.

Fixed costs are different. As the volume of output and sales increases:

(a)   total fixed costs are unchanged, but

(b)   the fixed cost per unit fall with increases in output and sales (because the fixed costs are spread over more units).

HOW IT WORKS

J R Grantham & Partners are considering expanding their business from its current production and sales of 100,000 units per annum. Market research suggests that it will almost certainly be possible to increase sales to 150,000 and possibly even to 180,000 units per annum.

The business produces a single product that sells for £20 and has variable costs of production of £15 per unit. The fixed costs are currently £400,000 per annum and are not expected to increase.

We will look at the contribution per unit, full production cost per unit and profit per unit at each activity level. (There are no changes in inventory levels, so marginal costing and absorption costing will report the same profit.)

Activity level	100,000 units	150,000 units	180,000 units
	£	£	£
Sales	2,000,000	3,000,000	3,600,000
Variable costs	1,500,000	2,250,000	2,700,000
Contribution	500,000	750,000	900,000
Fixed costs	400,000	400,000	400,000
Profit	100,000	350,000	500,000
Contribution per unit (£20 – £15)	£5	£5	£5

Full production cost per unit:

	£	£	£
Variable	15.00	15.00	15.00
Fixed: £400,000/100,000	4.00		
Fixed: £400,000/150,000		2.67	
Fixed: £400,000/180,000			2.22
Full cost per unit	19.00	17.67	17.22
Sales price per unit	20.00	20.00	20.00
Unit profit, absorption costing	£1.00	£2.33	£2.78

There is a fall in the full production cost per unit as the activity level rises, because of the fixed costs being spread over a larger number of units. This also therefore means that there is a significant increase in profit per unit as the activity level increases.

However, the increase in profit is caused entirely by the increase in total contribution. Contribution per unit has remained constant. The profit increases by £250,000 between 100,000 units and 150,000 because sales are higher by 50,000 units and at contribution of £5 per unit, this means that profits are higher by £250,000. Similarly the increase in total profit by £150,000 between 150,000 units and 180000 units is due entirely to the increase in total contribution by £150,000 (= 30,000 units × £5 contribution per unit).

Analysing contribution helps us to understand changes in total profit when activity changes. This is a reason why, for decision making purposes, contribution per unit is a much more meaningful figure than profit per unit.

HOW IT WORKS

A company produces a single product at a variable cost per unit of £20. During the year the company expects to make 100,000 units, all of which can be sold to existing customers for £30 per unit. The total fixed costs for the period are expected to be £4 per unit.

(i) How much profit will the company make?

(ii) A customer has offered to buy an extra 5,000 units as a one-off order at a price of £23. Should the company accept (assuming it has spare capacity)?

(iii) What would the profit be if the company only made and sold 80,000 units? (Ignore the one-off order for this purpose.)

We shall take each point in turn.

(i) The full cost per unit is £20 + £4 = £24

The profit per unit is £30 − £24 = £6 per unit, so the total profit from 100,000 units is £600,000.

Another way of reaching the same result is as follows:

Contribution per unit = £30 – £20 = £10.

Total contribution = 100,000 units × £10 = £1,000,000.

Total fixed costs = 100,000 units × £4 = £400,000.

Therefore profit = £1,000,000 - £400,000 = £600,000.

(ii) The full absorption cost of the product is £24 so on the face of it at a selling price of £23 the product would make a loss. However, absorbed cost is misleading for decision-making purposes, and we should look at changes in total contribution (and any *changes* in *total* fixed costs).

The additional revenue and costs involved in the order are:

	£
Sales (5,000 × £23)	115,000
Variable costs (5,000 × £20)	100,000
Additional contribution	15,000

Since the fixed costs will be unchanged by the order, the company would increase profit by £15,000 by accepting the order. Unless there is any other reason why accepting the order might be undesirable, the company should accept the one-off order and increase profit by £15,000.

However the company would not want to accept £23 as a regular selling price in the long term for the units that it sells, because it needs to cover its fixed overhead costs.

Note: It is possible that the company might incur additional fixed costs relating specifically to the additional order, in which case these would need to be taken into account in determining whether or not to accept the order.

(iii) The profit from 80,000 units would not be 80,000 × £6 = £480,000. This is because if only 80,000 units are made (instead of 100,000 units) the fixed overhead per unit would increase from £4 to £5.

This is an important concept that you need to grasp. Questions may tell you the fixed cost **per unit** but don't let this confuse you. Fixed costs are a set **total** amount. Every time the level of activity changes, the fixed cost **per unit** also changes. You need to multiply the fixed cost per unit that you are given by the expected number of production units to obtain the **total fixed cost**. In this case, the expected total fixed costs are £400,000, as calculated earlier.

Spread over 80,000 units this gives a fixed cost of £5 per unit and a new profit per unit of £30 – £25 = £5.

Hence total profit from 80,000 units of sales would be 80,000 × £5 = £400,000.

An alternative (and easier) way of reaching the same conclusion is with marginal costing.

Contribution per unit = £30 – £20 = £10

Total contribution = 80,000 × £10 = £800,000, less fixed costs £400,000 = profit £400,000

Thus, for decision making purposes, you should always treat total profit as having two distinct elements:

1	Total contribution (= contribution per unit × units)	X
	Less	
2	Fixed costs	(X)
		X

Element **1** (total contribution) varies proportionately with volume, while element **2** (fixed costs) is a lump-sum period deduction.

As fixed costs in total are assumed to be constant for the period, whatever volume of products is made, the most amount of profit will be achieved if the amount of contribution is maximised. However, if total fixed costs change, the changes should be included in the analysis of the effect on profit.

COST-VOLUME-PROFIT ANALYSIS

COST-VOLUME-PROFIT ANALYSIS (CVP analysis) is a term for the analysis of the relationship between activity levels, costs and profit. It is based on contribution analysis. A common application of CVP analysis is BREAK-EVEN ANALYSIS to determine the break-even point for business operations.

The BREAK-EVEN POINT is the level of activity where the sales revenue is equal to the total costs of the business, meaning that all costs are covered by sales revenue but no profit is made. The business 'breaks even' and makes neither a profit nor a loss. This is an important point for managers of a business to be aware of, because if the activity level falls below the break-even point then there will be a loss. The breakeven volume of sales is the minimum amount of sales needed to avoid a loss.

So the break-even point activity level can be expressed as the point where:

Sales revenue = Variable costs + Fixed costs

We can re-arrange this simple formula to state that break-even is where:

Sales revenue – Variable costs = Fixed costs

Remember that sales revenue minus variable costs is equal to contribution. So the break-even point is where:

Total contribution = Fixed costs

Contribution per unit × Break-even point units = Fixed costs

We saw in an earlier example in this chapter that provided selling price and variable costs remain constant at different levels of activity, contribution per unit will also remain constant. We can therefore use this to calculate the break-even point.

$$\text{Break even point} = \frac{\text{Fixed costs}}{\text{Contribution per unit}}$$

The arithmetic is quite simple, but break-even analysis and CVP analysis have many useful applications.

HOW IT WORKS

Reardon Enterprises sells a single product with a selling price of £10 per unit. The variable costs of producing the product are £6 per unit and the total annual fixed costs of the business are £200,000.

What is the break-even point in units?

$$\text{Break-even point} = \frac{£200,000}{£10 - £6}$$

$$= 50,000 \text{ units}$$

We can prove that this is the point where no profit or loss is made:

	£
Sales (50,000 × £10)	500,000
Variable costs (50,000 × £6)	(300,000)
Contribution (50,000 × £4)	200,000
Fixed costs	(200,000)
Profit	0

Therefore the management of Reardon Enterprises know they must achieve a sales volume in excess of 50,000 units per annum in order for the business to cover its total costs and make any profit.

Task 1

A business has a single product that it sells for £28. The variable costs of producing the product are £19 per unit and the fixed costs of the business are £360,000.

What is the break-even point in units?

☐ units

Target profit

It is also possible to extend the CVP analysis using contribution per unit in order to determine the level of sales that is necessary in order not only to cover all of the costs but also to make a particular amount of profit, a 'target profit'.

Thus we want:

Total contribution	X
Less: fixed costs	(X)
Target profit	X

Total contribution = contribution per unit x target number of units (activity level)

This needs to cover fixed costs and generate the target profit.

Working back this gives us:

$$\text{Activity level} = \frac{\text{Fixed costs} + \text{target profit}}{\text{Contribution per unit}}$$

HOW IT WORKS

Returning to Reardon Enterprises the managing director, Anna Reardon, would like to ensure a profit of £100,000 for the coming year. What level of sales is required for this profit to be made?

$$\text{Activity level} = \frac{£200,000 + £100,000}{£10 - £6}$$
$$= 75,000 \text{ units}$$

Therefore if the business sells 75,000 units of the product a profit of £100,000 will be made. Again we can check this:

	£
Sales (75,000 × £10)	750,000
Variable costs (75,000 × £6)	(450,000)
Contribution	300,000
Fixed costs	(200,000)
Profit	100,000

Task 2

A business has fixed costs of £250,000. It sells just one product for a price of £80 and the variable costs of production are £60.

How many units of the product must be business sell in order to make a profit of £150,000?

| | units
|---|

Margin of safety

Another measure that might interest management is the MARGIN OF SAFETY.

(a) The budgeted margin of safety is the difference between budgeted sales and break-even sales. It may be measured in units, but is more commonly measured as a percentage of budgeted sales.

(b) The actual margin of safety is the difference between actual sales and break-even sales. It may be measured in units, but is more commonly measured as a percentage of actual sales.

(In your assessment, make sure you express the margin of safety as a percentage of the budgeted, forecast or actual sales, and **not** as a percentage of break-even sales.)

HOW IT WORKS

The break-even sales volume for a business is 50,000 units. If the budgeted sales for the forthcoming year is 70,000 units, what is the margin of safety?

Margin of safety   =   70,000 units – 50,000 units

=   20,000 units

This can be expressed as a percentage of budgeted sales, which should be used as the denominator in calculations.

$$\text{Margin of safety} = \frac{20,000}{70,000} \times 100$$

$$= 28.6\%$$

This tells management that sales can drop below the budgeted figure by 28.6% before losses are made.

Task 3

A business has budgeted to sell 75,000 units of its single product in the next year. The product sells for £32 and the variable costs of production are £24. The fixed overheads of the business are £480,000.

What is the margin of safety as a percentage?

☐ %

Contribution to sales ratio

When calculating the break-even point above, we used contribution per unit in the calculations. There is another method of calculating break-even or the sales volume needed to achieve a target profit. This method uses the CONTRIBUTION TO SALES (C/S) ratio. (This ratio can also be called the PROFIT VOLUME (P/V) ratio, but this term is a bit misleading. Contribution/sales ratio is a more exact and understandable term.)

$$\text{Contribution to sales ratio} = \frac{\text{Contribution}}{\text{Sales}} \times 100\%$$

Thus the C/S ratio measures contribution per £ sales revenue rather than contribution per sales unit.

Total contribution can be calculated as:

Total sales × Contribution/sales ratio.

Thus, at break-even sales revenue

Total contribution (C/S ratio × break-even sales revenue)	X
Less fixed costs	(X)
Profit	0

The break-even point in terms of sales revenue can be calculated as:

$$\text{Break-even point (in £ sales revenue)} = \frac{\text{Fixed costs}}{\text{C/S ratio}}$$

HOW IT WORKS

Reardon Enterprises sell their product for £10 and the variable costs are £6 per unit. Total fixed costs are £200,000.

$$\text{C/S ratio} = \frac{£10 - £6}{£10} \times 100$$

$$= 40\%$$

$$\text{Break-even point (£)} = \frac{200,000}{0.40}$$

$$= £500,000$$

(which corresponds to units of sales of $\frac{£500,000}{£10} = 50,000$, as before)

Task 4

A business has a single product that it sells for £36. The variable costs of producing the product are £27 per unit and the fixed costs of the business are £360,000.

What is the break-even point in terms of sales revenue?

£ [   ]

Contribution to sales ratio and target profit

The C/S ratio can also be used to calculate the sales revenue required to achieve a target profit.

Target profit + Fixed costs = Target contribution

$$\text{Sales revenue required} = \frac{\text{Target contribution}}{\text{C / S ratio}}$$

HOW IT WORKS

Reardon Enterprises sell their product for £10 and the variable costs are £6 per unit. Total fixed costs are £200,000 and the managing director wants to achieve profit of at least £450,000.

C/S ratio = £4/£10 = 40%

Target contribution = £200,000 + £450,000 = £650,000.

Sales required to achieve target profit = £650,000/40% = £1,625,000.

Proof:	£
Sales	1,625,000
Variable costs (60%)	(975,000)
Contribution (40%)	650,000
Fixed costs	(200,000)
Profit	450,000

Task 5

A business has a single product that it sells for £18. The variable costs of producing the product are £12 per unit and the annual fixed costs of the business are £1,000,000.

What sales revenue is required to achieve a profit of £500,000 for the year?

£ [   ]

LIMITING FACTOR ANALYSIS

Obviously the managers of a business will wish to produce and sell more than the break-even number of units in order to cover fixed costs. They should want to make a profit. As a basic assumption, we normally assume that a business should try to sell as much as it possibly can in order to maximise profits and available sales demand is the factor that sets a limit on the amount of sales and profits that can be achieved.

However, in practice sales, the amount of units that customers are prepared to buy may not be the factor that limits sales revenue and profits. The quantity that a business can produce and sell may be limited by one or more production factors, such as a limited amount of labour time available or a limited amount of machine time. When there is a limited supply of a production factor, we call it a LIMITING FACTOR.

The problem for management is then to decide how to use the limiting factor in the most profitable way. In other words, how do we maximise profit when there is a limited supply of labour, machine time or a key item of direct materials?

When the business makes just one product, the solution is straightforward. Profit is maximised by making and selling as many units of the products as possible with the available limited supply of the key production factor.

The solution is not quite as simple when the business makes and sells more than one product. The problem now is to decide how many units of each different product to make with the limited production resource available in order to maximise profit.

Profit is maximised in these circumstances by looking at the contribution that each different product earns per unit of the scarce production resource. In order to maximise profit, we **maximise the contribution earned per unit of limiting factor**.

HOW IT WORKS

A business sells a single product for £35. The variable costs of the product are:

    Direct materials   3 kg per unit @ £3 per kg

    Direct labour   2 hours per unit @ £7.50 per hour

The annual fixed costs of the business are £800,000.

Materials as limiting factor

Let's begin by assuming that direct materials are in limited supply. The business sells just one product, so in order to maximise profit, we should make as many units as possible with the limited supply of materials.

So if the annual supply of materials is limited to 360,000 kg, how many units can the business produce and how much profit will be made?

    Number of units that can be produced   = 360,000 kg/3 kg per unit
                                                 = 120,000 units

	£
Sales (120,000 × £35)	4,200,000
Variable costs (120,000 × (£9 + £15))	2,880,000
Contribution	1,320,000
Fixed costs	800,000
Profit	520,000

Labour hours as limiting factor

Let's now assume that direct labour time is a limiting factor. If materials are now not restricted, but the business only has 280,000 labour hours available for production, how many units can be made and what is the profit?

    Number of units that can be produced   = 280,000 hrs/2 hrs per unit
                                                 = 140,000 units

	£
Sales (140,000 × £35)	4,900,000
Variable costs (140,000 × £24)	3,360,000
Contribution	1,540,000
Fixed costs	800,000
Profit	740,000

More than one product

We will now make the position a bit more complicated by looking at a business that makes more than one product. If the availability of either materials or labour hours is a limiting factor, then it will be necessary to determine the optimum

production mix – which product or products should be made and sold in order to maximise profit?

Total fixed costs are assumed to be constant whatever combination of products is made. Profit is therefore maximised by maximising total contribution. Total contribution is maximised by maximising the contribution that is earned with each unit of the limiting production factor.

If a business has more than one product, and one limiting factor, the technique to use in order to maximise contribution is to determine the contribution per unit of the limiting factor (or scarce resource) and concentrate on making and selling the product with the highest contribution per unit of limiting factor.

HOW IT WORKS

Farnham Engineering makes three products A, B and C. The costs and selling prices of the three products are:

	A	B	C
	£	£	£
Direct materials @ £4 per kg	8	16	12
Direct labour @ £7 per hour	7	21	14
Variable overheads	3	9	6
Marginal cost	18	46	32
Selling price	22	54	39
Contribution per unit	4	8	7

Sales demand for the coming period is expected to be as follows:

Product A	3,000 units
Product B	7,000 units
Product C	5,000 units

The supply of materials is limited to 50,000 kg during the period and the labour hours available are 28,000.

Step 1 First, we have to decide if there is a limiting factor other than sales demand. There is a limit to the materials available and a limit to the number of labour hours. But do these limits prevent the business from meeting the available sales demand for the three products? Consider the materials usage for each product if the maximum sales demand is produced. (You are not given the actual usage of materials of each product but you can work it out – for example the materials cost for A is £8; as the materials are £4 per kg, product A must use 2 kg etc.)

	A	B	C	Total required
Materials (2/4/3kg)	6,000 kg	28,000 kg	15,000 kg	49,000 kg
Labour (1/3/2hrs)	3,000 hours	21,000 hours	10,000 hours	34,000 hours

50,000 kg of materials are available for the period and only 49,000 kg are required for the maximum production level. Materials are therefore not a limiting factor.

However, only 28,000 labour hours are available whereas 34,000 hours are required in order to produce enough output to meet the total sales demand. Therefore labour hours are a limiting factor.

Step 2 The next step is to calculate the contribution per limiting factor unit – in this case, the contribution per labour hour – for each product. We then rank the products in descending order of contribution per unit, giving top priority to the product that earns the most per direct labour hour and least priority to the product that earns the least contribution per labour hour.

	A	B	C
Contribution	£4	£8	£7
Labour hours per unit	1 hour	3 hours	2 hours
Contribution per labour hour:			
£4/1	£4.00		
£8/3		£2.67	
£7/2			£3.50
Ranking	1	3	2

Product A makes the most contribution per unit of limiting factor (labour hours) and therefore in order to maximise contribution, we must concentrate first on production of A up to its maximum sales demand, then on C, and finally, if there are any remaining hours available, on B.

The optimal production plan in order to maximise contribution is:

	Units produced	Labour hours required
A	3,000	3,000
C	5,000	10,000
		13,000
B (balance)	5,000*	15,000 (balancing figure)
		28,000

* **Working**: After making A and C there are 15,000 hours left. Each unit of B needs 3 hours so there is sufficient to make 15,000/3 = 5,000 units.

The contribution earned from this production plan is:

		£
A	(3,000 × £4)	12,000
B	(5,000 × £8)	40,000
C	(5,000 × £7)	35,000
Total contribution		87,000

Task 6

A business produces four products and the details are:

	P	Q	R	S
Contribution per unit	£12	£15	£9	£14
Materials per unit	3 kg	4 kg	1 kg	2 kg
Maximum sales demand (units)	2,000	6,000	1,000	4,000

Fixed costs amount to £30,000 each period, and the materials supply is limited to 30,000 kg.

(a) Complete the following table in order to determine the production plan that will maximise profit.

Product	Units produced

(b) The profit earned from this production plan will be

£ [   ]

MAKE OR BUY DECISIONS

A make or buy problem involves a decision by a business about whether it should make a product itself or whether it should pay another organisation to do so. Here are some examples of applications of make or buy decisions.

(a) Whether a company should manufacture its own components, or buy the components from an outside supplier.

(b) Whether a construction company should do some work with its own employees, or whether it should sub-contract the work to another company.

(c) Whether a service should be carried out by an internal department or whether an external organisation should be employed.

'Make or buy' decisions are therefore decisions about whether to 'outsource' production work to a sub-contractor.

Essentially the choice is between whether to do something in-house – 'make', or contract it out – 'buy'. The 'make' option should give management more direct control over the work, but the 'buy' option often has the benefit that the external organisation has a specialist skill and expertise in the work. Make or buy decisions should certainly not be based exclusively on cost considerations.

If an organisation has the freedom of choice about whether to make internally or buy externally and has no scarce resources that put a restriction on what it can do itself, the relevant costs for the decision will be the differential costs between the two options.

HOW IT WORKS

Shellfish Co makes four components, W, X, Y and Z, for which costs in the forthcoming year are expected to be as follows.

	W	X	Y	Z
Production (units)	1,000	2,000	4,000	3,000
Unit marginal costs	£	£	£	£
Direct materials	4	5	2	4
Direct labour	8	9	4	6
Variable production overheads	2	3	1	2
	14	17	7	12

Directly attributable fixed costs per annum and committed fixed costs:

	£
Incurred as a direct consequence of making W	1,000
Incurred as a direct consequence of making X	5,000
Incurred as a direct consequence of making Y	6,000
Incurred as a direct consequence of making Z	8,000
Other fixed costs (committed)	30,000
	50,000

A sub-contractor has offered to supply units of W, X, Y and Z for £12, £21, £10 and £14 respectively. Should Shellfish Co make or buy the components?

(a) The relevant costs are the differential costs between making and buying, and they consist of differences in unit variable costs plus differences in

directly attributable fixed costs. Sub-contracting will usually result in some directly attributable fixed costs being saved.

	W £	X £	Y £	Z £
Unit variable cost of making	14	17	7	12
Unit variable cost of buying	12	21	10	14
Differential variable cost	(2)	4	3	2
Annual requirements (units)	1,000	2,000	4,000	3,000

	W £	X £	Y £	Z £
Extra variable cost/(saving) of buying (per annum)	(2,000)	8,000	12,000	6,000
Fixed costs saved by buying	(1,000)	(5,000)	(6,000)	(8,000)
Extra total cost/(saving) of buying	(3,000)	3,000	6,000	(2,000)

(b) The company would save £3,000 each year by sub-contracting component W (where the purchase cost would be less than the marginal cost per unit to make internally) and would save £2,000 pa by sub-contracting component Z (because of the saving in fixed costs of £8,000). Financially it would not appear to be viable to sub-contract component X and Y, since this would increase costs.

(c) In this example, relevant costs are the variable costs of in-house manufacture, the variable costs of sub-contracted units, and the saving in fixed costs. Normally relevant costs are only variable costs but in instances like this, the savings in fixed costs must be taken into consideration as incremental costs as well. This is because they are incurred as a direct consequence of making the components.

(d) **Further considerations**

Other issues may need to be considered when reaching a make-or-buy decision.

(i) If components W and Z are sub-contracted, the company will have spare capacity. How should that spare capacity be profitably used? Are there hidden benefits/costs to be obtained from sub-contracting? Would the company's workforce resent the loss of work to an outside sub-contractor, and might such a decision cause an industrial dispute? Alternatively can the spare capacity created be used for productive and profitable purposes?

71

(ii) Would the sub-contractor be reliable with delivery times, and would it supply components of the same quality as those manufactured internally?

(iii) Does the company wish to be flexible and maintain better control over operations by making everything itself?

(iv) Are the estimates of fixed cost savings reliable? In the case of product W, buying is clearly cheaper than making in-house. In the case of product Z, the decision to buy rather than make would only be financially beneficial if it is feasible that the fixed cost savings of £8,000 will really be 'delivered' by management. All too often in practice, promised savings fail to materialise!

Task 7

A business produces three products with the following costs per unit:

	A £	B £	C £
Direct materials	1.60	2.00	0.80
Direct labour	3.20	3.60	1.60
Direct overheads	0.80	1.20	0.40
Fixed overheads	1.60	2.00	0.80

An external firm has offered to make these components and sell them to the company at the following prices:

A   £5.50
B   £8.40
C   £4.00

On the basis of cost alone which if any products should be purchased from the external firm?

A   A only
B   B only
C   C only
D   None of the products

CLOSURE OF A BUSINESS SEGMENT

'Shutdown' decisions are another type of decision that can be made with the same approach to analysing costs and profits.

Discontinuance or shutdown problems involve the following decisions:

(a) Whether or not to close down a product line, department or other activity, either because it is making losses or because it is too expensive to run.

(b) If the decision is to shut down, whether the closure should be permanent or temporary.

In practice, shutdown decisions may often involve longer-term considerations, and consideration of capital expenditures and revenues.

(a) A shutdown should result in savings in annual operating costs for a number of years into the future.

(b) Closure will probably release unwanted non-current assets for sale. Some assets might have a small scrap value, but other assets, in particular property, might have a substantial sale value.

(c) Employees affected by the closure must be made redundant or relocated, perhaps after retraining, or else offered early retirement. There will be lump sum payments involved which must be taken into account in the financial arithmetic. For example, suppose that the closure of a regional office would result in annual savings of £100,000, non-current assets could be sold off to earn income of £2 million, but redundancy payments would be £3 million. The shutdown decision would involve an assessment of the net capital cost of closure (£1 million) against the annual benefits (£100,000 pa).

It is possible, however, for shutdown problems to be simplified into short-run decisions, by making one of the following assumptions.

(a) Non-current asset sales and redundancy costs would be negligible.

(b) Income from non-current asset sales would match redundancy costs and so these capital items would be self-cancelling.

In such circumstances the financial aspect of shutdown decisions would be based on short-run relevant costs.

HOW IT WORKS

A company manufactures three products, Pawns, Rooks and Bishops. The present net annual income from these is as follows:

	Pawns £	Rooks £	Bishops £	Total £
Sales	50,000	40,000	60,000	150,000
Variable costs	30,000	25,000	35,000	90,000
Contribution	20,000	15,000	25,000	60,000
Fixed costs	17,000	18,000	20,000	55,000
Profit/loss	3,000	(3,000)	5,000	5,000

The company is concerned about its poor profit performance, and is considering whether or not to cease selling Rooks. It is felt that selling prices cannot be raised or lowered without adversely affecting net income. £5,000 of the fixed costs of Rooks are direct fixed costs which would be saved if production ceased (ie there are some attributable fixed costs). All other fixed costs, it is considered, would remain the same.

By stopping production of Rooks, the consequences would be a £10,000 fall in profits.

	£
Loss of contribution	(15,000)
Savings in fixed costs	5,000
Incremental loss	(10,000)

Suppose, however, it were possible to use the resources realised by stopping production of Rooks and switch to producing a new item, Crowners, which would sell for £50,000 and incur variable costs of £30,000 and extra direct fixed costs of £6,000. A new decision is now required.

	Rooks £	Crowners £
Sales	40,000	50,000
Less variable costs	25,000	30,000
	15,000	20,000
Less direct fixed costs	(5,000)	(6,000)
Contribution to shared fixed costs and profit	10,000	14,000

It would be more profitable to shut down production of Rooks and switch resources to making Crowners, in order to boost profits by £4,000.

Timing of shutdown

An organisation may also need to consider the most appropriate timing for a shutdown. Some costs may be avoidable in the long run but not in the short run. For example, office space may have been rented and three months' notice to

quit may be required. This cost is therefore unavoidable for three months. In the same way supply contracts may require notice of cancellation. A month-by-month analysis of when notice should be given and when savings will be made will help the decision making process.

Qualitative factors

With any business decision, the decision is not merely a matter of choosing the best financial option. Qualitative (non-financial) factors must always be taken into consideration.

(a) What impact will a shutdown decision have on employee morale?

(b) What signal will a shutdown decision give to competitors? How will they react?

(c) How will customers react? Will they lose confidence in the company's products?

(d) How will suppliers be affected? If one supplier suffers disproportionately there may be a loss of goodwill and damage to future relations.

Transferring production overseas

In some cases management of an organisation may be considering shutting its UK operations and transferring its production operations overseas. This may be the case if key resources such as materials and labour are significantly cheaper in the foreign country. The quantitative and qualitative factors to be taken into account will tend to be very similar to those for a closure of a business segment. However there will also be other issues which are specific to setting up operations in a foreign country including:

- Administrative/legal issues in setting up the operations

- The attitude of the host government to foreign investment

- The tax system in the country

- Transportation issues involved in getting the products to their final destination

Mechanisation decisions

In a similar way to decisions about closing a segment of the business, management may face a decision about changing the technology that is used in production. For example as technology plays a greater part in manufacturing, a business may be considering changing from a labour intensive production process to a machine intensive one.

There will be a number of aspects of costs that will need to be considered here:

- As with a closure of a business segment moving to a machine intensive production process will naturally mean a number of redundancy/early retirement costs.

- However the reduction in the labour force will create savings in short term direct labour costs.

- The investment in machinery will be very large and the methods of financing this investment should be considered.

- In a machine based environment, it is likely that overheads in general will be much higher including costs of machine maintenance, depreciation, power etc.

- Many of the additional overheads may be fixed overheads which may have an effect on the break-even point for the business. In order for the increased fixed overheads to be covered by contribution then more units may need to be sold. Break-even analysis may be needed to determine whether the business can sell enough products to cover the additional fixed costs.

- If the level of fixed costs in the business increases as a proportion of total cost, the profits of the business will become more sensitive to changes in sales volumes. This is because if the sales of a business fall and its costs are mainly variable, the reduction in sales will lead to a corresponding reduction in costs. However if a business has mainly fixed costs, when sales volumes fall, the cost base remains largely the same and as a result there is a bigger impact on profits.

- There will also be qualitative factors to take into consideration, including the effect on the morale of the remaining workforce and any environmental issues involved in the mechanisation process.

HOW IT WORKS

A business is considering the purchase of machines which would cost £475,000 per year to rent. The machine will allow the business to reduce the labour required to manufacture its product by 1.5 hours per unit. Currently the business makes and sells 4,000 units pa at £125 each and total annual fixed costs are £180,000.

The product's standard cost card shows the following variable costs:

		£
Direct material	3kg @ £5	15
Direct labour	6hrs @ £10	60
		75

Assuming the business continues to make and sell 4,000 units we will consider the impact the machine purchase will have on the break-even point, the margin of safety, the profit for the year and the ratio of fixed costs to total costs.

Currently:

Contribution per unit = £125 – £75 = £50

Break-even = £180,000/£50 per unit = 3,600 units.

Margin of safety = (4,000 – 3,600)/4,000 = 10%

Profit = (4,000 × £50) – £180,000 = £20,000

Fixed costs/Total costs = £180,000/(£180,000 + (4,000 @ £75)) = 37.5%

With machine:

The labour cost is now 4.5 hours @ £10 = £45

Contribution per unit becomes (£125 – £15 – £45) = £65

Fixed costs increase by £47,500 (rental costs) to £227,500 pa.

Break-even = £227,500/£65 per unit = 3,500 units.

Margin of safety = 4,000 – 3,500/4,000 = 12.5%

Profit = (4,000 × £65) – £227,500 = £32,500

Fixed costs/Total costs = 227,500/(227,500 + (4,000 @ £60)) = 48.7%

Here, the saving in direct labour (4,000 units at 1.5hrs × £10) £60,000 is greater than the increase in fixed costs due to the machine rental costs.

The break-even point is lower and the margin of safety is higher but the business becomes more risky due to the increased proportion of fixed costs. This is known as having higher 'operating gearing' or 'operational gearing'.

DISCOUNTED CASH FLOWS

So far in this chapter we have looked at short-term decision making. This is decision making where the financial benefits or costs or a decision can be assessed by looking at annual costs, or 'one off' short-term changes in cost.

With many decisions, the costs and benefits will occur over a much longer period of time, and may vary from one year to the next. For example, a decision whether or not to buy a new machine will involve a large capital expenditure 'now' but will provide benefits over the life of the machine.

Decisions that affect the long-term should take into consideration the time value of money. We usually do this by means of DISCOUNTED CASH FLOW analysis, or DCF analysis.

So what is the time value of money?

If we are offered £100 now or £100 in one year's time we are not comparing like with like. If interest rates are, say, 10% per annum then if the £100 received now were invested it would earn interest for a year at 10%. After one year we would have:

£100 × 1.10 = £110

Therefore we would definitely prefer the £100 now because it offers us an investment opportunity to earn £110 in one year's time.

Another way of looking at this is to say we would be indifferent between £100 now and £110 in one year's time. The value of £110 in one year has the same value as £100 now. So we can say that the 'present value' of £110 in one year's time is £100.

The present value of any cash flow in a future year is calculated by discounting the future cash flow by the interest that could be earned during the time between 'now' and the time that the future cash flow will occur.

The present value of a future cash flow is calculated by applying a discount factor to the cash flow. The discount factor can be calculated as:

$$\frac{1}{(1+r)^n}$$

where: $r =$ the periodic interest rate or discount rate (expressed as a decimal)

  $n =$ the number of periods before the cash flow occurs

Fortunately you do not need to remember the formula as there are present value tables which have calculated the discount factors for each time period and each discount rate. Note that the interest rate or discount rate is often referred to as the cost of capital.

HOW IT WORKS

A company is to invest in a project with an immediate cash outflow of £20,000. The receipts from this project are £10,000 in one year's time, £14,000 in two years' time and finally £6,000 in three years' time.

The interest rate applicable to the company is 8% and the discount factors at this rate are given below.

Period	Discount factor @ 8%
1	0.926
2	0.857
3	0.794

What is the present value of each of these cash flows?

Note that an immediate cash flow is taken as occurring at Time 0, a cash flow in one year's time as Time 1 etc. The discount factor for cash flows in Year 0 is always 1.000, whatever the cost of capital.

Time	Cash flow	Discount factor @ 8%	Present value
	£		£
0	(20,000)	1.000	(20,000)
1	10,000	0.926	9,260
2	14,000	0.857	11,998
3	6,000	0.794	4,764

Discounted cash flow and project appraisal

When we compute a present value, we are discounting a future cash flow to its present value equivalent. This is why the technique is called 'discounted cash flow'. We are finding the discounted present value of the cash flows in each future year that would occur as a consequence of the decision taken now.

The cash flows that are relevant to a capital expenditure decision are the future incremental cash flows that will arise as a result of the investment project that is being considered.

Note that for decision making we use cash flow and not profits. Investment is about spending cash and earning cash returns. Notional accounting costs such as depreciation are not cash flows and they should be ignored for decision-making. As a result, if you are given the expected profits from a capital investment project you will need to add back any depreciation in order to estimate the annual cash flows.

The financial impact of any investment decision must ALWAYS consider cash flows, not profits. There should never be any exception to this rule.

Discounted cash flow (DCF): net present value method

The most common method of discounted cash flow or DCF analysis is called the NET PRESENT VALUE method or NPV method. Using this method, we calculate the present value of the cash flow for each year of the investment project and then add them up. If there is a cash outflow in any year, this is a negative present

value. In a typical investment project, there is a cash outflow at the beginning of the project in Year 0, and then a series of net cash inflows in each subsequent year. The total of the present values of the cash inflows minus the present value of cash outflows is the project's net present value.

(a) If the net present value (NPV) is positive, then the project should be accepted because after taking having taken account of the time value of money, the value of the cash inflows from the project exceed the cash outflows.

(b) If however the net present value is a negative figure, then the project should be rejected. The future benefits do not justify the current capital spending in Year 0.

HOW IT WORKS

Returning to our previous example:

A company is to invest in a project with an immediate cash outflow of £20,000. The receipts from this project are £10,000 in one year's time, £14,000 in two years' time and finally £6,000 in three years' time.

The interest rate applicable to the company is 8% and the discount factors at this rate are given below.

Period	Discount factor 8%
1	0.926
2	0.857
3	0.794

What is the net present value of this project and should the company invest in it?

Here is the DCF analysis.

Time	Cash flow £	Discount factor	Present value £
0	(20,000)	1.000	(20,000)
1	10,000	0.926	9,260
2	14,000	0.857	11,998
3	6,000	0.794	4,764
Net present value			6,022

The project has a positive net present value and therefore the company should invest in it.

Note. A **convention in DCF analysis** is that if cash flows are earned throughout the course of a year, we assume that they occur at the end of the year. All cash flows occur at the end of the year.

So if we incur a cash expenditure 'now' at the beginning of the first year of a project, we assume that it happens at the end of Year 0. Any cash flow that will occur at the beginning of a year is assumed to occur at the end of the previous year. All other cash flows occur at the year-end.

Net present cost

In some instances you may be required just to calculate the present value of the costs of an operation or decision. This is done in exactly the same way as above but simply deals with costs rather than revenues. This technique is often used to calculate the life cycle cost of a machine that is regularly used by a business.

HOW IT WORKS

A company is to invest in a machine with an immediate cash outflow of £100,000. The machine will have annual running costs of £20,000 for the next three years paid in arrears. At the end of its three year life the machine will have an estimated residual value of £30,000.

The interest rate applicable to the company is 8% and the discount factors at this rate are given below.

Period	Discount factor @ 8%
1	0.926
2	0.857
3	0.794

What is the net present cost (life cycle cost) of this machine?

Time	Cash flow £	Discount factor @ 8%	Present value £
0	(100,000)	1.000	(100,000)
1	(20,000)	0.926	(18,520)
2	(20,000)	0.857	(17,140)
3 (30,000 – 20,000)	10,000	0.794	7,940
Net present cost			(127,720)

Net terminal value

The DCF method of analysing investment decisions brings all future cash flows down to a present value.

Another method of looking at the cash flows of projects, which produces the same investment decision, is to calculate the NET TERMINAL VALUE of a project. This is the value at the end of the project's life. Using net terminal value is much less common in practice than NPV, but you need to know what it is.

The terminal value method takes the cash flow in each year of a project and treats it as an investment earning interest each year at the cost of capital. Each annual cash flow is compounded at the cost of capital to measure what its investment value would be at the end of the project. The value of each cash flow at the end of the project life is its terminal value.

For example, suppose that £10,000 is received at the end of Year 1 for a three-period project with a discount rate of 10%.

The terminal value of this cash receipt is calculated by compounding the £10,000 at 10% per year to the end of project's life, which is the end of Year 3 (two years later). The terminal value would be £10,000 × 1.10 × 1.10 = £12,100. In other words, if the cash receipt of £10,000 at the end of Year 1 is invested for the remainder of the project life at 10% per year, then it would have a terminal value of £12,100.

The net terminal value of a project is calculated by adding the terminal values for all the years of the investment project. Years when there is a negative cash flow have a negative terminal value.

(a) If the net terminal value is positive, the project earns more than the cost of capital and should be accepted on financial considerations.

(b) If the net terminal value is negative, the project earns less than the cost of capital and should be rejected on financial considerations.

HOW IT WORKS

Returning to our previous example:

A company is to invest in a project with an immediate cash outflow of £20,000. The receipts from this project are £10,000 in one year's time, £14,000 in two years' time and finally £6,000 in three years' time.

The interest rate applicable to the company is 8%.

Calculate the net terminal value of the project.

This will involve calculating the terminal value (the value at the end of Year 3) of each individual cash inflow and then deducting the terminal value of the cash outflow.

			Terminal value at Time 3
Cash inflow at end of Year 1	£10,000 × 1.08 × 1.08	=	£11,664
Cash inflow at end of Year 2	£14,000 × 1.08	=	£15,120
Cash inflow at end of Year 3		=	£6,000
			£32,784
Less: initial outflow (£20,000 × 1.08 × 1.08 × 1.08)			(£25,194)
Net terminal value			£7,590

Task 8

A business is considering replacing one of its current machines with a new machine.

Using the table below, calculate the discounted life cycle cost of purchasing the machine based on the following:

- Purchase price £400,000

- Annual running costs of £45,000 for the next four years paid annually in arrears

- Residual value of £150,000 from selling the machine at the end of the four years

The discount factors at 5% are as follows:

Year 0	1.000
Year 1	0.952
Year 2	0.907
Year 3	0.864
Year 4	0.823

Year	0	1	2	3	4
Cash flow					
Discount factor					
Present value					
Net present cost					

CHAPTER OVERVIEW

- Due to the nature of fixed costs, total unit costs fall as activity levels increase. This is because the fixed costs are spread over more units of production

- However if selling price and variable costs remain constant then contribution per unit will remain constant as activity levels change

- As total fixed costs are assumed to be constant for the period, whatever the volume of production, profits are maximised by maximising contribution

- Therefore for 'short-run' decision making purposes we concentrate on marginal costing and contribution

- The break-even point in units is found by dividing the fixed costs by the contribution per unit

- If a target profit is required, the target contribution is the fixed costs plus the target profit. The unit sales to achieve this target profit can be found by dividing the fixed costs plus target profit (= target contribution) by the contribution per unit

- The difference between budgeted or actual sales and the break-even point is the margin of safety. This is often expressed as a percentage of budgeted sales or actual sales

- The contribution to sales ratio can be used to find the break-even point in terms of sales revenue:

  Break-even point (sales revenue £) = Fixed costs/C/S ratio

- Normally output in any period is limited by sales demand. However occasionally a factor of production such as the availability of material, labour hours or machine hours may be a limiting factor on output and profitability

- Where there is more than one product and a limiting factor, overall profit is maximised by concentrating production on the products with the highest contribution per limiting factor unit

- In a make or buy decision with no limiting factors, the relevant costs to consider are the differential costs between the two options, make in-house or buy externally ('outsource'). Typically the relevant costs are any variable costs incurred/saved as a result of the decision and any savings in attributable fixed costs

- Shutdown/discontinuance problems can be simplified into short-run relevant cost decisions

- Whether or not to move from a labour intensive production process to a machine intensive production process will also have many short and some long term effects
- Discounted cash flow is used in decision making for long-term investment decisions, to take account of the time value of money
- Time value of money recognises that £1 today is worth more than £1 at a future time, because money can be reinvested to earn more money over time

Keywords

Contribution – sales revenue less variable costs

Cost-volume-profit analysis – analysis of the relationships between activity levels, costs and profits using marginal costing

Break-even analysis – calculations to determine the break-even point

Break-even point – level of sales where sales revenue and total costs are equal, so that there is no profit and no loss

Margin of safety – excess of budgeted sales or actual sales over the break-even point sales, which may be measured as a percentage of budgeted or actual sales

Contribution to sales (C/S) ratio – ratio of contribution to sales revenue

Profit volume (P/V) ratio – alternative name for the contribution to sales ratio

Limiting factor – a factor of that limits the amount of a product that can be produced or sold: it is often sales demand but may be a production factor in limited supply

Net present value – the net total of the present values of a set of annual cash flows for an investment project

Net terminal value – the value of all cash flows for an investment project as though invested until the end of the project

TEST YOUR LEARNING

Test 1

If selling prices and variable costs remain constant at differing levels of activity, explain why unit cost will tend to fall as activity levels increase.

Test 2

A business making a single product has budgeted sales of 38,000 units. The selling price per unit is £57 and the variable costs per unit of production are £45. The fixed costs of the business are £360,000.

The break-even point is [   ] units

The margin of safety is [   ] %

Test 3

A business has fixed costs of £910,000. It sells a single product at a selling price of £24 and the variable costs of production and sales are £17 per unit.

How many units of the product must the business sell in order to make a profit of £500,000?

71,428 units [ ]

82,941 units [ ]

130,000 units [ ]

201,429 units [ ]

Test 4

A business sells its single product for £40. The variable costs of this product total £32 per unit. The fixed costs of the business are £100,000.

The sales revenue required in order to make a profit of £200,000 is

£ [   ]

Test 5

A business produces three products, the production and sales details of which are given below:

	Product		
	R	S	T
Direct materials @ £2 per kg	£16	£12	£10
Direct labour @ £9 per hour	£18	£36	£9
Selling price	£40	£60	£25
Machine hours per unit	6	4	3
Maximum sales demand	10,000 units	20,000 units	5,000 units

During the next period the supply of materials is limited to 250,000 kgs, the labour hours available are 120,000 and the machine hours available are also 120,000. Fixed costs are £50,000 per period.

(a) The limiting factor of production resources is materials/labour hours/machine hours. Select the appropriate answer.

(b) Complete the following table to show the production plan which will maximise profit.

Product	Units produced

(c) The profit that will be earned under this production plan is £ ☐

Test 6

A business has two products, X and Y, with the following costs per unit.

	X Cost per unit	Y Cost per unit
	£	£
Direct materials	2.50	3.00
Direct labour	8.00	6.00
Fixed overheads	3.00	1.50

The business could buy in X from an external supplier at a cost £ 11 per unit, and it could buy in Y at £10 per unit, but this would not save any fixed overheads.

On the basis of cost alone which if any products should be bought in?

Both X and Y ☐

X only ☐

Y only ☐

Neither X nor Y ☐

Test 7

A business is considering investment in new machinery at a cost of £340,000 on 1 April 20X4. This machinery will be used to produce a new product which will give rise to the following net cash inflows:

31 March 20X5	£80,000
31 March 20X6	£70,000
31 March 20X7	£90,000
31 March 20X8	£120,000
31 March 20X9	£60,000

The new machinery is to be depreciated at 20% per annum on cost. The cost of capital is 7%.

Complete the table below to calculate the net present value of this project.

Year	Cash flows £	Discount factor at 7%	Present value £
0		1.000	
1		0.935	
2		0.873	
3		0.816	
4		0.763	
5		0.713	
Net present value			

Test 8

A business is considering investment in new plant and machinery on 1 January 20X6 at a cost of £90,000. The company has a cost of capital of 11%. The cash cost savings are estimated to be:

31 December 20X6	£23,000
31 December 20X7	£31,000
31 December 20X8	£40,000
31 December 20X9	£18,000

(a) Complete the table below to determine the net present value of this project.

Year	Cash flows £	Discount factor at 11%	Present value £
0		1.000	
1		0.901	
2		0.812	
3		0.731	
4		0.659	
Net present value			

(b) Advise the business as to whether it should invest in the new plant and machinery and justify your advice.

chapter 4:
STATISTICAL METHODS

chapter coverage 📖

In this chapter we will look at some basic statistical methods that you may need to use for this unit.

The topics that are to be covered are:

- ✍ Predicting future costs and revenues from historical data
- ✍ Time series analysis
- ✍ Additive model
- ✍ Trend and seasonal variations
- ✍ Index numbers
- ✍ Linear regression

PREDICTING FUTURE COSTS AND REVENUES FROM HISTORICAL DATA

A business may collect data about its previous activities, costs and sales revenues and use it to estimate future levels of activity, costs or sales. This chapter considers a number of statistical techniques that can be used in this way to produce forecasts from historical data.

By analysing historical information, a business may be able to make valid predictions about the future. Sometimes a sample of historical data is used, because of the time and effort involved in examining all the available historical data. In order to provide a reasonable estimate, the sample of data on which such forecasts are made needs to be as representative as possible.

Techniques can be used to adjust the data for seasonal variations (time series) and also for changes in price levels (indexing).

TIME SERIES ANALYSIS

If we have collected data about costs or income over a number of time periods, such as sales revenue or production costs, this is known as a time series. Such historical data may be used as a basis for forecasting future values. For example, historical data about sales revenue may be used to prepare a forecast of future sales. One of the key elements of information that management might look for in a time series is an indication of the TREND. The trend is a feel for how the figure in question is changing over time – is it increasing or is it decreasing and is the rate of increase or decrease rapid or slow?

The techniques for determining the trend and other underlying components of a time series of figures are known as TIME SERIES ANALYSIS.

Elements of a time series

When considering results or costs over time there are four main elements that are likely to influence the figures:

- **Trend**

    The trend is the underlying movement of the figures over time. For example, sales may be erratic from month to month but in general terms there may be a gradual rising trend.

- **Cyclical variations**

    Most economies tend to have cycles between periods of growth and periods of recession. Economic cycles typically take place over a seven to nine year period. Such long term economic cycles may cause alterations in the pattern of actual results over time, such as the volume of sales. Changes in results caused by changes in the economic cycle are called CYCLICAL VARIATIONS. If the economy is growing then sales are likely increase more rapidly but if the economy is in recession then sales growth may slow down or even go into decline.

- **Seasonal variations**

    Most businesses experience some fluctuations up and down due to the seasonality of their business. This does not necessarily mean the actual seasons, summer, winter etc but some regular cycles for the particular business, repeated within a time frame of less than a year. These cycles are known as SEASONAL VARIATIONS. For example, a restaurant that is open six nights a week, Monday to Saturday, may experience peak numbers of customers on Friday and Saturday nights with lows on Monday and Tuesday.

- **Random variations**

    The actual results over time will also be influenced by random factors. For example in a manufacturing business if 30% of the workforce is affected by flu over a two week period then production will probably drop during this time. These RANDOM VARIATIONS are totally unpredictable.

Task 1

What is the difference between a cyclical variation and a seasonal variation?

TREND ONLY

For the purpose of your assessment, you may be given a time series where there is a linear trend, and no seasonal variation or other type of variation. When the historical trend shows that the value of an item is increasing in a linear trend, you can assume that the same linear trend will continue in the future. In this way, you can make a forecast of what the value of the item will be at a future time.

HOW IT WORKS

Suppose that the historical cost of an item has been as follows:

Date	Cost
	£
January	1,367.82
February	1,525.46
March	1,683.10

What should be the forecast cost of the item in June, three months later?

The first step in producing a forecast is to measure the historical increase in cost each month from January to March.

Date	Cost	Cost increase
	£	£
January	1,367.82	-
February	1,525.46	157.64
March	1,683.10	157.64

The historical costs show a rising linear trend in cost of £157.64 per month. If we assume that this trend will continue in the future, the forecast of cost in June is (in £):

1,683.64 + (3 × 157.64) = 2,156.02

ADDITIVE MODEL

In practice, a simple linear trend is unusual. The trend may not be exactly linear, and there may be seasonal and other variations. Under the additive model of time series analysis, it is assumed that the actual figure for each period of a time series is made up of the trend, the cyclical variation, the seasonal variation and any random variation added together. This can be expressed as follows:

Actual figure = T + C + S + R

where:

T	=	The underlying trend
C	=	The cyclical variation
S	=	The seasonal variation
R	=	The random variation

You do not have to be concerned about calculations involving cyclical variation or random variation. You only need to concern yourself with the underlying trend and seasonal variations above or below this trend. Therefore we are left with the simpler expression:

Actual figure = T + S

Note. There is also another model that can used in time series analysis, the multiplicative model. However the multiplicative model is not relevant for this syllabus and we shall concentrate on the additive model.

TREND AND SEASONAL VARIATIONS

A trend is an underlying movement in the value of an item over time, ignoring seasonal variations.

A simple way of detecting the trend from historical observations over time is to take averages over each seasonal cycle. If these averages change over time then there is evidence of a trend in the series.

Thus the technique that will be used is to take the actual figures from the time series and from these, determine the trend using a technique of moving averages.

Once the trend in a value is calculated as a moving average, the trend value for each time period can be compared to the actual figure. The difference between the trend value and the actual value is the seasonal variation.

Since: Actual figure = T + S

   Actual figure – T = S

We will look at the calculation of a trend first, and then go on to consider seasonal variations later.

Moving averages to calculate a trend

The technique of calculating a MOVING AVERAGE is a key tool in time series analysis. There are three elements to calculating a moving average.

(a)   We calculate the average value of an item, such as average daily sales, over a number of time periods. If there are seasonal variations, we calculate an average over one cycle of values, such as the average of daily sales for a week.

(b)   The average is associated with the middle of the time period. For example, if we calculate average daily sales over a five day week starting on Monday and ending on Friday, the average is associated with the Wednesday, which is the middle of the five-day period.

(c)   Moving averages are averages calculated in this way for each day (or week or month, etc) over a longer period of time. For example, having calculated an average of daily sales from Monday to Friday in Week 1 and attributing this average to Wednesday of Week 1, we next calculate the average daily sales for Tuesday to Friday in Week 1 and Monday in Week 2, and attribute this average to Thursday of Week 1. Then we calculate the average daily sales for Wednesday to Friday in Week 1 and Monday/Tuesday in Week 2, and attribute this average to Friday of Week 1. In this way we can build up a trend of moving averages over time.

Moving averages are a trend of averages for each successive unit of time (each day, or week or month etc) over a long period of time.

HOW IT WORKS

Suppose that the sales figures for a business for the first six months of the year are as follows:

	£
January	33,000
February	39,000
March	36,000
April	44,000
May	35,000
June	49,000

It is decided to calculate a moving average trend line of monthly sales, using moving averages for three months. We begin with the average monthly sales for the period January to March.

$$\frac{33,000 + 39,000 + 36,000}{3} = £36,000$$

This average is associated with February.

Then we move on one month, and the average for February, March and April sales are calculated:

$$\frac{39,000 + 36,000 + 44,000}{3} = £39,667$$

This average is associated with March.

Then the average for March, April and May, which is associated with April:

$$\frac{36,000 + 44,000 + 35,000}{3} = £38,333$$

Then finally the average for April, May and June, which is associated with May:

$$\frac{44,000 + 35,000 + 49,000}{3} = £42,667$$

Now we can show these moving averages together with the original figures.

	Actual data £	Moving average £
January	33,000	
February	39,000	36,000
March	36,000	39,667
April	44,000	38,333
May	35,000	42,667
June	49,000	

Task 2

Given below are the production costs for a factory for a six month period.

Complete the table to show the three month moving average for these figures.

Month	Actual £	Three month moving average £
March	226,504	
April	251,600	
May	238,200	
June	247,600	
July	240,500	
August	262,800	

Centred moving averages

The trend for a time series is the trend in the moving averages for a time series. However, if the number of time periods used to calculate each average value is an even number, such as the four quarters of the year, then there is a further calculation to make – the CENTRED MOVING AVERAGE. The reason for this is that if the moving average is based on an even number of periods, then there is no central time period to place the moving average against – a further average, the centred average, is required in order to find the trend.

For example, if we calculate the average quarterly sales in a time series, the average quarterly sales for the four quarters of Year 1 will be associated with Quarter 2½. The next moving average would be the average for quarters 2 – 4 in Year 1 and Quarter 1 of Year 2: this will be associated with Quarter 3½ of Year 1. We need to calculate the average of the moving averages for Quarter 2½ and Quarter 3½ to obtain a moving average (trend line) value for quarter 3.

HOW IT WORKS

The quarterly sales figures for Wrigley Partners for the last three years are given below:

			£
20X6	Quarter 1		88,900
	Quarter 2		100,300
	Quarter 3		63,800
	Quarter 4		75,200

		£
20X7	Quarter 1	91,600
	Quarter 2	103,700
	Quarter 3	66,100
	Quarter 4	76,400
20X8	Quarter 1	95,400
	Quarter 2	106,000
	Quarter 3	68,800
	Quarter 4	77,100

By inspection, it would appear the sales figures exhibit seasonal variations over the four quarters of the year, for example Quarter 2 is always the highest and Quarter 3 the lowest. In order to find the trend of the time series a four quarterly centred moving average must first be calculated. Start with the four quarterly moving average:

First average: $\dfrac{88,900+100,300+63,800+75,200}{4} = 82,050$

Second average: $\dfrac{100,300+63,800+75,200+91,600}{4} = 82,725$

and so on.

		ACTUAL	Moving average
		£	£
20X6	Quarter 1	88,900	
	Quarter 2	100,300	
			82,050
	Quarter 3	63,800	
			82,725
	Quarter 4	75,200	
			83,575
20X7	Quarter 1	91,600	
			84,150
	Quarter 2	103,700	
			84,450
	Quarter 3	66,100	
			85,400
	Quarter 4	76,400	
			85,975
20X8	Quarter 1	95,400	
			86,650
	Quarter 2	106,000	
			86,825
	Quarter 3	68,800	
	Quarter 4	77,100	

As the moving average being calculated is an even number, a four quarter moving average, then it is shown in between the second and third quarter for each quarterly average – the middle of the four quarters.

In order to obtain a trend line the centred moving average must now be calculated. To do this we take each consecutive pair of moving average figures and in turn average them and showing them against the third quarter.

First average:
$$\frac{82,050+82,725}{2} = 82,388$$

Second average:
$$\frac{82,825+83,575}{2} = 83,150$$

and so on.

		ACTUAL £	Moving average £	Centred moving average TREND £
20X6	Quarter 1	88,900		
	Quarter 2	100,300		
			82,050	
	Quarter 3	63,800		82,388
			82,725	
	Quarter 4	75,200		83,150
			83,575	
20X7	Quarter 1	91,600		83,863
			84,150	
	Quarter 2	103,700		84,300
			84,450	
	Quarter 3	66,100		84,925
			85,400	
	Quarter 4	76,400		85,688
			85,975	
20X8	Quarter 1	95,400		86,313
			86,650	
	Quarter 2	106,000		86,738
			86,825	
	Quarter 3	68,800		
	Quarter 4	77,100		

Calculating seasonal variations

Having calculated a trend line, we can measure seasonal variations above or below the trend. Remember that the relationship between the actual figures, the trend and the seasonal variation in our simplified model is:

Actual figure – Trend = Seasonal variation

We now include a final column in our table to show the seasonal variation for each quarter that can be directly compared to the trend. The seasonal variation is negative when the actual value is less than the trend line value. It is positive when the actual value is more than the trend line value.

For example, the centred moving average (the trend) for 20X6 Quarter 3 is 82,388 but the actual observation for the same period is 63,800. The difference, which is due to seasonal variation, is – 18,588 (63,800 – 82,388).

			Moving average	Centred moving average	Seasonal variation
		ACTUAL		TREND	ACTUAL-TREND
		£	£	£	£
20X6	Quarter 1	88,900			
	Quarter 2	100,300			
			82,050		
	Quarter 3	63,800		82,388	–18,588
			82,725		
	Quarter 4	75,200		83,150	–7,950
			83,575		
20X7	Quarter 1	91,600		83,863	+7,737
			84,150		
	Quarter 2	103,700		84,300	+19,400
			84,450		
	Quarter 3	66,100		84,925	–18,825
			85,400		
	Quarter 4	76,400		85,688	–9,288
			85,975		
20X8	Quarter 1	95,400		86,313	+9,087
			86,650		
	Quarter 2	106,000		86,738	+19,262
			86,825		
	Quarter 3	68,800			
	Quarter 4	77,100			

We should expect the seasonal variation to be positive or negative for the same season in each cycle. In this example, the seasonal variation is negative in Quarters 1 and 2 each year, and positive in Quarters 3 and 4 each year.

The next stage is to find an average seasonal variation for each quarter, to get a representative seasonal variation for forecasting purposes. This is done by grouping the seasonal variations together, by quarter, in a table:

	Quarter 1	Quarter 2	Quarter 3	Quarter 4
20X6	–	–	–18,588	–7,950
20X7	+7,737	+19,400	–18,825	–9,288
20X8	+ 9,087	+ 19,262	–	–
Total	+ 16,824	+ 38,662	– 37,413	– 17,238
Average = total/2	+8,412	+19,331	–18,707	–8,619

Seasonal variations above and below the trend line should, by definition, add up to 0 over each cycle, if we assume that each seasonal variation is a constant value over every cycle.

The next stage is therefore to ensure that the total seasonal variations add up to zero. In our example, they do not, and we have an imbalance of + 417 in the seasonal variations:

+ 8,412 + 19,331 – 18,707 – 8,619 = +417

To reduce this to 0 we must make a minor adjustment to each of the seasonal variations by dividing the difference by 4:

417/4 = +104 (rounded)

Since we are trying to get rid of a positive imbalance, we deduct this figure from each of the seasonal variations we calculated from the trend line and actual figures.

	Quarter 1 £	Quarter 2 £	Quarter 3 £	Quarter 4 £
Unadjusted seasonal variation	+8,412	+19,331	–18,707	–8,619
Adjustment	–104	–104	–104	–105
Adjusted seasonal variation	+8,308	+19,227	–18,811	– 8,724

Here we have deducted 105 from Quarter 4, because we must reduce seasonal variations to 0, but it would be just as acceptable to deduct 105 instead of 104 from any one of the other Quarters. The essential requirement is that the seasonal variations must add up to 0.

We now have seasonal variations that total to zero:

+ 8,308 + 19,227 – 18,811 – 8,724 = 0

Task 3

Given below are the annual sales figures for a business for the last eight years. Complete the table to calculate a four-year moving average and trend using the centred moving average.

	Actual £	Four year moving average £	Centred moving average = trend £
20X1	226,700		
20X2	236,500		
20X3	240,300		
20X4	242,500		
20X5	240,100		
20X6	245,600		
20X7	247,600		
20X8	248,200		

Graphing the time series and trend

Let's return to our previous example. Wrigley Partners, at this stage it might be useful to draw the actual figures and the trend line onto a graph of the time series. When drawing a graph of a time series the time scale is always shown on the horizontal x axis and the figures on the vertical y axis.

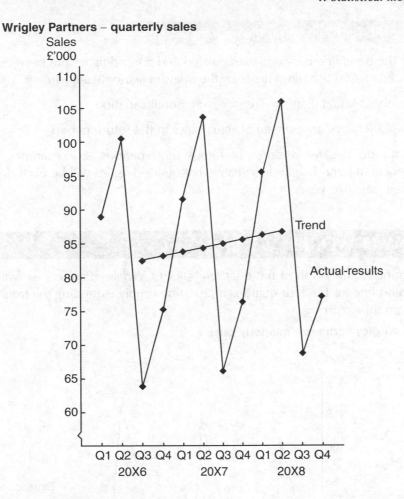

Wrigley Partners – quarterly sales

Using the trend to make forecasts

As you can see in the graph, the sales of Wrigley Partners are irregular – quite high in Quarters one and two, low in Quarter three and higher again in Quarter 4 (but still below the trend line). This is known as a seasonal business.

The trend line, taken from the centred moving averages, smoothes out the seasonal elements and shows how the sales are generally increasing over the three years.

We can use a trend line of historical figures to make a forecast for the future.

In this example of Wrigley Partners, the trend line can be extended into the future and the likely trend value of sales in future periods can be read off from the graph as estimates. This process of estimating a future figure from a trend line on a graph is known as EXTRAPOLATION.

Using the seasonal variations in forecasting

Once the trend line has been extrapolated and a trend figure has been estimated, we should adjust the trend figure by the relevant seasonal adjustment.

Remember: Actual figure = Trend +/– Seasonal variation

This will then give an estimate of actual sales in the future period.

We can do this for a series of future time periods. For example, we can extrapolate a trend line and estimate what quarterly sales will be each quarter for the next, say, two years.

HOW IT WORKS

Returning to the graph of the quarterly sales of Wrigley Partners we will extend the trend line for the four quarters in 20X9 by simply extending the trend line by hand on the graph.

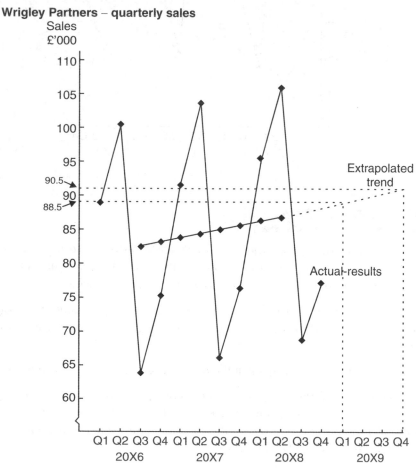

Wrigley Partners – quarterly sales

BPP
LEARNING MEDIA

Once the trend line has been extended the estimated trend figures can then be read off from the graph. (This will be easier if the graph is drawn on graph paper.):

20X9	Quarter 1	£88,500
	Quarter 2	£89,200
	Quarter 3	£89,900
	Quarter 4	£90,500

These figures however are not the expected sales for each quarter but the expected trend figure for each quarter. Quarters 1 and 2 are seasonally higher than the trend and Quarters 3 and 4 lower. Therefore we must apply the seasonal variation to the expected trend in order to produce the forecast sales figure.

		Trend	Seasonal variation	Forecast sales
		£	£	£
20X9	Quarter 1	88,500	+8,308	96,808
	Quarter 2	89,200	+19,227	108,427
	Quarter 3	89,900	−18,811	71,089
	Quarter 4	90,500	−8,724	81,776

Task 4

A manufacturing business has used its production costs for the last two years to identify a trend and monthly seasonal variations. Extrapolating the trend line has produced estimates of the trend in costs for the months of January to March 20X9, and time series analysis has provided monthly seasonal variations.

	Estimated trend	Seasonal variations
	£	£
January	205,600	+23,200
February	208,600	+9,230
March	209,200	−3,500

Complete the table to calculate the anticipated production costs for January to March 20X9.

Month	Cost £
January	
February	
March	

INDEX NUMBERS

We have seen how we can estimate how a time series of values is changing over time by plotting a trend line. Another simple and convenient method of measuring a trend is to convert the actual historical figures to a series of INDEX NUMBERS.

Index numbers measure the change in value of a figure over time, by reference to its value at a fixed starting point in time.

This is done by selecting a BASE PERIOD. The value for this base period is given an index value of 100. The value for each subsequent time period is then converted into an index value using the following formula:

$$\text{Index} = \frac{\text{Current period's figure}}{\text{Base period figure}} \times 100$$

HOW IT WORKS

The sales figures for a business for the first six months of the year are as follows:

	£
January	136,000
February	148,000
March	140,000
April	130,000
May	138,000
June	145,000

We will set the January figure as the base period, with an index of 100.

This means that the index for February is calculated as:

$$\frac{\text{Current period's figure}}{\text{Base period figure}} \times 100 = \frac{148,000}{136,000} \times 100 \qquad = 109$$

The index for March is:

$$\frac{140,000}{136,00} \times 100 \qquad = 103$$

The index for April is:

$$\frac{130,000}{136,000} \times 100 \qquad = 96$$

The index for May is:

$$\frac{138,000}{136,000} \times 100 \qquad = 101$$

The index for June is:

$$\frac{145,000}{136,000} \times 100 \qquad = 107$$

Interpreting an index

If the index for a period is greater than 100, this means that the current period figure is larger than the base period figure and if it is less than 100, the figure is lower than the base period figure. If the index figures are rising over time this means that the underlying values are also increasing. If the index is falling, the underlying values are also falling.

Remember when interpreting an index that it represents the current period figure compared to the base period, not compared to the previous period. For example, if the base period is January Year 1 and the index for January Year 5 is 150, this means that the value of the underlying item has risen by 50 index points (= 50%) between the base period January Year 1 and January Year 5.

HOW IT WORKS

We can show the actual sales together with the index for the previous example.

	£	Index
January	136,000	100
February	148,000	109
March	140,000	103
April	130,000	96
May	138,000	101
June	145,000	107

The index shows that although sales start to increase in February, they then fall again with April being lower than January. However by June the sales are again increasing, almost to the February level.

Task 5

The profit of a business for the last eight quarters is given below. Complete the table below to show the index for the profit figures using Quarter 1 20X7 as the base period. Give your answers to one decimal place.

		Profit £	Index
20X7	Quarter 1	86,700	
	Quarter 2	88,200	
	Quarter 3	93,400	
	Quarter 4	90,500	
20X8	Quarter 1	83,200	
	Quarter 2	81,400	
	Quarter 3	83,200	
	Quarter 4	85,000	

Retail prices index

The Retail Prices Index (RPI) is a measure of general price changes for retail goods in the UK. It is published each month by the government's statistics department and it provides a good indication of the general level of inflation in the economy. Since December 2003 the government has also used the Consumer Prices Index (CPI) to measure inflation in the economy.

A business can use the RPI (or CPI) to determine the extent to which its income and its costs have changed in line with general inflation.

HOW IT WORKS

A business has had the following sales for the last eight years:

	£
20X1	513,600
20X2	516,300
20X3	518,400
20X4	522,400
20X5	530,400
20X6	535,200
20X7	549,800
20X8	558,700

If we use 20X1 as the base year and then index the sales figures on that basis, the index will be as follows:

		Index
20X1	100.0	
20X2	516,300/513,600 × 100	100.5
20X3	518,400/513,600 × 100	100.9
20X4	522,400/513,600 × 100	101.7
20X5	530,400/513,600 × 100	103.3
20X6	535,200/513,600 × 100	104.2
20X7	549,800/513,600 × 100	107.0
20X8	558,700/513,600 × 100	108.8

This index shows a small but steady increase in annual sales revenue over the years. But is this due to an increase in sales volume, or simply the effects of inflation increasing the selling price?

We can consider the general increases in prices over the period by looking at the average Retail Prices Index (RPI) for each of the years:

	RPI
20X1	140.7
20X2	144.1
20X3	149.1
20X4	152.7
20X5	157.5
20X6	162.9
20X7	165.4
20X8	170.2

We apply the RPI to the annual sales figures in order to show the RPI adjusted figures. This is done by using the following formula:

$$\text{Sales for current year} \times \frac{\text{RPI for year 1}}{\text{RPI for current year}}$$

20X1	Adjusted sales figure	=	513,600 × 140.7/140.7	=	£513,600
20X2	Adjusted sales figure	=	516,300 × 140.7/144.1	=	£504,118
20X3	Adjusted sales figure	=	518,400 × 140.7/149.1	=	£489,194

and so on:

	Sales £	Adjusted sales £
20X1	513,600	513,600
20X2	516,300	504,118
20X3	518,400	489,194
20X4	522,400	481,347
20X5	530,400	473,824
20X6	535,200	462,263
20X7	549,800	467,696
20X8	558,700	461,863

In 'real' terms, i.e. without inflationary effects, sales have fallen. This could be due to:

- Falling sales volumes
- Selling prices failing to keep up with general inflation

or a combination of these.

What has been done here is to turn each period's actual sales values into a value at 20X1 price levels, to 'compare like with like' in real terms. The analysis in this example shows that annual sales in real terms have fallen over the time period under review.

We can now calculate an index based upon these price-adjusted sales figure which shows a very different picture from the earlier index:

20X2   Amended index   =   504,118/513,600 × 100   =   98.2

and so on:

	Sales £	Adjusted sales (20X1 price levels) £	Index
20X1	513,600	513,600	100.0
20X2	516,300	504,118	98.2
20X3	518,400	489,194	95.2
20X4	522,400	481,347	93.7
20X5	530,400	473,824	92.3
20X6	535,200	462,263	90.0
20X7	549,800	467,696	91.1
20X8	558,700	461,863	89.9

This shows that the sales for the last eight years have in fact dramatically failed to keep up with the general rise in prices, as shown by the sales index adjusted for changes in the RPI.

Task 6

Given below are the monthly production costs for a business for the last year, together with the Retail Prices Index for each month. Complete the table to show the adjusted production cost figures for the year based on the Retail Prices Index, in terms of June 20X7 prices.

		Costs £	RPI	Restated costs £
20X7	June	133,100	171.1	
	July	133,800	170.5	
	Aug	133,600	170.8	
	Sept	134,600	171.7	
	Oct	135,800	171.6	
	Nov	135,100	172.1	
	Dec	135,600	172.1	
20X8	Jan	134,700	171.1	
	Feb	135,900	172.0	
	Mar	136,200	172.2	
	April	136,500	173.1	
	May	136,700	174.2	

Restating costs and income in current prices

In the previous example we took a series of sales figures and restated them in terms of prices prevailing in the earliest year of the time series. Another way of using the Retail Prices Index is to re-state earlier period's figures in terms of today's prices. In other words, instead of adjusting values to the price level at Index = 100, we can adjust historical values to today's prices.

HOW IT WORKS

We will use the figures for sales which have been used earlier:

	£
20X1	513,600
20X2	516,300
20X3	518,400
20X4	522,400
20X5	530,400
20X6	535,200
20X7	549,800
20X8	558,700

The average Retail Prices Index for each of these years was:

	RPI
20X1	140.7
20X2	144.1
20X3	149.1
20X4	152.7
20X5	157.5
20X6	162.9
20X7	165.4
20X8	170.2

In order to restate the sales in terms of year 20X8 prices the following formula is applied:

$$\text{Sales in current year} \times \frac{\text{RPI for 20X8}}{\text{RPI for the current year}}$$

The restated figures would appear as follows:

	Actual £	In year 20X8 prices £
20X1	513,600 × 170.2/140.7	621,284
20X2	516,300 × 170.2/144.1	609,814
20X3	518,400 × 170.2/149.1	591,762
20X4	522,400 × 170.2/152.7	582,269
20X5	530,400 × 170.2/157.5	573,169
20X6	535,200 × 170.2/162.9	559,184
20X7	549,800 × 170.2/165.4	565,756
20X8	558,700 × 170.2/170.2	558,700

We have now shown each year's sales in terms of year 20X8 prices. Again this shows that in real terms annual sales have decreased over the period.

Task 7

Given below are the monthly production costs for a business for the last year, together with the Retail Price Index for each month. Complete the table to show the adjusted production cost figures for the year based upon the Retail Prices Index, in terms of May 20X8 prices.

		Costs £	RPI	Restated costs £
20X7	June	133,100	171.1	
	July	133,800	170.5	
	Aug	133,600	170.8	
	Sept	134,600	171.7	
	Oct	135,800	171.6	
	Nov	135,100	172.1	
	Dec	135,600	172.1	
20X8	Jan	134,700	171.1	
	Feb	135,900	172.0	
	Mar	136,200	172.2	
	April	136,500	173.1	
	May	136,700	174.2	

LINEAR REGRESSION

Another technique that can be used in forecasting is LINEAR REGRESSION analysis. Linear regression analysis involves the prediction of the value of one variable, for example total cost, given the value of another variable, such as the volume of output, on the assumption that there is a linear relationship (straight line on a graph) between the two variables.

The equation of a straight line

Given below is a straight line drawn on to a graph

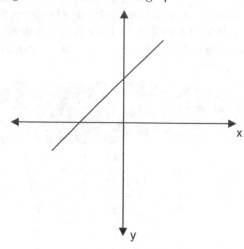

Any such straight line will have a defining equation in the following form:

$$y = a + bx$$

Both a and b are constants and represent specific figures:

- a is the point on the graph where the line intersects the y axis
- b represents the gradient of the line (how steep it is)

We can now show a and b on the previous graph.

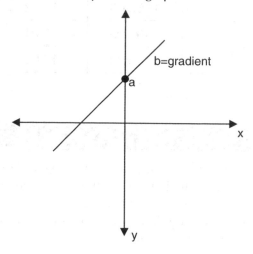

Using the equation of a straight line

The straight line drawn on the graphs above should remind you of two other straight line graphs that you have met earlier:

- The graph of a semi-variable cost
- The graph of a linear trend in a time series analysis

We can therefore use the equation for a straight line, or LINEAR REGRESSION EQUATION, in two possible ways in forecasting:

- To forecast the amount of a semi-variable cost at a given production level. In the linear equation $y = a + bx$:

  a = Fixed costs

  b= Variable cost per unit

  y = Total cost

  x = Number of units of activity or output

- To forecast future sales volumes or sales revenue using the linear regression equation as the equation for the trend line in sales. In the linear equation $y = a + bx$:

  y − Total sales

  x = The time period in the time series (for example, the year number)

  b = The increase in sales each time period (for example, each year)

  a = A constant value, which has no specific meaning

In assessments you will not be required to derive the linear regression equation for a straight line. Either you will be given this equation and asked to find values of x and y, or you will be given values of x and y and asked to determine the values of a and b. However some care must be taken with what the variables x and y, and the constants a and b represent.

Dependent and independent variables

Given the equation of a straight line: $y = a + bx$:

- y is always the DEPENDENT VARIABLE

  (plotted on the vertical axis)

  The dependent variable is the variable whose value depends on the value of the independent variable x

- x is always the INDEPENDENT VARIABLE

  (plotted on the horizontal axis)

The dependent variable y can be calculated using the linear regression equation, provided that a value is known for the independent variable x.

HOW IT WORKS

(a) A linear regression equation expresses the relationship between the costs of producing a product and the quantity of production.

Which is the dependent variable and which the independent variable?

The cost of production is the dependent variable as this will depend upon the quantity produced. Therefore x represents the quantity of production and y represents the costs of production.

(b) A linear regression equation expresses the trend line for a time series of sales volumes.

Which is the dependent variable and which the independent variable?

The volume of sales depends on the time period in which the sales were made, so volume is represented by y and time is represented on the x axis. (Note, time is ALWAYS an independent variable!).

Task 8

A linear regression equation expresses the relationship between advertising costs and sales volume. Which is the dependent variable and which is the independent variable?

If we have established, using linear regression analysis, that total costs each month are (in £):

$550,000 + 20x$

where x = the number of direct labour hours worked, then we can calculate the expected monthly costs when:

(a) 10,000 direct labour hours are worked

(b) 12,000 direct labour hours are worked

When 10,000 direct labour hours are worked, total costs (in £)

$= 550,000 + (20 \times 10,000) = 750,000$

When 10,000 direct labour hours are worked, total costs (in £)

$= 550,000 + (20 \times 12,000) = 790,000$

Similarly, if we have estimated that annual sales will be (in £) $800,000 + 25,000x$

where x is the year and 20X2 is Year 1, then we can forecast sales in 20X7 and 20X8.

In 20X7 (= Year 6), forecast sales = 800,000 + (6 × 25,000) = 950,000

In 20X8 (= Year 7), forecast sales = 800,000 + (7 × 25,000) = 975,000

HOW IT WORKS

The linear regression equation for the canteen costs (y) of a business for a month is as follows:

$$y = 20,000 + 45x$$

The variable x represents the number of employees using the canteen – the independent variable.

It is anticipated that the number of employees using the canteen in the next three months will be as follows:

	Number of employees
January	840
February	900
March	875

What are the forecast canteen costs for each period?

		£
January	20,000 + (45 × 840)	57,800
February	20,000 + (45 × 900)	60,500
March	20,000 + (45 × 875)	59,375

Task 9

The linear regression equation for production costs (y) for a business is:

$$y = 63,000 + 3.20\,x$$

If production is expected to be 44,000 units in the next quarter, what are the anticipated production costs?

£ [   ]

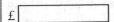

Determining x in a linear regression equation

Instead of calculating the value of y given values for a, b and x, we can calculate a value for x given values for a, b and y.

HOW IT WORKS

A business has been monitoring its monthly production costs and next year budgeted production costs are £2,500,000. Budgeted annual fixed costs are £1,600,000 and the variable costs are £12 per direct labour hour.

How many direct labour hours are budgeted next year?

Since we know total costs and fixed costs, we can calculate budgeted variable costs.

	£
Budgeted total costs	2,500,000
Budgeted fixed costs	1,600,000
Budgeted total variable costs	900,000

We know the variable cost per direct labour hour (£12), so we can calculate the budgeted number of direct labour hours as:

£900,000/£12 per direct labour hour = 75,000 direct labour hours.

Determining a and b in a linear regression equation

If you are given a number of figures for x and y, then it is possible to draw the linear regression line on a graph and determine the amounts represented by a and b. Alternatively, you can calculate x and y using the high-low method.

HOW IT WORKS

A business has been monitoring its monthly production costs and has discovered the following:

- If production is 2,000 units then the cost of production is £7,000

- If production is 3,000 units then the cost of production is £9,000

If we assume that this relationship is linear, then the quantity of production will represent x and the cost of production will represent y. We can now plot these figures on a graph with the quantity of production on the x axis and the cost of production on the y axis.

- The first point to plot is where x = 2,000 units of production and y = production costs of £7,000

- The second point to plot is where x = 3,000 units of production and y = production costs of £9,000

Once these two points have been plotted, then a line can be joined between them.

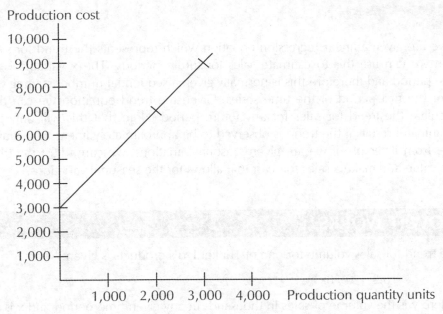

We can now easily read off the graph the figure for a in the linear regression equation. This is the point where the regression line meets the y axis, so in this case £3,000.

The figure for b requires a little more thought. This is the gradient of the line. We can see from our two points plotted that the cost of production increases by £2,000 (from £7,000 to £9,000) with a 1,000 unit increase in production (2,000 to 3,000). Therefore for every 1,000 increase in units there is £2,000 increase in costs giving a gradient of 2,000/1,000 = 2, therefore the figure for b is 2.

A graph does not have to be used to find a and b. **We can use the high-low method**.

	Output units	Cost £
High	3,000	9,000
Low	2,000	7,000
Difference (variable costs)	1,000	2,000

So variable cost per unit = £2,000/1,000 = £2 per unit.

Substitute this value in either High or Low figures. Here the High figures are used:

	£
Total cost of 3,000 units	9,000
Variable cost of 3,000 units (× £2)	6,000
Difference = Fixed costs (variable costs)	3,000

So fixed costs are £3,000 and variable costs are £2 per unit.

Forecasting sales

If we are given a linear regression equation which represents the trend for sales, then we can use this to estimate sales for future periods. The x variable is the time period and therefore this is normally given a sequential number starting with 1 for the first period of the time series. Given the trend equation we can then calculate the trend for sales for any future period. Note that this will only give meaningful results if the trend is observed to be approximately linear, ie a straight line, from its graph. If we are given seasonal variations, we can adjust the trend line value and make a sales forecast that allows for the seasonal variations.

HOW IT WORKS

The trend for sales volume for one of Trinket Ltd's products is given:

$$y = 16.5 + 0.78x$$

Where y is the volume of sales in thousands in any given time period and x is the time period.

The time series is based on quarterly sales volumes starting in Quarter 1 of 20X1.

The seasonal variations for each quarter are:

Quarter 1	−2,660
Quarter 2	+4,250
Quarter 3	+2,130
Quarter 4	−3,720

Estimate the sales volume for each quarter of 20X4.

Step 1   Find the values of x for the four quarters in 20X4.

Q1	20X1	x = 1
Q2	20X1	x = 2
Q3	20X1	x = 3
Q4	20X1	x = 4
Q1	20X2	x = 5

and so on until

Q1	20X4	x = 13

Step 2   Calculate the trend for each quarter before seasonal adjustments using the linear regression equation.

20X4	x value	y = 16.5 + 0.78 x ('000 units)
Q1	13	26.64
Q2	14	27.42
Q3	15	28.20
Q4	16	28.98

Step 3   Adjust the trend figures for the seasonal variations to find the seasonally adjusted sales volume.

Quarter	Trend ('000 units)	Seasonal adjustment volume (units)	Seasonally adjusted sales (units)
Q1	26.64	−2,660	23,980
Q2	27.42	+4,250	31,670
Q3	28.20	+2,130	30,330
Q4	28.98	−3,720	25,260

Interpolation and extrapolation

We need to remember that interpolation, an estimation within the historical range, is more reliable than extrapolation, an estimation beyond the historical range.

When using linear regression analysis to estimate future sales from a trend line, this is **always extrapolation** and this means that there is an underlying assumption that the current trend will continue into the future.

Task 10

The linear regression equation for the trend of sales in thousands of units based upon time series analysis of the monthly figures for the last two years is:

$y = 4.8 + 1.2x$

What is the estimated sales trend for each of the first three months of next year?

Month 1 [   ]

Month 2 [   ]

Month 3 [   ]

CHAPTER OVERVIEW

- A series of cost or income data collected over a number of periods, such as sales revenue or production costs, is known as a time series. Such historical data may be used as a basis for forecasting future values

- The four elements that make up the actual figures in a time series are the trend, cyclical variations, seasonal variations and random variations

- The additive model for time series is that the actual figure is made up of the trend plus the cyclical variation plus the seasonal variation plus the random variation – for this Unit only the trend and seasonal variation need be considered, so Actual figure = T + S

- The trend is found by calculating a moving average for actual historical figures. If the moving averages are calculated from an even number of time periods, then the trend line is found by calculating a centred moving average

- The seasonal variation for each period is calculated as the actual figure minus the trend – the average seasonal variation is then found for each period and adjustments are made to ensure that the total seasonal variation adds up to zero

- The actual figures and the trend can be plotted on a time series graph with the time scale always shown on the horizontal axis

- Forecasts of future figures can be found by extending the trend line on the graph, reading off the estimated trend figure for the future period and then adjusting for the seasonal variation in that future period

- Another fairly simple method of showing whether income or expenditure has increased or decreased is to calculate an index. This is done by comparing each period's figures with those of the designated base period – the base period has an index of 100 and the index value for each period relates to the base index value of 100

- If the index for a period is above 100 then the income or expense is greater than the base period, but if it is below 100 then it is lower than in the base period – a rising index shows growth in the figures and a falling index indicates decline

- The Retail Prices Index can be used to determine whether income or costs have changed in line with general changes in inflation by adjusting each period's figures for changes in the RPI

- The RPI can be used to adjust historical values to the same cost or price level. Figures can be converted to values as at the base date (index = 100 costs or prices) or prices based on the current year (or any year in between for that matter). The resulting trend in 'real values' will always be the same

- Regression analysis involves the prediction of one variable eg cost, from another variable eg volume of output, on the assumption that there is a linear relationship between the two variables

- Linear regression analysis can be used to estimate either semi-variable costs at a particular activity level or future sales volumes at a particular point in time, based on the assumption of a linear trend in sales

- The linear regression line, $y = a + bx$, will always be given to you in an assessment and you will not need to derive it. However care should be taken with the variables x and y: x is always the independent variable and y is the dependent variable

- You may also need to calculate y given values for a, b and x, or a value for x given values for a, b and y. You may also be required to apply the high low method to calculate values for a and b given two pairs of values for x and y

Keywords

Time series – a series of income or expense figures recorded for a number of consecutive periods

Trend – the underlying movements of the time series over the period

Time series analysis – a method of calculating the trend and other relevant figures for a time series

Cyclical variations – the effect on figures due to long term economic cycles

Seasonal variations – the regular short-term pattern of increases or decreases in figures that repeats regularly due to the nature of the business

Random variations – the effects on the figures due to totally random events or circumstances

Moving average – the calculation of an average figure for the results of consecutive periods of time

Centred moving average – the average of two consecutive moving averages when the period for the moving average is an even number

Extrapolation – estimation of a future figure outside the range of data previously observed eg predicting future sales from a line on a graph

Index number – conversion of actual figures compared to a base period where the base year period is expressed as 100

Base period – the period for which the index is expressed as 100 and against which all other period figures are compared

Retail Prices Index (RPI) – a measure of general price changes, which is published each month by the government

Linear regression – a technique for forecasting semi-variable costs or future sales using the equation for a straight line

Linear regression equation $y = a + bx$

where: a is the point on the graph where the line intersects the y axis

           b is the gradient of the line

Dependent variable – y is always the dependent variable

Independent variable – x is always in the independent variable

TEST YOUR LEARNING

Test 1

Given below are the production cost figures for a business for the last year. Complete the table to calculate a three month moving average for these figures.

	Actual £	Three month moving average £
July	397,500	
August	403,800	
September	399,600	
October	405,300	
November	406,100	
December	408,500	
January	407,900	
February	410,400	
March	416,000	
April	413,100	
May	417,500	
June	421,800	

Test 2

Given below are the quarterly sales figures for a business for the last three and a half years. Complete the table to calculate a four quarter moving average, the trend using a centred moving average and the seasonal variations. Then adjust the seasonal variations as necessary.

		Actual	Four quarter moving average	Centred moving average = TREND	Seasonal variations
		£	£	£	£
20X5	Quarter 1	383,600			
	Quarter 2	387,600			
	Quarter 3	361,800			
	Quarter 4	328,600			
20X6	Quarter 1	385,900			
	Quarter 2	392,400			
	Quarter 3	352,500			
	Quarter 4	338,800			
20X7	Quarter 1	392,500			
	Quarter 2	410,300			
	Quarter 3	368,900			

		Actual	Four quarter moving average	Centred moving average = TREND	Seasonal variations
		£	£	£	£
	Quarter 4	344,400			
20X8	Quarter 1	398,300			
	Quarter 2	425,600			

Seasonal variations:

	Quarter 1 £	Quarter 2 £	Quarter 3 £	Quarter 4 £
20X5				
20X6				
20X7				
Average				
Adjustment required				

	Quarter 1 £	Quarter 2 £	Quarter 3 £	Quarter 4 £
Unadjusted				
Adjustment				
Seasonal variation				

Test 3

Given below are the direct materials costs of business operations for the last six months. Complete the table to calculate the index for each month's costs using January as the base month. Give your answers to one decimal place.

	Cost £	Index
January	59,700	
February	62,300	
March	56,900	
April	60,400	
May	62,400	
June	66,700	

Test 4

(a) Given below are the wages costs of a business for the last six months together with the Retail Prices Index for those months. Complete the table to calculate the RPI adjusted wages cost figures for each of the six months, with all costs expressed in terms of June prices.

	Wages cost £	RPI	Adjusted cost £
January	126,700	171.1	
February	129,700	172.0	
March	130,400	172.2	
April	131,600	173.0	
May	130,500	172.1	
June	131,600	171.3	

(b) Using the adjusted RPI wages costs complete the table to calculate an index for the wages costs for each month with January as the base year.

	Adjusted cost £	Index
January		
February		
March		
April		
May		
June		

Test 5

The total production costs of a business are £15,000 if 1,000 units are produced, and £25,000 if 2,000 units are produced. The linear regression equation

y = a + bx

can be used to forecast the production costs where y is the total production cost and x is volume of production. Calculate a and b, and then the production costs if 1,400 units are produced.

Test 6

The linear regression equation for costs of the stores department of a business is given as follows:

y = 13,000 + 0.8x

where x is the number of units produced in a period.

The anticipated production levels for the next six months are given below. Complete the table to calculate the forecast stores department costs for the next six months.

	Production Units	Costs £
January	5,400	
February	5,600	
March	5,700	
April	6,000	
May	5,500	
June	6,100	

Test 7

A time series analysis of sales volumes each quarter for the last three years, 20X6 to 20X8, has revealed that the trend can be estimated by the equation:

y = 2,200 + 45x

Where y is the sales volume and x is the time period.

The seasonal variations for each quarter have been calculated as:

Quarter 1   −200
Quarter 2   +500
Quarter 3   +350
Quarter 4   −650

Use the table below to estimate the sales volume for each quarter of 20X9.

	Value of x	Trend	Seasonal variation	Forecast sales
Quarter 1 20X9				
Quarter 2 20X9				
Quarter 3 20X9				
Quarter 4 20X9				

chapter 5:
STANDARD COSTING

chapter coverage 📖

In this chapter we will introduce the important concept of standard costing. We will look at how standards are developed and their uses in a management control system. We will then move on to the calculation of all of the basic variances, before considering further aspects of calculating variances in the next chapter.

The topics that are to be covered are:

- ✍ Introduction to standard costing systems
- ✍ How standard costs are set
- ✍ Types of standard
- ✍ Calculating variances
- ✍ Direct materials variances
- ✍ Direct labour variances
- ✍ Variable overhead variances
- ✍ Fixed overhead variances
- ✍ Fixed overhead efficiency and capacity variances
- ✍ Fixed overhead variances – absorption costing
- ✍ Reconciliation of total standard cost to total actual cost: standard absorption costing
- ✍ Deriving actual data from standard cost details and variances
- ✍ Marginal costing variances
- ✍ Standard cost bookkeeping

INTRODUCTION TO STANDARD COSTING SYSTEMS

A STANDARD COSTING SYSTEM is one in which a business produces a limited number of standard products. Every unit of a standard product is expected to use the same quantity of direct materials and requires the same amount of time to make. This expected cost or standard cost of each unit of standard product is set out in a standard cost card.

The actual costs of units produced are compared in detail with the standard cost and the differences between actual and standard costs are reported as VARIANCES. Variance reports can be used by management to help them run the business efficiently.

There are several aspects to standard costing and variances.

- Setting the standards – see below

- Calculating the variances – we will concentrate on this aspect in this chapter

- Interpreting the variances – this will be considered in the next chapter

- Reporting variances to management and management action – again this will be considered in the next chapter

Uses of a standard costing system

Many manufacturing organisations and some service industries make use of standard costing systems, as they can help management in a variety of different ways and can provide management with information to aid their tasks of planning, decision making and controlling the business operations.

- The standard quantities of materials and labour required for production, and variable overhead costs, can be useful when planning future operations and setting cost budgets.

- The standard costs of production can be useful for decision making – for example in comparing the costs of two similar products or setting selling prices.

- Standard costing variances aid control by analysing in detail the reasons for differences between actual costs and standard or expected costs. The variances between actual costs and standard costs can provide management with information about areas of the business which require monitoring or where some remedial action should be taken.

Introduction to variances

The variances to be calculated for this Unit are set out in the diagram below:

Summary of variances: standard absorption costing

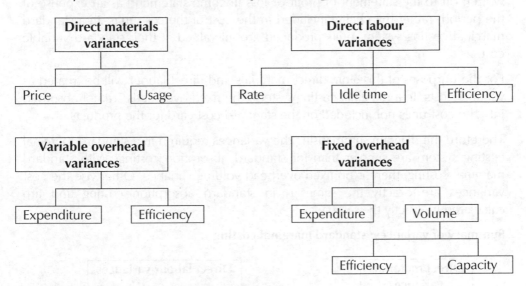

Absorption costing and standard costs

In a system of absorption costing the overheads of the business are absorbed into the cost units on the basis of a pre-determined overhead absorption rate. The cost of the unit of production is a 'full' cost including its share of production overheads. Absorption costing and marginal costing were explained in Chapter 2.

In standard costing, every unit produced is recorded in the cost accounting system at its standard cost per unit. So if the standard cost of a product is £10, every unit produced will be recorded in the cost accounting system at £10.

Standard costing may be based on either absorption costing or marginal costing. If it is based on absorption costing, there will be under- or over-absorbed overheads, and the under- or over-absorbed overhead is analysed as fixed overhead variances.

Marginal costing and standard costs

In a marginal costing accounting system the cost of cost units is made up of their variable costs only. The fixed overheads are treated as period costs and are written off to the statement of profit or loss (income statement) as an expense of the period, rather than being included in the cost of the cost units. In a standard marginal costing system, units produced are all valued at their standard variable cost.

For the purposes of this Unit, direct materials and direct labour will be treated as variable costs. In a marginal costing system, the fixed overheads are not absorbed into the cost units nor included on the standard cost card for the products.

Therefore the diagram summarising the variances required in a standard marginal costing system are simpler than for standard absorption costing. With standard marginal costing, there is no fixed overhead volume variance. Otherwise the cost variances are exactly the same as in standard absorption costing and are calculated in exactly the same way.

Summary of variances: standard marginal costing

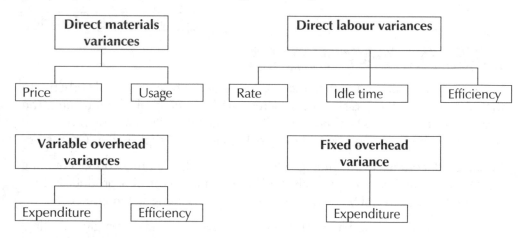

HOW STANDARD COSTS ARE SET

Standard costs

A standard cost is the planned unit cost of a standard product or service. This is usually recorded in a standard cost card.

A standard cost card shows full details of the standard cost of each product. An example is shown below.

STANDARD COST CARD – PRODUCT 1234

	£	£
Direct materials		
Material X – 3 kg at £4 per kg	12	
Material Y – 9 litres at £2 per litre	18	
		30
Direct labour		
Grade A – 6 hours at £7 per hour	42	
Grade B – 8 hours at £8 per hour	64	
		106
Standard prime cost		136
Variable production overhead: 14 hours at £0.50 per hour		7
Standard marginal cost		143
Fixed production overhead – 14 hours at £4.50 per hour		63
Standard full production cost		206

Notice how the total standard cost is built up from standards for each cost element: standard quantities of materials at standard prices, standard quantities of labour time at standard rates and so on. It is therefore determined by management's estimates of the following.

- The expected prices of materials, labour and expenses
- Efficiency levels in the use of materials and labour
- Budgeted overhead costs and budgeted volumes of activity

We will now think about how each of the standard costs on the standard cost card are set.

Direct materials standard cost

The standard cost for the direct materials in a product is made up of two elements:

- The expected or standard amount of material for one unit
- The price of the material per unit of material (per kg, litre etc)

The amount of material required for each unit of a product can be found from the original product specification – the amount originally considered necessary for each unit.

This figure may however be amended over time as the actual amount used in production is monitored.

The basic price of the material can be found from suppliers' quotations or invoices. However when setting the standard, the following should also be taken into account:

- General inflation rates

- Any foreseen increases in the price of this particular material

- Any seasonality in the price

- Any discounts available for bulk purchases

- Any anticipated scarcity of the material which may mean paying a higher price

A standard product may contain several different direct materials.

Direct labour standard cost

The standard cost of the direct labour for a product will be made up of:

- The expected or standard amount of labour time to make each unit of the product
- The hourly wage rate for the employees working on the product

The information for the amount of labour time for each unit may come from time sheets, clock cards, computerised recording systems on the machines being used or from formal observations of the operations, known as work study or more commonly a 'time and motion' study. Factors that should be taken into account when setting the standard for the amount of labour time include:

- The level of skill or training of the labour used on the product
- Any anticipated changes in the grade of labour used on the product
- Any anticipated changes in work methods or productivity levels
- The effect on productivity of any bonus scheme to be introduced

The hourly rate for the direct labour used on the product can be found from the payroll records. However consideration should be given to:

- Anticipated pay rises

- Any anticipated changes of the grade of labour to be used

- The effect of any bonus scheme on the labour rate

- Whether any overtime is anticipated and whether the premium should be built into the hourly rate

A product may be worked on by different types of worker who are paid a different rate per hour. A standard cost may therefore include more than one 'grade' of direct labour employee.

Variable production overhead standard cost

There may be variable production overhead in the standard cost. (Alternatively, all overheads may be fixed costs and there are no variable production overheads.)

When there are variable production overheads, it is usually assumed that variable overhead costs vary with the number of direct labour hours worked (excluding hours recorded as idle time).

Fixed production overhead standard cost

In standard absorption costing there is a standard fixed overhead cost per unit. An overhead absorption rate is calculated from the budgeted figures for fixed overhead expenditure and budgeted activity. This is usually an absorption rate per direct labour hour, but it may possibly be a machine hour absorption rate.

The standard fixed overhead cost per unit is derived as:

Standard direct labour hours per unit × Absorption rate per direct labour hour

So the estimate of the standard fixed overhead cost per unit depends on budgeted estimates of:

- Number of units produced
- Total direct labour hours (or direct machine hours)
- Labour hours (or machine hours) per unit

The information for determining the total budgeted fixed overhead will come from bills or invoices for past periods plus any anticipated price changes, either based upon specific indices or a general measure of inflation such as the Retail Prices Index.

TYPES OF STANDARD

There are different approaches to establishing a standard cost. The approach that is selected will affect the standard costs themselves and also the variances between actual costs and standard costs.

Ideal standards

IDEAL STANDARDS are standard costs that are set on the basis that ideal working conditions apply. Therefore there is no allowance for wastage, inefficiencies or idle time when setting the materials and labour cost standards.

There are two main problems with ideal standards:

Planning – If ideal standards are used for planning purposes, it is likely that the plans will be inaccurate and unreliable, because the standard does not reflect the current reality of the working conditions. Therefore if a labour cost standard is set with no allowance for any inefficiency or idle time in the operations, the reality is that the operations will take longer or will require more employees than the standard amount. For this reason, ideal standard costs should not be used for planning.

Control – If ideal standards are compared with actual costs, there will always be adverse variances, because actual levels of efficiency and spending will never be 'ideal' and there will be some inefficiencies and wastage. This can demotivate managers and employees who will feel that the standards can never be met and therefore they may stop trying to meet them. A further problem with the reported adverse variances is that they may be considered 'normal' and 'only to be expected' so that management do not see any reason to take corrective action on the basis of variance reports.

Target standards

TARGET STANDARDS (sometimes called attainable standards) are standards that are more efficient than the level of performance that is currently achieved. It contains some element of 'improvement' - greater efficiency, or lower prices or less spending; but the improvements are considered achievable and reasonable to expect. Target standards allow for some wastage and inefficiency; so they are not 'ideal'. Although a target standard is one that is achievable, it will only be met if operations are carried out efficiently and cost-effectively.

If target standards are well set, then the variances that result should be a mixture of favourable and adverse variances, since sometimes the standard will be exceeded and sometimes it will not quite be met. Target standards may be considered as motivating for managers and employees. The standards are not out of reach in the way that ideal standards are, and they can be met if all goes to plan.

Normal standards

NORMAL STANDARDS (sometimes called current standards) are standards based on **current working conditions** (allowing for current levels of wastage and current inefficiencies). The main disadvantage of normal standards is that they do not attempt to improve on current levels of efficiency. Standards set are on a short term basis and frequent revisions may be necessary.

Basic standards

BASIC STANDARDS are unusual in practice. They are a historical standard cost, probably set when the product was first produced. As such, they are likely to be out of date, as they will not have taken account of inflation or any changes in working practices.

If basic standards are used to compare to actual costs, then this will tend to result in large variances, both adverse and favourable, depending upon how out of date the basic standard is. These variances will therefore be little more than meaningless. For this reason basic standards are rarely used for variance analysis but may still be kept as historical information alongside other more up-to-date standards.

Variances calculated with a basic standard may show by how much operations have improved in terms of efficiency and cost since the standard cost was first established.

Task 1

What are the potential problems with using ideal standards to calculate variances?

CALCULATING VARIANCES

You need to be able to calculate all the variances shown earlier and each of the variances will now be explained in detail.

It may help to remember that variances for variable cost items – direct materials, direct labour and variable production overheads – are all calculated in a similar way. Fixed overhead variances, however, are different.

Variances are either favourable or adverse (unfavourable).

(a)   A FAVOURABLE VARIANCE is usually shown as a value followed by (F). This indicates that actual costs or performance were more favourable than the standard. For example, the actual time to complete the units produced might be less than the standard expected time for their production.

(b)   An ADVERSE VARIANCE is usually shown as a value followed by (A). It may be called an unfavourable variance, and shown as the value of the variance followed by (U). This indicates that actual costs or performance were less favourable than the standard.

DIRECT MATERIALS VARIANCES

The total DIRECT MATERIALS VARIANCE is the difference between the actual cost of the materials used in production and the standard direct materials cost for the actual number of units produced.

Note that we are using the standard cost for the actual number of units produced (actual level of production) for comparing standard and actual costs. For variable costs such as direct materials, we ignore the budgeted volume of production. (Using the standard cost of actual output for comparison with actual costs is an example of flexing a budget.)

For example, suppose that budgeted production is 1,000 units of a product with a total standard direct material cost of £1,000 (= £1 per unit). If 1,500 units are actually produced with a total direct material cost of £1,400 it would be meaningless to compare the actual cost of £1,400 with the original budget of £1,000, because they are costs for different numbers of units. Only by flexing the budget, to show the standard cost of the actual production of 1,500 units (£1,500), can a meaningful comparison be made.

(a) The total direct material variance is adverse (A) if the actual cost of the materials is more than the standard cost for the actual volume of production.

(b) The total direct material variance is favourable (F) if the actual cost of the materials is less than the standard cost for the actual volume of production.

In the example above the standard direct material cost for 1,500 units of production is £1,500 and the actual cost is £1,400. This means that there is a favourable variance of £100.

The total direct material variance can then be split into the MATERIALS PRICE VARIANCE and the MATERIALS USAGE VARIANCE.

Direct materials price variance

The calculation of a direct materials price variance starts with the quantity of direct materials used. (Alternatively, the price variance may start with the quantity of direct materials purchased in the period.)

The price variance is the difference between the standard price that **should have** been paid for the materials and the amount that was **actually paid** for them. It is the difference between the standard and actual price per unit of direct materials, for the quantity of materially actually used.

The price variance can therefore be expressed as follows:

	£
Actual quantity of materials should have cost ($\times$ standard price)	X
But did cost (actual quantity at actual price)	X
Direct materials price variance	X

(a) If the actual amount paid for the materials is more than their standard price, the variance is adverse.

(b) If the actual amount paid for the materials is less than their standard price, the variance is favourable.

You may prefer to think of variances in terms of a formula:

Direct materials price variance = AQM $\times$ (AP – SP)

where

AQM is the actual quantity of materials used.

AP is the actual price paid per unit of direct materials.

SP is the standard price paid per unit of direct materials.

Direct materials usage variance

The direct materials usage variance indicates whether the amount of materials actually used in the production is more or less than the standard usage for the actual number of units produced. In standard costing, all efficiency or usage variances are valued at standard price or standard rate.

To calculate the usage variance in quantities of direct materials, compare the actual and the standard material usage for actual production. Having calculated the variance as a quantity of materials, convert it into a cost or value by applying the standard price per unit of the direct material.

The usage variance can be expressed as follows:

	kg
Actual number of units produced should have used ($\times$ standard quantity of materials per unit)	X
But did use	X
Direct materials usage variance, as a quantity of materials	X
$\times$ Standard price per unit of the material	$\times$ £p
Direct materials usage variance in £	= £ Xp

(a) If the actual quantity of materials used is more than the standard quantity that should have been used, the usage variance is adverse.

(b) If the actual quantity used is less than standard, the usage variance is favourable.

You may prefer to think of variances in terms of a formula:

Direct materials usage variance = (AQM – SQM) × SP

where

AQM is the actual quantity of materials used.

SQM is the standard quantity of materials for the units produced.

SP is the standard price paid per unit of direct materials.

HOW IT WORKS

The standard cost card for one of Lawson Ltd's products, the George, is shown below:

	£
Direct materials 4 kg @ £2.00 per kg	8.00
Direct labour 2 hours @ £7.00 per hour	14.00
Fixed overheads 2 hours @ £3.00 per hour	6.00
Total standard absorption cost	28.00

The budgeted level of production for July was 20,000 units but in fact only 18,000 units were produced.

The actual quantity of materials used in July was 68,000 kg and the total cost of the materials was £142,800.

We will now determine the direct materials cost variances.

Total materials cost variance

	£
Standard materials cost for actual production	
18,000 units should have cost × 4 kg × £2.00	144,000
But did cost	142,800
Total materials cost variance	1,200 (F)

The actual cost is less than the total standard cost (based on the flexed budget for actual production of 18,000 units) so the variance is favourable.

Materials price variance

	£
68,000kg of materials should have cost (× £2.00)	136,000
But did cost	142,800
Materials price variance	6,800 (A)

The actual price paid for the materials is more than the standard price, so the price variance is adverse.

The 68,000 kg were actually purchased for a price of £142,800 which is £2.10 per kg (£142,800/68,000) whereas the standard price is only £2.00 per kg.

So price variance = 68,000 × £(2.10 – 2.00) = £6,800 (A)

Materials usage variance

	kg
18,000 units should have used (× 4 kg)	72,000
But did use	68,000
Materials usage variance in kg	4,000 (F)
× Standard price per kg of materials	×£2
Material usage variance in £	£8,000 (F)

The actual quantity of materials used is less than the expected or standard quantity, so the usage variance is favourable.

For the production of 18,000 units the requirement should have been for 72,000 kg (18,000 × 4 kg), whereas the production level was achieved using only 68,000 kg.

We can finally just check our variance calculations by ensuring that the sum of the price and usage variances equals the total materials cost variance:

	£
Materials price variance	6,800 (A)
Materials usage variance	8,000 (F)
Total materials cost variance	1,200 (F)

In the assessment you may be asked to prepare a reconciliation of the budgeted material cost with the actual material cost using the material cost variances. This should be set out as below:

Standard cost of materials for actual production			£144,000
Variances	Favourable	Adverse	
Direct materials price		£6,800	
Direct materials usage	£8,000		
Total variance			(£1,200) Fav
Actual cost of materials for actual production			£142,800

Task 2

A product has a standard usage of 12 litres of material, at a standard price of £20.50 per litre. The production of the product during the last month was 24,000 units, for which 312,000 litres were used at a total cost of £6,240,000.

(a)   What is the total materials cost variance?

Total materials cost variance £ [   ]

(b)   What is the materials price variance?

Materials price variance £ [   ]

(c)   What is the materials usage variance?

Materials usage variance £ [   ]

Material inventory

Sometimes a business will purchase more materials than it uses in production for the period which results in an addition to material inventory. In this situation the material price variance in the period is based on the quantity of material **purchased** whereas the usage variance is based on the quantity actually used in production.

HOW IT WORKS

Studley Ltd makes a product that requires 3 kg of material at £5 per kg. During March 4,000 kg of material were purchased at a price of £19,200. In the period 1,200 units of product were made using 3,800 kg of the material.

We will now determine the direct materials cost variances.

Materials price variance

	£
4,000 kg purchased should have cost (× £5.00)	20,000
But did cost	19,200
Materials price variance	800 (F)

The actual price is less than the standard, so the price variance is favourable.

Materials usage variance

	kg
1,200 units should have used (× 3 kg)	3,600
But did use	3,800
Materials usage variance in kg	200 (A)
× Standard price per kg	× £5
Materials usage variance in £	£ 1,000 (A)

As the actual quantity total is more than the standard quantity total, the variance is adverse.

Note: The difference between the actual quantity purchased and used is an increase in inventory of 200 kg (4,000 – 3,800). By calculating the price variance on quantities purchased, closing inventory of materials is valued at their standard cost, not their actual cost.

Task 3

A company manufactures a product that requires 5 kg of material at £10 per kg. During June 8,000 kg of material were purchased at a price of £75,000.
In the period 1,500 units of product were made using 7,700 kg of the material.

(a)   What is the materials price variance?

Materials price variance £ [   ]

(b)   What is the materials usage variance?

Materials usage variance £ [   ]

DIRECT LABOUR VARIANCES

The total DIRECT LABOUR VARIANCE is the difference between the actual cost of direct labour and the standard cost of labour for the actual number of units produced in the period. Note again, that as with the materials cost, we are comparing the actual cost to the standard cost for the actual quantity of production (the flexed budget).

The total direct labour cost variance can then be split into the LABOUR RATE VARIANCE and the LABOUR EFFICIENCY VARIANCE. The rate variance is very similar to the materials price variance and the efficiency variance is very similar the materials usage variance, and therefore the calculations of these variances are the same as for the equivalent materials variances.

There is one possible difference to remember. If there are any records of idle time for direct labour, this is calculated as a separate variance. For the purpose of calculating a direct labour efficiency variance, we take the hours actively worked, which is the number of hours paid for, minus the number of hours of idle time.

Labour rate variance

The direct labour rate variance shows the difference between the actual cost of direct labour (for the hours actually worked, including any recorded as idle time) and the standard cost for those hours worked. As the actual rate of pay and the standard rate of pay are being compared, the hours used must remain constant – the actual hours paid.

The variance can be expressed as follows:

	£
Actual hours should have cost (at standard rate)	X
But did cost	X
Labour rate variance	X

(a) If the actual rate paid is higher than the standard rate, the rate variance is adverse.

(b) If the actual cost is less than the standard cost for the paid hours, the variance is favourable.

If you prefer to think of variances in terms of a formula:

Direct labour rate variance = AH × (AR – SR)

where

AH is the actual hours worked and paid for

AR is the actual rate paid per direct labour hour

SP is the standard rate per direct labour hour

Labour efficiency variance

The direct labour efficiency variance compares the hours that were taken to produce the actual output and the quantity of hours that should have been taken. This is calculated initially as a difference in hours of work (favourable or adverse) and it is then converted into a cost or value at the standard rate per direct labour hour. The direct labour efficiency variance is therefore a measure of whether the labour force worked efficiently or not.

The direct labour efficiency variance can be calculated as follows:

	Hours
Actual number of units produced should have taken	X
But did take	X
Labour efficiency variance in hours	X
× Standard rate per hour	× £R
Labour efficiency variance in £	= £XR

(a) If the actual hours worked are more than the standard hours for the actual number of units produced, then the efficiency variance is adverse.

(b) If the actual hours are less than the standard hours for the number of units produced, then the employees have worked efficiently and the variance is favourable.

If you prefer to think of variances in terms of a formula:

Direct labour efficiency variance = (AH – SH) × SR

where

AH is the actual number of hours worked (excluding any time recorded as idle time).

SH is the standard hours for the actual units produced.

SR is the standard rate of pay per direct labour hour.

HOW IT WORKS

The standard cost card for the George is given again below:

	£
Direct materials 4 kg @ £2.00 per kg	8.00
Direct labour 2 hours @ £7.00 per hour	14.00
Fixed overheads 2 hours @ £3.00 per hour	6.00
Total standard absorption cost	28.00

Remember that the actual production was 18,000 units, rather than the 20,000 units originally budgeted for.

The total cost of the labour for the month was £254,600 for 38,000 hours.

Total direct labour cost variance

	£
18,000 units should have cost (× 2 hours × £7.00)	252,000
But did cost	254,600
Total direct labour cost variance	2,600 (A)

As the actual cost is greater than the standard total cost, the variance is adverse.

Labour rate variance

	£
38,000 hours should have cost (× £7.00)	266,000
But did cost	254,600
Labour rate variance	11,400 (F)

The hours 'paid for' cost less than expected, therefore the rate variance is favourable.

The actual labour rate per hour paid was £6.70 per hour (£254,600/38,000) compared to the standard rate of £7.00 per hour.

So Rate variance = 38,000 × £(6.70 – 7.00) = £11,400 (F).

Labour efficiency variance

	Hours
18,000 units should have taken (× 2 hours)	36,000
But they did take	38,000
Labour efficiency variance in hours	2,000 (A)
× Standard rate per hour	× £7
Labour efficiency variance in £	£14,000 (A)

The actual number of hours worked is more than the standard time for the work, so the variance is adverse.

Production of 18,000 units should have taken 36,000 hours (18,000 × 2) whereas in fact the production was inefficient and took 38,000 hours.

Finally, a check to ensure that the sub-variances total back to the total labour cost variance.

	£
Labour rate variance	11,400 (F)
Labour efficiency variance	14,000 (A)
Total direct labour cost variance	2,600 (A)

In the assessment you may be asked to prepare a reconciliation of the budgeted labour cost with the actual labour cost using the labour cost variances. This should be set out as below:

Standard cost of labour for actual production			£252,000
Variances	**Favourable**	**Adverse**	
Direct labour rate	£11,400		
Direct labour efficiency		£14,000	
Total variance			£2,600(A)
Actual cost of labour for actual production			£254,600

Task 4

A product has a standard requirement of 4 hours of direct labour per unit at a standard hourly rate of £6.50. During the last month production was 12,000 units using 45,000 hours at a total cost of £306,000.

(a)   What is the total direct labour cost variance?

   Total direct labour cost variance £ [ ]

(b)   What is the labour rate variance?

   Labour rate variance £ [ ]

(c)   What is the labour efficiency variance?

   Labour efficiency variance £ [ ]

Idle time variance

A company may operate a costing system in which idle time is recorded. Idle time may be caused by machine breakdowns, or by not having work to give to employees, perhaps because of bottlenecks in production or a shortage of orders from customers. When idle time occurs, the labour force is still paid wages for time at work, but no actual work is done. Time paid for without any work being done is unproductive and therefore inefficient.

When idle time is recorded separately, it is helpful to provide control information which identifies the cost of idle time separately, and in variance analysis, we calculate an idle time variance as a separate part of the total labour efficiency variance. The remaining efficiency variance will then relate only to the productivity of the labour force during the hours spent actively working.

In other words:

(a) Idle time variance = Hours of idle time × Standard rate per direct labour hour

(b) Efficiency variance: this is calculated by taking the actual hours worked as total hours paid for, minus idle time hours.

HOW IT WORKS

The standard direct labour cost of product X is as follows.

2 hours of grade Z labour at £5 per hour = £10 per unit of product X.

During the period, 1,500 units of product X were made and the cost of grade Z labour was £17,500 for 3,080 hours. However, there was a shortage of customer orders and 100 hours were recorded as idle time.

Calculate the following variances.

(a) The direct labour total variance
(b) The direct labour rate variance
(c) The idle time variance
(d) The direct labour efficiency variance

Variances

(a) **The direct labour total variance**

	£
1,500 units of product X should have cost £10 per unit	15,000
But did cost	17,500
Direct labour total variance	2,500 (A)

Actual cost is greater than standard cost. The variance is therefore adverse.

(b) **The direct labour rate variance**

The rate variance is a comparison of what the hours paid should have cost and what they did cost.

	£
3,080 hours of grade Z labour should have cost £5 per hour	15,400
But did cost	17,500
Direct labour rate variance	2,100 (A)

Actual cost is greater than standard cost. The rate variance is therefore adverse.

(c) **The idle time variance**

The idle time variance is the hours of idle time, valued at the standard rate per hour.

Idle time variance = 100 hours (A) × £5 = £500 (A)

For this Unit you can assume that the idle time will always be an adverse variance.

(d) **The direct labour efficiency variance**

The efficiency variance considers the hours actively worked (the difference between hours paid for and idle time hours). In our example, there were (3,080 − 100) = 2,980 hours when the labour force was not idle. The variance is calculated by taking the amount of output produced (1,500 units of product X) and comparing the time it should have taken to make them, with the actual time spent actively making them (2,980 hours). Once again, the variance in hours is valued at the standard rate per labour hour.

1,500 units of product X should take 2hrs each	3,000 hrs
But did take (3,080 − 100)	2,980 hrs
Direct labour efficiency variance in hours	20 hrs (F)
× Standard rate per hour	× £5
Direct labour efficiency variance in £	100 (F)

(e) **Summary**

	£
Direct labour rate variance	2,100 (A)
Idle time variance	500 (A)
Direct labour efficiency variance	100 (F)
Direct labour total cost variance	2,500 (A)

VARIABLE OVERHEAD VARIANCES

When the standard cost includes variable production overheads, there will be VARIABLE PRODUCTION OVERHEAD VARIANCES. These are calculated in a similar way to direct materials and direct labour variances.

There is a total variable production overhead cost variance. This is split into a variable production overhead expenditure variance and a variable production overhead efficiency variance.

The total variable overhead cost variance is the difference between the actual variable overhead cost and the standard cost for the actual number of units produced.

151

Variable overhead expenditure variance

It is assumed that variable overheads vary with the number of direct labour hours actively worked (= direct labour hours paid for minus any idle time).

The variable overhead expenditure variance shows the difference between the actual cost for the hours worked and what the cost should have been for those hours.

The variable overhead expenditure variance can be expressed as follows:

	£
Actual hours should have cost (at standard rate per hour for variable overhead)	X
But did cost	X
Variable overhead expenditure variance	X

(a) If the actual rate or cost per hour is higher than the standard rate, the expenditure variance is adverse.

(b) If the actual rate or cost per hour is less than the standard rate for the active worked hours, the expenditure variance is favourable.

Variable overhead efficiency variance

The variable overhead efficiency variance is exactly the same in hours as the direct labour efficiency variance. It is valued at the standard rate per hour for variable overhead.

If the work force is inefficient, there is an adverse variance not only for labour costs but also for variable overheads. Similarly, if the work force is efficient and there is a favourable labour efficiency variance, there will be a cost benefit with variable overheads as well as labour costs.

HOW IT WORKS

The standard direct labour cost of product Z is as follows.

2 hours of grade 2 labour at £15 per hour = £30 per unit of product Z.

During the period, 1,000 units of product Z were made in 1,960 hours. The cost of variable production overhead was £30,750.

Calculate the following variances:

(a) The variable production overhead total cost variance
(b) The variable production overhead expenditure variance
(c) The variable production overhead efficiency variance

Variances

(a) **The variable production overhead total cost variance**

	£
1,000 units of product Z should have cost £30 per unit	30,000
But did cost	30,750
Variable production overhead total variance	750 (A)

Actual cost is greater than standard cost. The variance is therefore adverse.

(b) **The variable overhead expenditure variance**

The expenditure variance is a comparison of what the hours should have cost in variable overheads and what they did cost.

	£
1,960 hours of work should have cost £15 per hour	29,400
But did cost	30,750
Variable overhead expenditure variance	1,350 (A)

Actual cost for the hours worked is more than standard cost. The rate variance is therefore adverse.

(d) **The variable overhead efficiency variance**

1,000 units of product Z should take 2 hrs each	2,000 hrs
But did take	1,960 hrs
Direct labour efficiency variance in hours	40 hrs (F)
× Standard rate per hour for variable overheads	× £15
Variable overhead efficiency variance in £	600 (F)

(e) **Summary**

	£
Variable production overhead expenditure variance	1,350 (A)
Variable production overhead efficiency variance	600 (F)
Variable production overhead total cost variance	750 (A)

FIXED OVERHEAD VARIANCES

Fixed overhead variances in a system of standard absorption costing

In an absorption costing system fixed overheads are absorbed into the actual units of production on the basis of a pre-determined overhead absorption rate.

In standard absorption costing, the standard fixed overhead cost per unit is made up from:

Direct labour hours per unit × Standard fixed overhead absorption rate per hour.

(a)   The amount of fixed overhead cost included in every unit produced is the standard fixed overhead cost per unit.

(b)   For fixed production overheads the total variance is the difference between actual fixed overhead expenditure and absorbed fixed overheads (= units produced multiplied by standard fixed cost per unit).

(c)   This total under- or over-absorbed overhead is then analysed into an expenditure variance and a volume variance and the volume variance in turn can be analysed into an efficiency variance and a capacity variance.

So fixed overhead variances are different from variable overhead cost variances.

Fixed overhead variances: total cost variance

As stated above, the total fixed overhead cost variance in a system of standard absorption costing is the total amount of fixed overheads over-absorbed or under-absorbed.

	£
Actual fixed overhead expenditure	X
Absorbed fixed overheads	
= Actual units produced × Standard fixed overhead cost per unit	X
Fixed production overhead total cost variance	X

 (a)   If actual fixed overhead costs are higher than the standard costs (= absorbed fixed overheads), there is under-absorption. Under-absorption is an adverse variance.

(b)   If standard fixed overhead costs (= absorbed fixed overheads) are higher than the actual fixed costs, there is over-absorption. Over-absorption is a favourable variance.

Any under- or over-absorption of fixed overheads will be due to either (or both) of two reasons:

(a)   Actual fixed overhead expenditure is different from the budgeted fixed overhead expenditure.

(b)   The actual number of units produced is more or less than the budgeted volume of production.

So the total fixed overhead cost variance can be split into a FIXED OVERHEAD EXPENDITURE VARIANCE and a FIXED OVERHEAD VOLUME VARIANCE.

Fixed overhead expenditure variance

Remember that fixed overhead spending is not expected to change if the actual volume of production is different from that which is budgeted. So any difference between the budgeted fixed overhead expenditure and the actual fixed overhead

expenditure must be caused by the fact that the level of fixed spending is higher or lower than budgeted.

The difference will also result in some under- or over-absorbed fixed overheads. For example, if actual fixed overhead spending is more than budgeted fixed costs, this is likely to cause some under-absorption of overheads. It should be apparent however, that if actual fixed costs are higher than budgeted fixed costs, the fixed overhead expenditure variance must be adverse.

If actual fixed cost expenditure is lower than budget, the fixed overhead expenditure variance is favourable.

The fixed overhead expenditure variance is therefore simply:

	£
Budgeted fixed overhead	X
Actual fixed overhead	X
Fixed overhead expenditure variance	X

Fixed overhead volume variance

The second reason why there might be over- or under-absorbed fixed overheads is that the actual volume of production is higher or lower than the budgeted volume.

(a) If actual production volume is less than the budgeted volume, there will be under-absorption and an adverse fixed overhead volume variance.

(b) If actual production volume is more than the budgeted volume, there will be over-absorption and a favourable fixed overhead volume variance.

In standard absorption costing, fixed overheads are absorbed at a rate per unit produced. To measure the volume variance, we therefore look at units of production.

Since fixed overheads are absorbed at a standard rate per unit produced, the fixed overhead volume variance is calculated as follows:

	£
Actual production in units	X
Budgeted production in units	X
Fixed overhead volume variance in units of production	X
Standard fixed overhead cost per unit	£F
Fixed overhead volume variance in £	£XF

HOW IT WORKS

Lawson Ltd produces a standard product, the George.

The standard cost card for the George is given below:

	£
Direct materials 4 kg @ £2.00 per kg	8.00
Direct labour 2 hours @ £7.00 per hour	14.00
Fixed overheads 2 hours @ £3.00 per hour	6.00
Total standard cost (full cost)	28.00

Actual production was 18,000 units rather than the budgeted figure of 20,000 and the production work took a total of 38,000 labour hours.

The actual fixed overhead incurred in the period was £115,000.

Calculate:

(a) The total fixed overhead cost variance

(b) The fixed overhead expenditure variance

(c) The fixed overhead volume variance

Total fixed overhead variance

	£
Fixed overhead expenditure incurred	115,000
Fixed overhead absorbed (18,000 units × £6.00 per unit)	108,000
Total cost variance = Fixed overhead under-absorbed	7,000 (A)

There is under-absorption of overhead and under-absorption is an adverse variance.

Fixed overhead expenditure variance

In order to find the fixed overhead expenditure variance, we must calculate the budgeted fixed overhead. By returning to the standard cost card and the budgeted production information we can calculate what this figure is.

The standard cost card shows the standard fixed overhead absorption rate to be £6.00 per unit. This was based upon planned production of 20,000 units therefore the budgeted fixed overhead must have been:

20,000 units × £6.00 per unit = £120,000

The fixed overhead expenditure variance is therefore:

	£
Budgeted fixed overhead	120,000
Actual fixed overhead	115,000
Fixed overhead expenditure variance	5,000 (F)

As the actual fixed overhead expenditure is less than the budgeted amount, this is a favourable variance. It will result in over-absorption of fixed overhead, which is another way of deciding that the variance is favourable.

Fixed overhead volume variance

As fixed overheads in standard absorption costing are absorbed on a unit basis the calculation is as follows:

	Units
Actual production in units	18,000
Budgeted production in units	20,000
Fixed overhead volume variance in units	2,000 (A)
Standard fixed overhead cost per unit	£6
Fixed overhead volume variance in £	12,000 (A)

The variance is adverse, as actual production is less than budgeted production. This results in under-absorption, which is adverse.

We will now check that the fixed overhead expenditure and volume variances add up to the fixed overhead total variance:

	£
Fixed overhead expenditure variance	5,000 (F)
Fixed overhead volume variance	12,000 (A)
Fixed overhead total variance	7,000 (A)

In the assessment you may be asked to prepare a reconciliation of budgeted fixed overheads with actual fixed overheads using fixed overhead variances. This should be set out as below:

Standard fixed cost for actual production			£108,000
Variances	Favourable	Adverse	
Fixed overhead expenditure	£5,000		
Fixed overhead volume		£12,000	
Total variance			£7,000 Adv
Actual fixed cost for actual production			£115,000

Task 5

A manufacturing company makes a single product and uses a system of standard absorption costing. The standard fixed overhead cost per unit is £10, consisting of 2 hours of direct labour at a fixed overhead rate of £5 per hour.

During the month of September budgeted fixed overheads were £26,000 and budgeted production was 2,600 units. The actual production was 2,500 units, which took 5,500 hours to make. Actual fixed overhead expenditure in the month was £24,500.

Calculate the following figures:

(a) The total fixed overhead variance

Total fixed overhead variance £ [ ]

(b) The fixed overhead expenditure variance

Fixed overhead expenditure variance £ [ ]

(c) The fixed overhead volume variance

Fixed overhead volume variance £ [ ]

FIXED OVERHEAD EFFICIENCY AND CAPACITY VARIANCES

A standard fixed overhead volume variance can be split into a FIXED OVERHEAD EFFICIENCY VARIANCE and a FIXED OVERHEAD CAPACITY VARIANCE.

This analysis of the fixed overhead volume variance helps to explain the causes of the volume variance:

- Was the volume variance due to the workforce working more or less efficiently than expected? – the efficiency variance

- Was the volume variance due to the workforce working for more or fewer total hours than budgeted? – the capacity variance

There are two reasons why actual production volume and budgeted production volume may differ:

(a) The work force was more or less efficient than expected. The difference between actual and standard levels of efficiency are an efficiency variance, which is exactly the same in hours as the direct labour efficiency variance and the variable overhead efficiency variance.

(b) The work force worked for more hours or fewer hours than budgeted. As a result, they should be expected to make more or fewer units of output. The effect of this difference on overhead absorption is measured as a fixed overhead capacity variance.

Fixed overhead efficiency variance

This variance considers how efficiently the workforce produced the goods by comparing the time the actual production should have taken to the time it actually took, all valued at the hourly absorption rate. It is calculated in hours in exactly the same way as the direct labour efficiency variance.

It is converted into a money value at the standard fixed overhead absorption rate per hour.

The calculation is:

	Hours
Actual units should take (× Standard hours per unit)	X
But did take	X
Fixed overhead efficiency variance in hours	X
× Standard fixed overhead absorption rate per hour	× £X
Fixed overhead efficiency variance in £	£ X

The efficiency variance is favourable or adverse, exactly the same as the direct labour efficiency variance and the variable overhead efficiency variance.

Fixed overhead capacity variance

The capacity variance measures whether the work force worked for more hours or less hours than budgeted. The capacity variance is first calculated in hours and is then converted into a money value at the standard fixed overhead rate per hour.

The calculation is:

	Hours
Budgeted hours of work	X
Actual hours of work	X
Fixed overhead capacity variance in hours	X
× Standard fixed overhead absorption rate per hour	× £X
Fixed overhead capacity variance in £	£ X

(a) If the actual hours worked are more than the budgeted hours then this should produce more output and more absorption of fixed overheads. It is therefore a favourable variance.

(b) If the actual hours worked are less than budget, this will cause under-absorption, so the variance is adverse.

HOW IT WORKS

Let's return to Lawson Ltd and the July production of the George.

The standard cost card is again shown:

	£
Direct materials 4 kg @ £2.00 per kg	8.00
Direct labour 2 hours @ £7.00 per hour	14.00
Fixed overheads 2 hours @ £3.00 per hour	6.00
Total standard absorption cost (full cost)	28.00

Budgeted production was 20,000 units and actual production was 18,000 units taking 38,000 hours. The fixed overhead incurred in the month was £115,000.

The fixed overhead variances calculated so far are:

	£
Fixed overhead expenditure variance	5,000 (F)
Fixed overhead volume variance	12,000 (A)
Total fixed overhead variance	7,000 (A)

We will now analyse the fixed overhead volume variance into its two constituent elements.

Fixed overhead efficiency variance

	Hours
18,000 units should take (× 2 hours)	36,000
But did take	38,000
Fixed overhead efficiency variance in hours	2,000 (A)
× Standard fixed overhead absorption rate per hour	×£3
Fixed overhead efficiency variance in £	£6,000 (A)

As the actual production of 18,000 units took more hours than the standard hours for 18,000 units, this is an adverse efficiency variance.

Fixed overhead capacity variance

For this calculation, the total budgeted hours must be calculated from the standard cost card. The budgeted production was for 20,000 units and each unit has standard hours of two direct labour hours. The the budgeted labour hours were therefore 40,000.

	Hours
Budgeted hours of work	40,000
Actual hours of work	38,000
Fixed overhead capacity variance	2,000 (A)
× Standard fixed overhead absorption rate per hour	×£3
Fixed overhead capacity variance in £	£6,000 (A)

Only 38,000 hours were worked although 40,000 hours were budgeted for. This is therefore an adverse capacity variance, since actual hours worked were less than budget and not all of the productive capacity has been used.

Now we can check that the efficiency and capacity variances add up to the volume variance:

	£
Fixed overhead efficiency variance	6,000 (A)
Fixed overhead capacity variance	6,000 (A)
Fixed overhead volume variance	12,000 (A)

The total fixed overhead variances for Lawson Ltd can now be presented as follows:

	£	£
Fixed overhead expenditure		5,000 (F)
Fixed overhead efficiency	6,000 (A)	
Fixed overhead capacity	6,000 (A)	
Fixed overhead volume		12,000 (A)
Total fixed overhead variance		7,000 (A)

Task 6

A manufacturing company makes a single product and uses a system of standard absorption costing. The standard fixed overhead cost per unit is £10, consisting of 2 hours of direct labour at a fixed overhead rate of £5 per hour.

During the month of September budgeted fixed overheads were £26,000 and budgeted production was 2,600 units The actual production was 2,500 units, which took 5,500 hours to make. Actual fixed overhead expenditure in the month was £24,500.

Calculate the following figures:

(a) the budgeted direct labour hours for the month

Budgeted direct labour hours [   ]

(b) the fixed overhead efficiency variance

Fixed overhead efficiency variance £ [   ]

(c) the fixed overhead capacity variance

Fixed overhead capacity variance £ [   ]

FIXED OVERHEAD VARIANCES – ABSORPTION COSTING

We can now summarise the fixed overhead variances that can be calculated under an absorption costing system using the figures from Lawson Ltd.

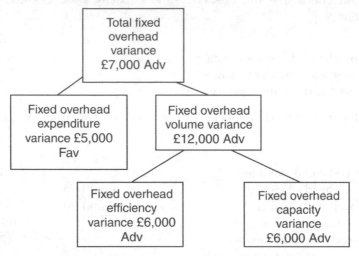

RECONCILIATION OF TOTAL STANDARD COST TO TOTAL ACTUAL COST: STANDARD ABSORPTION COSTING

All the cost variances together explain the difference between actual costs of production and the standard cost of production. A reconciliation between the standard cost and actual cost of production can be presented in a management report known as a RECONCILIATION STATEMENT (sometimes called an OPERATING STATEMENT).

It is usual practice to start with the total standard cost for the actual production, then adjust this for the variances calculated in order to finish with the total actual cost of production. This can be illustrated as follows:

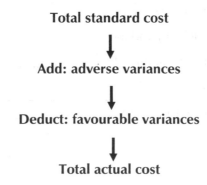

When preparing the operating statement or reconciliation statement, think about the addition and subtraction of variances. Adverse variances are added to the total standard cost, as this means that the actual cost is higher than the standard cost (or amount absorbed in the case of fixed overheads). Favourable variances are deducted from the standard cost, as this means that the actual cost is less than the standard/absorbed cost.

HOW IT WORKS

We will now summarise all of the variances calculated in the previous worked examples for Lawson Ltd.

	£
Materials price variance	6,800 (A)
Materials usage variance	8,000 (F)
Total materials cost variance	1,200 (F)

	£
Labour rate variance	11,400 (F)
Labour efficiency variance	14,000 (A)
Total labour cost variance	2,600 (A)

	£	£
Fixed overhead expenditure variance		5,000 (F)
Fixed overhead efficiency variance	6,000 (A)	
Fixed overhead capacity variance	6,000 (A)	
Fixed overhead volume variance		12,000 (A)
Fixed overhead total variance		7,000 (A)

The worked examples for Lawson Ltd do not include variable production overhead variances. However they can be included in a reconciliation statement in the same way as the other variances.

We will also need the standard cost card for the George:

	£
Direct materials 4 kg @ £2.00 per kg	8.00
Direct labour 2 hours @ £7.00 per hour	14.00
Fixed overheads 2 hours @ £3.00 per hour	6.00
Total standard absorption cost	28.00

The actual production costs for July were:

	£
Direct materials	142,800
Direct labour	254,600
Fixed overhead	115,000

We will now produce the reconciliation or operating statement.

First we must calculate the total standard cost for the actual production of 18,000 units:

	£
Direct materials 18,000 × £8.00	144,000
Direct labour 18,000 × £14.00	252,000
Fixed overhead 18,000 × £6.00	108,000
Total standard production cost	504,000

Alternatively this figure for total standard cost of production can be calculated as 18,000 × £28 which is the total standard cost per unit of product from the standard cost card.

We need to reconcile this figure to the total actual production cost:

	£
Direct materials	142,800
Direct labour	254,600
Fixed overhead	115,000
Total actual production cost	512,400

The reconciliation statement can be presented as follows:

Operating statement under absorption costing – July

	Favourable £	Adverse £	£
Total standard cost for actual production			504,000
Variances			
Variances:			
Materials price		6,800	
Materials usage	8,000		
Labour rate	11,400		
Labour efficiency		14,000	
Fixed overhead expenditure	5,000		
Fixed overhead efficiency		6,000	
Fixed overhead capacity		6,000	
Total variance	24,400	32,800	8,400 (A)
Total actual cost of actual production			512,400

Task 7

If you are producing an operating statement which reconciles the standard cost of production to the actual cost, explain whether favourable cost variances are added or subtracted and why.

DERIVING ACTUAL DATA FROM STANDARD COST DETAILS AND VARIANCES

Variances can be manipulated so as to derive actual data from standard cost details. In other words, we can 'work backwards':

(a)   From the variances and standard costs to calculate the actual cost, or

(b)   From the variances and actual costs to calculate the standard cost.

It is simply a matter of calculating a balancing figure.

HOW IT WORKS

The standard marginal cost card for the TR, one of the products made by P Co, is as follows.

	£
Direct material 16 kgs × £6 per kg	96
Direct labour 6 hours × £12 per hour	72
	168

P Co reported the following variances in control period 13 in relation to the TR.

Direct material price:	£18,840 favourable
Direct material usage:	£480 adverse
Direct labour rate:	£10,598 adverse
Direct labour efficiency:	£8,478 favourable

Actual direct wages cost £171,320. P Co paid £5.50 for each kg of direct material. There were no opening or closing inventories of the material.

Required

Calculate the following.

(a)   Actual units of output

(b)   Actual hours worked

(c)   Actual wage rate per hour

(d)   Actual number of kilograms purchased and used

Units of output

We can calculate the total direct labour cost variance, and we know the actual direct labour cost. So we can calculate the standard labour cost of production from this. We know the standard labour cost per unit, so we can then calculate the number of units of production.

	£
Actual cost of labour for actual production	171,320
Adjust for variances:	
Labour rate	(10,598)
Labour efficiency	8,478
Standard cost of labour for actual production	169,200

Actual output = Total standard cost of labour ÷ standard direct labour cost per unit

= £169,200 ÷ £72

= 2,350 units

Actual hours worked

To find the actual hours worked we can use the labour rate variance. We know what actual direct labour costs were, and the rate variance enables us to calculate the standard cost of the hours worked. We can then use the standard labour rate per hour of £12 to calculate the actual number of hours worked.

	£
Actual hours did cost	171,320.0
Less labour rate variance	10,598.0 (A)
Actual hours should have cost (x standard rate per hour)	160,722.0
÷ Standard rate per hour	÷ £12.0
Actual hours worked	13,393.5 hrs

Actual wage rate

Actual wage rate per hour   = Actual wages/actual hours

= £171,320/13,393.5

= £12.79 per hour

Actual materials usage

We have calculated the number of units produced. We know the standard direct materials cost and the materials price and usage variances. There were no opening or closing inventories of materials, therefore materials purchases and usage were the same. We can calculate actual materials purchases and usage in either of two ways.

We can use the materials usage variance:

The usage variance in £ = £480 (A)

The usage variance in kg = £480(A)/£6 per kg = 80 kg (A).

	kg	
2,350 units produced should use (× 16 kg)	37,600	
Usage variance	80	(A)
Therefore the units produced did use	37,680	

Alternatively we can reach the same answer using the materials price variance:

Let number of kg actually purchased and used = x

	£
x kgs should have cost (× £6)	6.0x
But did cost (× £5.50)	5.5x
Direct material price variance	0.5x

The price variance is £18,840 (F), therefore

$$£0.5x = £18,840$$
$$x = 37,680 \text{ kg}$$

Alternatively, P Co paid £5.50 per kg instead of the standard rate of £6.00 per kg, which is a favourable price variance of £0.50 per kg.

The total material price variance was £18,840.

So the actual kg purchased must have been £18,840/£0.50 = 37,680kg

Problems to find the missing figure with variances test your understanding of how variances are calculated, and the challenge is to identify how to find the solution with the information provided.

Task 8

XYZ Co uses standard costing. The following data relates to labour grade II.

Actual hours worked	10,400 hours
Standard allowance for actual production	8,320 hours
Standard rate per hour	£5
Rate variance (adverse)	£416

What was the actual rate of pay per hour?

- [ ] £4.95
- [ ] £4.96
- [ ] £5.04
- [ ] £5.05

Task 9

The standard material content of one unit of product A is 10kgs of material X which should cost £10 per kilogram. In June 20X4, 5,750 units of product A were produced and there was an adverse material usage variance of £1,500.

The quantity of material X used in June 20X4 is ▢ kg.

MARGINAL COSTING VARIANCES

In a standard marginal costing system the standard cost card includes only the variable costs of production. The fixed overheads are not included in the cost of the cost units, and are written off as a period cost.

The calculations of the materials and labour variances (and variable overhead variances) are exactly the same as in an absorption costing system. The only difference is that there is only one fixed overhead variance – the expenditure variance.

The presentation of a RECONCILIATION STATEMENT or OPERATING STATEMENT is slightly different for standard marginal costing than for standard absorption costing, to allow for the different treatment of fixed costs.

HOW IT WORKS

If Lawson Ltd operated a marginal costing system then the standard cost card for the George would appear as follows:

	£
Direct materials 4 kg @ £2.00 per kg	8.00
Direct labour 2 hours @ £7.00 per hour	14.00
	22.00

The actual production was 18,000 compared to budgeted production of 20,000 units. The budgeted fixed overhead was £120,000 and the fixed overhead incurred was £115,000.

The materials and labour variances would be calculated in exactly the same manner as before, giving the same figures:

	£
Materials price variance	6,800 (A)
Materials usage variance	8,000 (F)
Total materials cost variance	1,200 (F)

	£
Labour rate variance	11,400 (F)
Labour efficiency variance	14,000 (A)
Total labour cost variance	2,600 (A)

The fixed overhead expenditure variance is, as before, the difference between the budgeted and actual fixed overhead: £5,000 favourable (£120,000 – £115,000).

A reconciliation or operating statement can now be prepared between the standard marginal cost of production and the actual cost of production.

First we must calculate the standard production cost under marginal costing. This is the standard marginal cost of actual production.

	£
Direct materials 18,000 × £8.00	144,000
Direct labour 18,000 × £14.00	252,000
Marginal cost of production (18,000 x £22)	396,000

As before, the actual cost of production was £512,400.

The reconciliation statement or operating statement begins with the standard marginal cost of actual production, and the budgeted fixed costs. All the variances are then presented, and the total of these figures comes to total actual costs, as follows.

Note. The total variances come to a favourable amount. A favourable variance is deducted from standard cost to arrive at actual cost.

Operating statement marginal costing – July

	Favourable £	Adverse £	£
Standard variable cost for actual production			396,000
Budgeted fixed costs			120,000
Variances			
Variances:			
Materials price		6,800	
Materials usage	8,000		
Labour rate	11,400		
Labour efficiency		14,000	
Fixed overhead expenditure	5,000		
Total variance	24,400	20,800	(3,600) (F)
Actual cost of actual production			512,400

STANDARD COST BOOKKEEPING

When an organisation operates a standard costing system, the variances are recorded in the cost ledger accounts. This is known as standard cost bookkeeping.

The cost ledger includes the following accounts:

(a) Stores control (direct materials) account

(b) Wages control account

(c) Production overheads control account

(d) Work in progress control account

(e) Finished goods control account

(f) Variances account

'Control' means 'total', so a control account is simply a total cost account.

In a standard costing bookkeeping system variances are recorded as follows:

- The **materials price variance** is recorded in the stores control account.

  - A favourable variance is debited to the stores account

  - An adverse variance is credited to the stores account.

  The corresponding debit or credit entry is to the Variances account. In **the Variances account**:

  - A favourable variance is always credited.

  - An adverse variance is always debited.

- The **labour rate variance** is recorded in the wages control account.

  - A favourable variance is debited to the wages account.

  - An adverse variance is credited to the wages account.

  The corresponding double entry is to the Variances account. A favourable variance is credited to this account and an adverse variance is debited.

- The following variances are recorded in the work in progress control account:

  (a) **Materials usage variance**
  (b) **Labour efficiency variance**
  (c) **Idle time variance**

  - A favourable variance is debited to the work in progress account.

  - An adverse variance is credited to the work in progress account.

The corresponding double entry is to the Variances account. A favourable variance is credited to this account and an adverse variance is debited.

- The production overhead expenditure variance is recorded in the production overhead control account.

    - A favourable variance is debited to the overhead account.

    - An adverse variance is credited to the overhead account.

    The corresponding double entry is to the Variances account. A favourable variance is credited to this account and an adverse variance is debited.

- The production overhead volume variance is recorded either in the production overhead control account or in the work in progress control account.

- The balance of variances in the Variance account is transferred to the statement of profit or loss (income statement) at the end of the accounting period. A favourable variances balance will add to profit and an adverse variances balance will reduce profit.

HOW IT WORKS

Zed Co operates an integrated accounting system and a standard absorption costing system and prepares its accounts monthly.

The following variances have been calculated for the month of October.

Direct material price variance	£40 (F)
Direct material usage variance	£80 (A)
Direct labour rate variance	£45 (A)
Direct labour efficiency variance	£360 (F)
Fixed overhead expenditure variance	£100 (F)
Fixed overhead volume variance	£50 (A)

The journal entries to record these variances in the cost ledger are as follows. Remember that in the Variance account, adverse variances are debited and favourable variances are credited.

Direct material price variance

Debit	Stores control account	£40	
Credit	Variance account		£40

Direct material usage variance

Debit	Variance account	£80	
Credit	Work in progress control account		£80

Direct labour rate variance

Debit	Variance account	£45	
Credit	Wages control account		£45

Direct labour efficiency variance

Debit	Work in progress control account	£360	
Credit	Variance account		£360

Fixed overhead expenditure variance

Debit	Production overhead control account	£100	
Credit	Variance account		£100

Fixed overhead volume variance

DEBIT	Variance account	£50	
CREDIT	Production overhead control account		£50

In some accounting systems there is a separate account for each type of variance rather than a single variance account for all the different variances.

Task 10

A firm uses standard costing and an integrated accounting system. The double entry for an adverse material usage variance is

☐ DR Stores control account

   CR Work-in-progress control account

☐ DR Material usage variance account

   CR Stores control account

☐ DR Work-in-progress control account

   CR Material usage variance account

☐ DR Material usage variance account

   CR Work-in-progress control account

CHAPTER OVERVIEW

- In a standard costing system, all output is valued at a standard cost per unit

- The direct materials standard cost is set by determining the estimated quantity of material to be used per unit and the estimated price of that material

- The direct labour standard cost is set by determining the estimated labour time per unit and the estimated rate per hour

- The fixed overhead standard cost is determined by finding a realistic estimate of each of the elements of the fixed overhead

- The standards that can be set are an ideal standard, attainable standard, current standard and basic standard

- In a standard costing system, the standard cost of production is compared to the actual costs and the differences are reported as variances. Information about standard costs and variances can help management to perform their three main roles of decision making, planning and control

- For this Unit materials, labour, variable overhead and fixed overhead variances must be calculated and reconciliations of standard cost to actual cost prepared in both a standard absorption costing system and a standard marginal costing system

- The total direct materials cost variance can be split into a materials price variance and a materials usage variance

- The total direct labour cost variance can be split in a similar manner into the labour rate variance and the labour efficiency variance

- The total variable overhead variance can be split into an expenditure and an efficiency variance

- The total fixed overhead cost variance in an absorption costing system is the amount of fixed overhead that has been under- or over-absorbed in the period

- The total fixed overhead variance can then be analysed into the fixed overhead expenditure variance and fixed overhead volume variance

- The fixed overhead volume variance can be split into a fixed overhead efficiency variance and a fixed overhead capacity variance

- A reconciliation of the standard cost for the actual production to the actual cost of production can be performed by adding the adverse variances to the standard cost and deducting the favourable variances. This is also sometimes called an operating statement

- In a standard marginal costing system the materials and labour variances are calculated in exactly the same manner as in an absorption costing system – however there is only one fixed overhead variance, the fixed overhead expenditure variance

- The format for an operating statement is slightly different for standard marginal costing from an operating statement for standard absorption costing, to allow for the differing treatments of fixed costs

- In a standard cost bookkeeping system, the variances are recorded as follows:

  - The material price variance is recorded in the stores control account

  - The labour rate variance is recorded in the wages control account

  - The following variances are recorded in the work in progress account

    - Material usage variance
    - Idle time variance
    - Labour efficiency variance

  - The production overhead expenditure variance is recorded in the production overhead control account

  - The production overhead volume variance may be recorded in the fixed production overhead account. (Note. Alternatively, you may find the volume variance recorded in the work in progress account.)

- Adverse variances are debited to the relevant variance account and favourable variances are credited in the relevant variance account

- The balance of variances in the variance accounts at the end of a period is taken to the statement of profit or loss (income statement) adding to profit (favourable variances) or reducing profit (adverse variances)

Keywords

Standard costing system – a costing system where costs of production are recorded at a standard cost as set out in a standard cost card. Actual costs are compared in detail with this standard cost card and variances (differences) are recorded and reported

Standard cost card – document detailing the standard cost of a unit of a product

Ideal standards – standards based on perfect working conditions

Target standards – realistically achievable standards into which are built elements of normal wastage and inefficiency

Normal standards – standards based on current working conditions

Basic standards – historical standards that are normally set when the product is initially produced

Variances – the difference between the standard costs and the actual costs for a period

Adverse variance – where the actual cost is higher than the standard cost, or where actual performance is worse than expected

Favourable variance – where the actual cost is less than the standard cost, or where actual performance is better than expected

Total material variance – the difference between the standard materials cost for the actual production and the actual cost of the materials

Materials price variance – the difference between the standard price of the materials purchased and their actual purchase cost

Materials usage variance – the difference between the standard quantity of material for the actual production and the actual quantity used, valued at the standard price of the material

Total labour variance – the difference between the standard labour cost for the actual production and the actual cost of the labour

Labour rate variance – the difference between the standard rate of pay for the actual hours paid for and the actual cost of those hours

Labour efficiency variance – the difference between the standard hours for the actual production and the actual hours worked, valued at the standard labour rate per hour

Labour idle time variance – an adverse efficiency variance: the number of hours recorded as idle time, valued at the standard labour rate per hour

Under-absorption of overheads – where the amount of fixed overhead absorbed into cost units for the period is less than the overhead incurred. In standard costing under-absorption creates an adverse variance

BPP LEARNING MEDIA

Over-absorption of overheads – where the amount of fixed overhead absorbed into cost units for the period is more than the overhead incurred. In standard costing over-absorption creates a favourable variance

Total fixed overhead variance – the total under or over absorbed fixed overhead for the period

Fixed overhead expenditure variance – the difference between the budgeted fixed overhead and the actual fixed overhead expenditure

Fixed overhead volume variance – the difference between actual production level and budgeted production level in units, valued at the standard absorption rate per unit

Fixed overhead efficiency variance – the difference between the standard hours for the actual production and the actual hours, valued at the standard fixed overhead absorption rate per hour

Fixed overhead capacity variance – the difference between the actual hours worked and the hours budgeted to be worked, valued at the standard fixed overhead absorption rate per hour

Operating statement or reconciliation statement – a statement which uses the variances for the period to reconcile the standard cost for the actual production to the actual cost

TEST YOUR LEARNING

Test 1

Explain where the information for setting the direct labour cost standard would be found and what factors should be taken into consideration when setting it.

Test 2

Explain where the information for setting the direct material cost standard would be found and what factors should be taken into consideration when setting it.

Test 3

Explain the difference between ideal standards, target standards and basic standards.

Test 4

A business budgeted to produce 1,600 units of one of its products, the YG, during the month of October. The YG uses 7 kg of raw material with a standard cost of £6.00 per kg. During the month the actual production was 1,800 units of YG using 12,000 kg of raw materials costing £70,800.

Calculate the following figures:

(a) The total materials cost variance

Total materials cost variance £ [   ]

(b) The materials price variance

Materials price variance £ [   ]

(c) The materials usage variance

Materials usage variance £ [   ]

Test 5

Production of product FFD for the month of December in a manufacturing business was 15,400 units using 41,000 hours of direct labour costing £265,200. The standard cost card shows that the standard input for a unit of FFD is 2.5 hours at a rate of £6.80 per hour.

Calculate the following figures:

(a)   The total labour cost variance

Total labour cost variance £ [   ]

(b)   The labour rate variance

Labour rate variance £ [   ]

(c)   The labour efficiency variance

Labour efficiency variance £ [   ]

Test 6

A business produces a single standard product. The standard fixed overhead cost per unit is £7.50, consisting of 3 hours of work at an absorption rate of £2.50 per hour. Actual fixed overheads in the month of May were £56,000. The actual production during the month was 6,400 units although the budget was for 7,000 units. During the month 20,000 labour hours were worked.

Calculate the following figures:

(a)   The budgeted fixed overhead for the month

Budgeted fixed overhead £ [   ]

(b)   The fixed overhead expenditure variance

Fixed overhead expenditure variance £ [   ]

(c)   The fixed overhead volume variance

Fixed overhead volume variance £ [   ]

(d)   The fixed overhead efficiency variance

Fixed overhead efficiency variance £ [   ]

(e)   The fixed overhead capacity variance

Fixed overhead capacity variance £ [   ]

Test 7

The standard cost card for a business's product, the MU, is shown below:

	£
Direct materials 4.2 kg at £3.60 per kg	15.12
Direct labour 1.5 hours at £7.80 per hour	11.70
Fixed overheads 1.5 hours at £2.80 per hour	4.20
	31.02

The budgeted production was for 1,800 units of MU. The actual costs during the month of June for the production of 1,750 units of the MU were as follows:

	£
Direct materials 7,500 kg	25,900
Direct labour 2,580 hours	20,600
Fixed overheads	8,100

You are to:

(a) Calculate the materials price and usage variances

Materials price variance £ ⬚

Materials usage variance £ ⬚

(b) Calculate the labour rate and efficiency variances

Labour rate variance £ ⬚

Labour efficiency variance £ ⬚

(c) Calculate the fixed overhead expenditure, efficiency and capacity variances

Fixed overhead expenditure variance £ ⬚

Fixed overhead efficiency variance £ ⬚

Fixed overhead capacity variance £ ⬚

(d) Complete the table to prepare a reconciliation statement reconciling the standard cost of the production to the total cost

Operating statement – Absorption costing

			£
Standard cost of production			
Variances	**Favourable variances**	**Adverse variances**	
Materials price			
Materials usage			
Labour rate			
Labour efficiency			
Fixed overhead expenditure			
Fixed overhead efficiency			
Fixed overhead capacity			
Total variance			
Actual cost of production			

Test 8

A business operates a marginal standard costing system and the cost card for its single product is given below:

	£
Direct materials 12 kg @ £4.80	57.60
Direct labour 3 hours @ £8.00	24.00
	81.60

The budgeted output for the period was 2,100 units and the budgeted fixed overhead was £95,000.

The actual production in the period was 2,400 units and the actual costs were as follows:

	£
Direct materials 29,600 kg	145,000
Direct labour 6,900 hours	56,200
Fixed overhead	92,000

You are to:

(a) Calculate the total direct materials cost variance and the materials price and usage variances

Direct materials cost variance £ _____

Materials price variance £ _____

Materials usage variance £ _____

(b) Calculate the total direct labour cost variance and the labour rate and efficiency variances

Direct labour cost variance £ _____

Labour rate variance £ _____

Labour efficiency variance £ _____

(c) Calculate any relevant fixed overhead variances

Fixed overhead expenditure variance £ _____

(d) Complete the table to produce an operating statement reconciling the standard cost of the production to the actual cost.

			£
Standard variable cost of actual production			
Budgeted fixed overhead			
Variances	**Favourable variances**	**Adverse variances**	
Materials price			
Materials usage			
Labour rate			
Labour efficiency			
Fixed overhead expenditure			
Total variances			
Total actual cost			

Test 9

Which three of the following variances are recorded in the work-in-progress control account in a standard cost bookkeeping system?

- Material price variance
- Material usage variance
- Labour rate variance
- Variable overhead efficiency variance
- Idle time variance

chapter 6:
STANDARD COSTING – FURTHER ASPECTS

chapter coverage 📖

We will now take standard costing a little further and look at the reasons for variances and how to break down some variances further to determine their causes and in particular those causes that are controllable and those that are not.

The topics that are to be covered are:

✍ Reasons for variances

✍ Interdependence of variances

✍ Further analysis of variances

REASONS FOR VARIANCES

When reporting variances to management a simple operating statement (reconciliation statement) as illustrated in the previous chapter is a useful starting point. However management will also wish to know the reasons for the variances. Unless they know why variances happened, they cannot take control action to prevent them happening again (adverse variances) or to achieve the same results again in the future (favourable variances).

Before we look at a specific example we will consider some of the possible reasons for each type of variance:

Materials price variance – adverse

- An unexpected price increase from a supplier
- Loss of a previous trade discount or bulk buying discount from a supplier
- Purchase of a higher grade or better quality of materials

Materials price variance – favourable

- Negotiation of a better price from a supplier
- Negotiation of a trade discount or bulk purchase discount from a supplier
- Purchase of a lower grade of materials

Materials usage variance – adverse

- Greater wastage due to a lower grade of material
- Greater wastage due to use of a lower grade of labour or inexperienced labour
- Problems with machinery resulting in materials wastage

Materials usage variance – favourable

- Use of a higher grade of material which led to less wastage
- Use of more skilled labour leading to less wastage than normal
- New machinery which provides greater efficiency in material usage

Labour rate variance – adverse

- Unexpected increase in labour costs
- Use of a higher grade of labour than anticipated
- Unexpected high levels of overtime

Labour rate variance – favourable

- Use of a lower grade of labour than budgeted for
- Less overtime than budgeted for

Labour efficiency variance – adverse

- Use of a less skilled grade of labour
- Use of a lower grade of material which takes longer to work on
- More idle time than budgeted
- Poor supervision of the workforce
- Problems with machinery resulting in lost production time or slow working

Labour efficiency variance – favourable

- Use of a more skilled grade of labour
- Use of a higher grade of material which takes less time to work on
- Less idle time than budgeted
- Use of new more efficient machinery

Fixed overhead expenditure variance – adverse or favourable

- An unexpected increase or decrease in the cost of any element of fixed overheads (any item of expenditure in fixed overheads)

Fixed overhead volume variance – adverse or favourable

- An unexpected increase or decrease in production volume. If absorption is done on the basis of labour or machine hours, analysis of the volume variance into the efficiency and capacity variances can help to find reasons for the volume variance

Fixed overhead efficiency variance – adverse or favourable

- If the absorption basis is standard labour hours then the fixed overhead efficiency variance will be due to the same causes as the labour efficiency variance

- If the absorption basis is machine hours then the fixed overhead efficiency variance will reflect how efficiently the machinery has been used to produce the cost units

Fixed overhead capacity variance – adverse or favourable

- If the absorption basis is labour hours, this variance measures whether more or fewer hours were worked than originally budgeted

- If the absorption basis is machine hours, the capacity variance measures whether more or fewer machine hours were operated than originally budgeted

Task 1

If a business has a favourable labour rate variance of £2,500, which of the following might have been the cause of this?

more overtime paid than budgeted ☐

use of a lower grade of material which takes longer to work on ☐

more idle time than budgeted ☐

use of a lower grade of labour than anticipated ☐

INTERDEPENDENCE OF VARIANCES

You may have noticed from some of the possible causes of variances given above, that many of these are likely to be inter-related. This is known as the INTERDEPENDENCE OF VARIANCES.

For example, a favourable material price variance that is caused by purchasing a lower grade of material may lead directly to an adverse materials usage variance, as the lower grade of material means that there is greater wastage.

A further example might be the use of a lower grade of labour on a job than provided for in the standard cost, leading to a favourable labour rate variance but an adverse materials usage variance, as the less skilled workers cause more materials wastage.

Responsibility for variances

Investigating the causes of variances and determining any interdependence between the variances is an important aspect of management control, as in a system of RESPONSIBILITY ACCOUNTING the managers responsible for various elements of the business will be held accountable for the relevant variances.

Take the example of a favourable material price variance caused by purchasing a lower grade of material which leads directly to an adverse materials usage variance. The initial reaction might be to praise the purchasing manager for the favourable price variance and to lay blame for the adverse usage variance on the production manager. However, the true picture is that the responsibility for both variances may lie with the purchasing manager.

When asked to explain a variance, the budget holder may provide information that is inaccurate or ignores any interdependence between variances. In this case, the holder of the materials budget, the purchasing manager, may suggest that the favourable material price variance is due to better price negotiations with the supplier. However an independent assessment of quality by the production

manager may lead to the true cause of the variance (the lower grade of material) and its impact elsewhere in the business, in terms of adverse usage, being revealed.

Other reasons for variances

As well as the reasons suggested so far for variances that might occur, one fundamental reason for a variance, particularly one that recurs each period, may be that the standard cost is out of date. If the standard does not reflect the reality of the cost or usage of materials, labour or overheads then this will be a significant cause of any variances.

Standards should be regularly reviewed, at least annually, and kept up-to-date in terms of the costs of materials, labour and fixed overheads and in terms of the usage of materials and labour hours required for each product.

Further causes of variances may be one-off events such as a power cut, breakdown of machinery or annual staff holidays.

Alteration of standard costs

The decision to alter a standard cost should not be taken lightly and should only be done when there is a long term or permanent change in the cost of the resource or the usage.

For example, suppose a material price variance has been caused by a change of supplier due to the fact that the normal supplier was out of supplies. Purchases will continue to be made from the normal supplier in future. In this case the standard should not be changed. However if there is a general price increase for the material in question, no matter which supplier is used, then the standard direct materials cost should be revised.

HOW IT WORKS

Given below is the absorption cost reconciliation or operating statement for Lawson Ltd for the production of the George in July 20X8, showing all of the variances calculated in the previous chapter.

Reconciliation or operating statement – July

	Variances Adverse £	Favourable £	£
Total standard cost			504,000
Variances:			
Materials price	6,800		
Materials usage		8,000	
Labour rate		11,400	
Labour efficiency	14,000		
Fixed overhead expenditure		5,000	
Fixed overhead efficiency	6,000		
Fixed overhead capacity	6,000		
	32,800	24,400	
Add adverse variances			32,800
Less favourable variances			(24,400)
Total actual cost			512,400

Upon investigation of the variances, the following is discovered:

- The supplier of the materials has permanently increased its prices but has also significantly improved the quality of the material

- Some of the workforce used in the period were of a lower grade than normal and they were not as familiar with the production process as the normal labour force

- Lawson Ltd has recently reduced the amount of factory space that it rents but the standard rental cost has not been adjusted.

You are to write a report to the Operations Manager identifying possible causes of the variances and making any suggestions for action that should be taken.

REPORT

To: Operations Manager, Lawson Ltd
From: An Accountant
Date: August 20X8
Subject: Variances

The direct materials, direct labour and fixed overhead variances for the period have been calculated.

There is an adverse materials price variance, caused by the supplier of the materials permanently increasing its prices. However, the quality of the material has also been improved, which will have played a part in the favourable materials usage variance. We should consider other suppliers for the supply of our materials, but if their prices are the same as our supplier's, or the material quality is not as good, then the standard cost of the materials should be altered. If it can be shown that the higher quality material has caused the favourable usage variance then consideration should also be given to alteration of the direct materials usage per unit on the standard cost card.

The favourable labour rate variance will be due to the use of lower grade labour than normal for some of the period and this may also have partly caused the adverse labour efficiency variance. If it is anticipated that the lower grade of labour will now normally be used for the production, then the standard labour rate and hours should be changed.

The fixed overhead expenditure variance was favourable due to a reduction in factory rental. The reduction in rent is a permanent reduction and therefore the budgeted fixed overhead should be altered to reflect this in future periods.

The fixed overhead efficiency variance is due to the adverse labour efficiency variance and the factors that caused it, as discussed above. The adverse capacity variance shows that not all the available labour hours in the original budget were worked and the reasons for this should be investigated. One possible explanation may be that there are not enough employees who are skilled enough to produce the George.

Task 2

A business has recently taken on a new contract which required it to hire new workers. In its first period the results for the contract showed a favourable labour rate variance of £2,500, but an adverse labour efficiency variance of £6,250 and an adverse material usage variance of £5,750.

The manager responsible for hiring labour has suggested that the favourable labour rate variance was due to them managing to agree a lower rate per hour with the workforce.

What other possible explanations could there be for the favourable labour rate variance which might also explain the adverse labour efficiency and materials usage variances? What action could be taken to ascertain the true picture?

FURTHER ANALYSIS OF VARIANCES

In assigning responsibility for variances, managers should only be held accountable for factors that are within their control. Variances are caused by two basic factors:

- Planning factors – when setting standards and formulating budgets for how much will be produced, we are engaged in planning. A great deal of planning is actually (well-informed) guesswork, and it is useful to try to separate out a variance caused by a guess that turns out to be wrong (and therefore to an extent uncontrollable), from variances caused by other decisions.

- Control factors – as the production period goes on, managers must make a great many control decisions, such as buying material of a lower grade than planned, or taking advantage of a discount offered, which had not been anticipated at the planning stage. It is therefore useful to separate out variances caused by control decisions from those caused by planning assumptions.

It is sometimes the case that a variance can be split into two parts:

- The part that is caused by some particular factor that is known, such as actual change in materials prices (called a NON-CONTROLLABLE VARIANCE, or planning variance since it is attributable to a failure in planning, rather than an operational decision).

- The part that is caused by other factors that we do not specifically know about (called a CONTROLLABLE VARIANCE, since it is attributable to factors experienced in actual operations).

Examples of variances that might be split into controllable and non-controllable variances include the following:

- Materials price variance – analysed between the element due to a specific price change (non-controllable) and that due to other factors such as poor buying decisions (controllable).

- Materials price variance – analysed between the element due to a seasonal change in price of the material (non-controllable) and that due to other factors (controllable).

- Materials usage variance – analysed between the element due to the learning process for the workforce (non-controllable) and that due to other factors such as careless working practices (controllable).

- Labour rate variance – analysed between the element due to specific wage increases (non-controllable) and that due to other factors (controllable).

- Labour efficiency variance – analysed between the element due to the learning process or training period (non-controllable) and that due to other elements such as careless working practices (controllable).

Materials price changes

The standard materials cost will often be based on the anticipated materials price during the period. However the actual price of the materials may have been materially different during the period for a reason outside the control of the purchasing manager, meaning that the materials price variance may not show the true picture of what is happening for control purposes.

The materials price variance is calculated as follows:

	£
Actual kg should have cost	X
But did cost	X
Materials price variance	X

This can then be analysed into:

Price variance due to known price change (non-controllable variance)	£	Price variance due to other factors (controllable variance)	£
Standard price for actual quantity used	X	Price-adjusted cost for actual quantity used	X
Price-adjusted cost for actual quantity used	X	Actual cost	X
Non-controllable price variance	X	Controllable price variance	X

HOW IT WORKS

The standard direct materials cost for a business's product is:

4 kg @ £5.00 per kg = £20.00

During the month of October production was 12,000 units of the product and the actual materials cost was £248,000 for 45,600 kg. The market price of the materials has been unexpectedly increased to £5.50 per kg for the whole month, due to severe supply shortages.

Calculate the total materials price variance and then show how it can be analysed between the non-controllable element (caused by the price increase) and the controllable element (caused by other factors).

Total materials price variance

	£
45,600 kg should have cost (× £5.00)	228,000
But did cost	248,000
	20,000 (A)

Non-controllable variance due to price increase

	£
Standard price for actual quantity 45,600 kg × £5.00	228,000
Adjusted price for actual quantity 45,600 kg × £5.50	250,800
	22,800 (A)

Controllable variance due to other factors

	£
Adjusted price for actual quantity 45,600 × £5.50	250,800
Actual quantity at actual price	248,000
	2,800 (F)

```
                    ┌──────────────────────┐
                    │  Total materials price │
                    │  variance £20,000 (A)  │
                    └──────────────────────┘
                      ↙                    ↘
┌──────────────────────────┐      ┌──────────────────────────┐
│  Non-controllable variance │      │  Controllable variance due │
│    due to price increase   │      │     to other factors       │
│       £22,800 (A)          │      │        £2,800 (F)          │
└──────────────────────────┘      └──────────────────────────┘
```

The total materials price variance shows an adverse price variance of £20,000. However when we analyse the price variance, we can see that the problem was caused by the new higher price (the non-controllable variance) and that indeed the controllable variance caused by other factors was favourable. Therefore the purchasing manager should be praised for the favourable controllable variance and not blamed for the uncontrollable adverse planning variance.

Task 3

A business's product has a standard direct material cost of £24.60 (3 kg @ £8.20 per kg). During the month of September the total production of the product was 1,500 units using 4,600 kg of materials at a total cost of £40,800. During the month the price was unexpectedly increased due to a shortage of the material to £9.00 per kg.

(a)   The total materials price variance was £ [   ]

(b)   The non-controllable variance due to the price increase was

£ [   ]

The controllable variance due to other factors was

£ [   ]

Seasonal variations in price

In some businesses, material prices will tend to be different at different times of the year, due to availability or other factors. When considering the materials price variance, it may be useful to analyse this into the non-controllable price variance due to the seasonal effect and the controllable price variance due to any other factors.

HOW IT WORKS

A business makes a product which uses a raw material which has a standard price of £20.00 per kg. Each unit of the product requires 3 kg of this material. The price of the materials for the last 6 years has been subjected to a time series analysis and the following seasonal variations have been seen to occur.

Jan – Mar	–£2.00
Apr – Jun	+£1.00
Jul – Aug	+£3.00
Sep – Dec	–£2.00

During February 10,000 units of the product were made and the price paid for the 32,000 kg of material was £560,000.

What is the total materials price variance and how can this be analysed to show the non-controllable variance due to the season and the controllable variance due to other factors?

Total materials price variance

	£
32,000 kg should have cost (× £20)	640,000
But did cost	560,000
	80,000 (F)

Non-controllable variance due to seasonality

	£
Standard cost for actual quantity 32,000 kg × £20	640,000
Adjusted price for actual quantity 32,000 kg × (£20 – £2.00)	576,000
	64,000 (F)

Controllable variance due to other factors

	£
Adjusted price for actual quantity 32,000 kg × (£20 – £2.00)	576,000
Actual quantity at actual price	560,000
	16,000 (F)

```
              ┌─────────────────────────┐
              │   Total materials price  │
              │   variance £80,000 (F)   │
              └─────────────────────────┘
               ↙                        ↘
┌─────────────────────────┐   ┌─────────────────────────┐
│  Non-controllable variance│  │  Controllable variance due│
│  due to seasonality £64,000│  │     to other factors      │
│            (F)            │   │        £16,000 (F)        │
└─────────────────────────┘   └─────────────────────────┘
```

The total favourable price variance of £80,000 can now be seen to be due only partly to the seasonal factors. There is also £16,000 of favourable controllable variance due to other factors.

Task 4

The standard cost of direct materials for a product is made up of 5 kg of material at an average standard cost of £6.00 per kg. It has been noted over the years that the cost of the material fluctuates on a seasonal basis around the average standard cost as follows:

Jan – June   –£0.90

July – Dec   +£0.90

In the month of October the actual production was 2,000 units and 10,300 kg of material were used at a cost of £69,500.

(a) The total materials price variance was £ [   ]

(b) The non-controllable variance due to the seasonal price change was £ [   ]

The controllable variance due to other factors was £ [   ]

Labour efficiency variances

It is often the case that a labour force will have to learn how to make a new product, so their level of production will be lower in the early days of production and should increase in later periods. If the productivity of the workforce is affected by still being in this learning or training period, then the total labour efficiency variance may be misleading.

In exactly the same way as we did for the materials price variance, we can analyse the labour efficiency variance into the non-controllable element that has been caused by the learning process (and which should be anticipated at the planning stage) and the element caused by other controllable factors.

HOW IT WORKS

A business has just started production of a new product, with a long-run standard labour cost of 4 hours per unit at an hourly rate of £8.00.

However, in this first learning period of production, it is anticipated that each unit will take 20% longer to make than the long-run standard time.

The production in the first period was 2,000 units and the actual hours worked were 10,000 at a cost of £75,000.

What is the total labour efficiency variance, the non-controllable variance caused by the learning process and the controllable variance caused by other factors?

Total labour efficiency variance

2,000 units should have taken (× 4 hours)	8,000 hrs
But did take	10,000 hrs
Efficiency variance in hrs	2,000 hrs (A)
	× £8.00
Efficiency variance in £	16,000 Adv

Non-controllable variance due to learning process

	£
Standard hours for actual production at standard rate 2,000 × 4 hours × £8.00	64,000
Adjusted hours for actual production at standard rate 2,000 × (4 hours × 1.20) × £8.00	76,800
	12,800 (A)

Controllable variance due to other factors

	£
Adjusted hours for actual production at standard rate 2,000 × (4 hours × 1.20) × £8.00	76,800
Actual hours at standard rate 10,000 × £8.00	80,000
	3,200 (A)

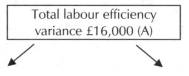

Total labour efficiency variance £16,000 (A)

Non-controllable variance due to learning process £12,800 (A)

Controllable variance due to other factors £3,200 (A)

The total adverse efficiency variance is made up of only £12,800 that relates to the learning process – the remaining £3,200 of adverse variance is due to other controllable factors.

Task 5

A business has just had its first month of production of a new product. During the period 12,000 units were produced in 48,000 hours costing £288,000 in direct labour. The standard labour cost has been set at 3.5 hours for each unit of production at a rate of £6.20 per labour hour. However it is anticipated that the first month's production will take 25% longer than the standard hours.

(a) The total labour efficiency variance was £ ⬚

(b) The non-controllable variance due to the early production problems was

£ ⬚

The controllable variance due to other factors was £ ⬚

Using indices to update standard costs

In some instances you may be given information about indices, either specific indices relating to the materials the business uses or indices regarding the labour rates. These index numbers can then be used to update an old standard cost.

HOW IT WORKS

A business has the following standard direct materials cost for its product:

10 kg @ £3.40 per kg = £34.00

The standard cost of the material was set when the price index for the material stood at 170. During the month of July, 4,000 units of the product were made, using 38,000 kg, at a total cost of £135,000. For July, the price index for the material was 185.

Calculate the total materials price variance and analyse it into the non-controllable variance that relates to the price increase and the controllable variance that is related to other factors.

Total materials price variance

	£
38,000 kg should have cost (× £3.40)	129,200
But did cost	135,000
	5,800 (A)

Non-controllable variance relating to price increase

	£
Standard price of actual materials 38,000 kg × £3.40	129,200
Adjusted price for actual materials	
38,000 kg × (£3.40 × 185/170)	140,600
	11,400 (A)

Controllable variance relating to other factors

	£
Adjusted price for actual materials	
38,000 × (£3.40 × 185/170)	140,600
Actual quantity at actual price	135,000
	5,600 (F)

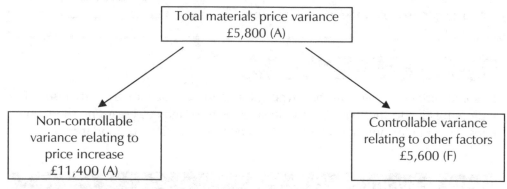

Although the price variance is only £5,800 adverse, this is due to the fact that there is a favourable controllable variance due to other factors of £5,600, which has been netted off against the £11,400 adverse non-controllable variance caused by the price increase.

Task 6

A business has a direct labour standard cost of 4 hours per product at a standard hourly rate of £7.50. This standard labour rate was set when the relevant labour index stood at 120. The labour rate index is now 130. During the period the actual production was 5,000 products using 21,000 hours costing £160,000.

(a)   The total labour rate variance was £ _____

(b)   The non-controllable variance due to the specific index of labour rate increases was £ _____

The controllable variance due to other factors was £ _____

CHAPTER OVERVIEW

- Each type of variance can have a variety of causes. Often the variances are interdependent, meaning that a factor that caused one variance is also the factor that causes other variances

- Once the reasons for the variances have been discovered, then responsibility for the variances, both favourable as well as adverse, can be assigned to the relevant managers

- A business may need to carry out an independent investigation of the reasons for a variance, in order to ascertain whether the explanation of the variance provided by the budget holder is reasonable. This may help them decide whether there is any interdependence and assess who should be held responsible

- Some variances may be due to the setting of the standard and therefore be uncontrollable by the relevant manager. In some circumstances the standard will need to be altered if there has been a long term or permanent change in the cost or usage of the resources

- If the actual price of materials is significantly different to standard price, due to a problem with the standard, then this can have an effect on materials price variance that can be misleading. In this situation, the materials price variance can be analysed into the non-controllable variance caused by the price increase (planning variance) and the controllable variance caused by other factors

- The materials price variance can also be affected by any seasonality of materials prices. Again the total price variance can be analysed into the non-controllable variance which is due to the seasonal element of the price and the controllable variance caused by other factors

- There may be occasions when the labour efficiency variance does not give a true picture of the situation, particularly in the early stages of manufacturing a new product when the workforce are still learning how to make the product. In such cases the labour efficiency variance can be analysed into the non-controllable variance caused by the learning process and the controllable variance caused by other factors

- If a standard cost is based on an index for a particular material or labour price then the standard cost can be updated using the current value of the index in order to analyse the materials price or labour rate variance into non-controllable and controllable variances

Keywords

Interdependence of variances – this is where the reasons for two or more variances may be the same, so that the variances are inter-related: the factor which causes one variance can also be the cause of another variance

System of responsibility accounting – a system where the managers responsible for various elements of the business will be held accountable for the variances within their control

Non-controllable variances – the part of a variance that is due to a cause outside the control of the manager responsible for the aspect of performance to which the variance relates

Controllable variances – the part of a variance that is due to controllable operational factors or decisions

TEST YOUR LEARNING

Test 1

Given below is the operating statement for one of the factories of a business for the month of November, reconciling the total standard cost to the total actual cost for the month.

Operating statement – November

	Variances		
	Adverse	Favourable	
	£	£	£
Total standard cost			634,200
Variances:			
Materials price	9,200		
Materials usage	14,600		
Labour rate		15,400	
Labour efficiency	13,200		
Fixed overhead expenditure	7,200		
Fixed overhead efficiency	11,500		
Fixed overhead capacity		6,000	
	55,700	21,400	
Add adverse variances			55,700
Less favourable variances			(21,400)
Total actual cost			668,500

You also discover the following information:

▪ Due to staff shortages a more junior grade of labour than normal, from one of the other factories, had to be used in the production process, giving rise to inefficiencies and additional wastage.

▪ The material price has been increased by all suppliers and it is doubtful that the materials can be purchased more cheaply than this in future.

▪ Due to its inventory-holding policy the factory has had to rent some additional space but this has not been recognised in the standard fixed overhead cost.

▪ Due to the inefficiencies of labour, more hours had to be worked than normal in the month.

Write a report to the Managing Director explaining the possible reasons for the variances for the month and making any suggestions about future actions that should be taken.

Test 2

What possible effect will the following scenarios have on variances? (You will need to create a table on a separate sheet of paper).

Scenarios	Possible effects
A business replaces machinery with new equipment	
A company has supply issues with a raw material	

Test 3

The standard direct materials cost for a product is:

12 litres @ £2.40 per litre = £28.80

During week 23, the total production was 1,200 units of the product which used 14,000 litres of material. The price of the material has suddenly increased to £2.80 per litre and the business paid £38,500 during the month for materials.

(a) The total materials price variance was £ ☐

(b) The non-controllable variance due to the price increase was £ ☐

The controllable variance caused by other factors was £ ☐

Test 4

A business makes a product that requires 6.5 kg of material input, which has been assigned a standard cost of £8.00 per kg. However the price of the material fluctuates throughout the year and the seasonal variations have been monitored over a number of years using time series analysis. The seasonal variations in price are:

Jan – Mar	–£1.84
Apr – June	–£0.40
July – Sept	+£0.64
Oct – Dec	+£1.60

During June the output was 1,800 units of finished product using 12,300 kg of material. The total material cost was £95,200.

(a) The total materials price variance was £ ☐

(b) The non-controllable variance due to the seasonal variation was £ ☐

The controllable variance due to other factors was £ ☐

Test 5

A business has just started to produce a new product which it is anticipated will require 11 direct labour hours per unit for the first month of production. However as the employees become used to making the product it is thought that the labour time per unit will reduce to 9 hours, which is the figure which has been used for the standard cost of the direct labour together with a labour rate of £6.80 per hour.

During the first month of production 2,400 units were produced, taking 27,000 hours to produce and the labour cost was £182,600.

(a)   The total labour efficiency variance was £ ⬚

(b)   The non-controllable variance due to the learning process in production was £ ⬚

The controllable variance due to other factors was £ ⬚

Test 6

A business set the standard cost for its materials at 7 kg per unit at a price of £6.50 per kg when the index for those particular material prices stood at 130. During the month of November 14,000 units of the product were produced using 100,000 kg of materials and the total cost was £670,000. In November the index for the materials price stood at 138.

(a)   The total materials price variance was £ ⬚

(b)   The non-controllable variance due to the price increase was £ ⬚

The controllable variance due to other factors was £ ⬚

chapter 7:
PERFORMANCE INDICATORS

---

chapter coverage 📖

In this chapter we will look at the calculation and meaning of a variety of performance indicators, both financial and non-financial.

The topics we shall cover are:

- Performance indicators
- Productivity
- Control ratios: efficiency, capacity and activity ratios
- Profitability measures
- Resource utilisation
- Working capital ratios
- Gearing
- Ratio analysis
- Limitations of ratio analysis
- The balanced scorecard
- Service organisations
- 'What if' analysis

PERFORMANCE INDICATORS

In the previous two chapters we considered standard costing as a method of providing information for management to allow them to control costs and hence performance. In this chapter we will consider other methods of summarising both financial and non-financial information about business performance, for the purposes of management's control of costs and enhancement of value. This information for management will be provided by calculating a variety of performance indicators.

PERFORMANCE INDICATORS are methods of summarising the performance of all or parts of a business for a period. Some performance indicators are expressed as absolute figures, such as the inventory holding period in days, whereas others are expressed as relative figures or percentages, for example, a gross profit percentage where gross profit is expressed as a percentage of sales revenue.

Financial and non-financial data

Some performance indicators are based on financial data. For example, gross profit margin is calculated using figures for gross profit and sales, both taken from the statement of profit or loss (income statement). However other performance indicators will be based on non-financial data, such as calculation of the number of units produced per hour.

Using the performance indicators

The performance indicators that we will consider in this chapter are vital tools of management as they serve as **summaries** of the performance of the business during the period. For example, a production director may be informed that output has been 50 units per hour for the month just ended: this would be a summary about the number of units produced and the number of hours worked in the form of a simple performance indicator, without the need for management to have the detailed production figures.

However performance indicators have little significance when considered on their own. They are only useful if they are compared to other figures. The comparisons that are useful are:

- Comparison to previous period's performance
- Comparison to budgeted performance measures or target measures
- Comparison to industry average performance measures
- Comparison to other similar organisations' measures

The latter three comparisons are all forms of BENCHMARKING. Benchmarking means comparing performance against something that the business should be trying to achieve or exceed. The item that is used for comparison purposes is a 'benchmark' for the organisation's performance.

Comparability

When performance indicators are used for comparison with another measure then it is important that we compare like with like. In general, performance indicators are a good method of providing consistent information. Provided the same formula is used in each period, the performance indicators can be compared over time in order to discover the trend of performance.

However, care must be taken to ensure that the figures used are properly comparable. For example, if the performance indicators of a business are compared with those of a competitor and the two businesses have different accounting policies regarding, say, depreciation, then the resulting comparison of costs and profit margins may be distorted.

A further problem may be when figures are compared over a period of time during which there has been an increase in prices. In such instances, before the performance indicators are calculated the figures should be made comparable by using an appropriate price index to adjust them to the same price level. (This was considered in detail in Chapter 4.)

PRODUCTIVITY

PRODUCTIVITY is a measure of how hard the employees are working or how productive they are being in their hours at work. Productivity, also called efficiency, is likely to be measured in terms of units of:

(a)   Output per hour or per minute

(b)   The average time required to perform an activity

As with many performance indicators, productivity can be measured in different ways but the basic calculation is to discover how many units of product or service are being produced either for a particular time period or by each employee.

Productivity is likely to be measured in different ways by different businesses. Examples of productivity performance measurements include:

- The number of vehicles manufactured per week (by a vehicle manufacturer)

- The number of operations undertaken per day (for a hospital)

- The number of rooms cleaned per hour (for a hotel)

- The average number of passengers transported per journey (for a passenger transport company)

HOW IT WORKS

Harris Engineering has two factories which each make a similar product. The production figures for the two factories for the month of June are given below:

	Factory A	Factory B
Units produced	285,000	146,000
Number of production workers	30	16
Hours worked	4,800	2,600

The productivity of the two factories could be expressed in two ways: productivity per hour or productivity per employee.

Method 1 – Productivity per labour hour

$$\text{Productivity per labour hour} = \frac{\text{Output in the period}}{\text{Hours worked in the period}}$$

Factory A	Factory B
$= \dfrac{285,000 \text{ units}}{4,800 \text{ hours}}$	$\dfrac{146,000 \text{ units}}{2,600 \text{ hours}}$
$=$ 59.4 units per hour	56.2 units per hour

Obviously the productivity of the two factories can be compared (provided that the units produced are similar) and these figures indicate that productivity per labour hour is slightly higher in Factory A than in Factory B.

This productivity level could also be compared with productivity in previous months and with budgeted figures.

Suppose that the budgeted figures for the month for Factory A were to produce 250,000 units in 4,400 labour hours.

$$\text{Budgeted productivity} = \frac{250,000 \text{ units}}{4,400 \text{ hours}}$$

$$= 56.8 \text{ units per labour hour}$$

In this case, the actual productivity during June (59.4 units per hour) is higher than the standard or budgeted productivity level.

Increase in productivity

An increase in productivity means that more units can be produced in one hour or by one employee. This will normally mean a reduction in costs, as the same number of units can be produced in fewer hours and therefore with reduced labour costs, machine costs and overheads.

HOW IT WORKS

Returning to Harris Engineering, in Factory B 146,000 units were produced in 2,600 hours in June resulting in productivity of 56.2 units produced per hour. Labour is paid at a rate of £10 per hour. If the productivity of Factory B could be increased to 59 units per hour (as in Factory A) what effect would this have on the labour cost of Factory B?

Suppose that 146,000 units are to be produced next month. If productivity increases to 59 units per hour then this production will take:

$$\frac{146,000}{59} = \text{approx 2,475 hours}$$

Time saving 2,600 – 2,475	=	125 hours
Cost saving 125 × £10	=	£1,250

An increase in productivity to 59 units per hour could therefore bring about a labour cost saving of £1,250.

Method 2 – Productivity per employee

Instead of measuring productivity as output per labour hour, we could measure it as output per employee per month.

$$\text{Productivity per employee} = \frac{\text{Output in the period}}{\text{No. of employees working on output}}$$

	Factory A	Factory B
=	$\dfrac{285,000}{30}$	$\dfrac{146,000}{16}$
=	9,500 units per employee	9,125 units per employee

Again a comparison can be made between the two factories, and also to productivity in previous periods or to the budgeted productivity level of output per employee per month.

Which method to use?

In a manufacturing situation, the most useful method of measuring productivity is normally method 1, productivity per labour hour, as on the factory floor each employee is likely to be doing different tasks. It is probably not the case, in the previous example, that each of the 30 production workers in Factory A actually produced 9,500 units.

However method 2, the productivity per employee, is most appropriate in a situation where each employee is doing an identical job and the job in question can take a varied amount of time.

An alternative way of measuring productivity, for standard repetitive tasks, is to measure the average length of time to complete an activity. For example, in a call centre we could measure the average number of calls answered per hour. Alternatively, we could measure the average time taken to deal with a call.

HOW IT WORKS

Harris Engineering has a sales department which processes all orders for goods. In June the six members of the telephone sales team processed 1,240 orders.

$$\text{Productivity per employee per month} = \frac{\text{Output} = \text{number of orders}}{\text{Number of employees}}$$

$$= \frac{1,240 \text{ orders}}{6 \text{ employees}}$$

$$= 207 \text{ orders per employee per month}$$

Task 1

An advertising company has produced 216 advertisements in the current quarter using 26 advertising executives. In the previous quarter only 188 advertisements were produced when there were 22 executives.

What is the productivity of the company for this quarter and the previous quarter?

Current quarter

Previous quarter

Value added

Another method of measuring productivity is to calculate the VALUE ADDED per employee.

When a business buys raw materials and services from suppliers, it is buying them at their value to the supplier. The business will then process or work on these raw materials, also incorporating any bought-in services, and it will aim to sell its finished goods for more than the cost of the materials and bought-in services, in order to cover its other costs and make a profit.

Value added is the difference between the value of the inputs in a business and the value of the outputs. The inputs are the cost of materials and bought in services and the value of the outputs is the sales revenue of the business.

Value added = Sales revenue − (cost of materials and bought in services)

The value added therefore is the extra value that the business has created through the work of its employees. The value of the materials and bought-in services was created by other businesses, but the employees of the business add to the value of the materials and bought-in services in order to create even more value in the finished goods that they produce and sell.

Value added can be used as a measure of overall company performance and often the **value added per employee** during a given period of time is a performance indicator used by management in order to measure productivity.

HOW IT WORKS

You are given the following information about a small manufacturing business for the year ending 30 June.

Sales revenue	£835,400
Cost of materials used	£466,700
Cost of bought in services	£265,000
Number of employees	12

What is the total value added and the value added per employee in the month?

Value added	=	Sales revenue − (cost of materials and bought in services)
	=	£835,400 − (466,700 + 265,000)
	=	£103,700
Value added per employee in the month	=	£103,700/12
	=	£8,642

Note. No deduction is made for the wages paid to the employees. Value added should be sufficient to cover labour costs and other expenses other than materials costs and the cost of bought-in services, and also make a profit.

CONTROL RATIOS: EFFICIENCY, CAPACITY AND ACTIVITY RATIOS

Another way of measuring output performance during a period is to calculate what are generally known as the CONTROL RATIOS. These are efficiency, capacity and activity ratios. (Note that the formulae for these ratios will be provided in assessment questions.)

You may remember from the earlier chapter on standard costs that the labour efficiency variance measures whether the work force had been more or less efficient than the standard level of efficiency. This was calculated by comparing:

- The standard hours for the actual production
- The actual hours worked

These three ratios of efficiency, capacity and activity are calculated using these same two figures, together with the budgeted total hours.

Efficiency ratio

As the name implies the EFFICIENCY RATIO is a measure of how efficiently the workforce has operated during a period and is expressed as a percentage. It is calculated as:

$$\text{Efficiency ratio} = \frac{\text{Standard hours for actual production}}{\text{Actual hours worked}} \times 100\%$$

If the ratio is 100% this means that the workforce has worked as efficiently as the standard that was set. If the ratio is more than 100% then they have worked more efficiently than expected. If the efficiency ratio is less than 100%, the work force has been less efficient than expected.

Capacity ratio

The CAPACITY RATIO is a measure of the hours worked compared with the budgeted hours. Has the work force worked more hours or fewer hours than expected or budgeted? The capacity ratio is calculated by comparing the actual hours worked to the hours that were budgeted and expressing this as a percentage.

$$\text{Capacity ratio} = \frac{\text{Actual hours worked}}{\text{Budgeted hours}} \times 100\%$$

If the capacity ratio is less than 100% then fewer hours were worked than budgeted. If the capacity ratio is more than 100%, more hours have been worked than budgeted.

If more hours are worked than budgeted (and the capacity ratio exceeds 100%), we should expect to produce more output. If fewer hours are worked than budgeted (and the capacity ratio is less than 100%), we should expect to produce less output than expected.

Activity ratio

The ACTIVITY RATIO is an indicator of how actual output compares to the budgeted output. It is calculated as:

$$\text{Activity ratio} = \frac{\text{Standard hours for actual production}}{\text{Budgeted hours}} \times 100\%$$

This ratio can also be calculated from actual and budgeted output levels, in which case it is sometimes known as the production volume ratio.

$$\text{Production volume ratio} = \frac{\text{Actual output}}{\text{Budgeted output}} \times 100\%$$

HOW IT WORKS

Harris Engineering has a third factory, Factory C, which makes a product from the components produced by Factories A and B. The production figures for June for this factory are as follows:

	Factory C
Budgeted production in units	4,800
Actual production in units	4,500
Labour hours worked	10,000
Standard hours for each unit	2

Efficiency ratio

$$\text{Efficiency ratio} = \frac{\text{Standard hours for actual production}}{\text{Actual hours worked}} \times 100\%$$

$$= \frac{4,500 \text{ units} \times 2 \text{ hours per unit}}{10,000} \times 100\%$$

$$= \frac{9,000}{10,000} \times 100\%$$

$$= 90\%$$

The workforce has worked well below standard levels, taking 10,000 hours to produce output that should have taken only 9,000 hours.

Capacity ratio

$$\text{Capacity ratio} \quad = \quad \frac{\text{Actual hours worked}}{\text{Budgeted hours}} \times 100\%$$

$$= \quad \frac{10,000}{4,800 \text{ units} \times 2 \text{ hours}} \times 100\%$$

$$= \quad \frac{10,000}{9,600} \times 100\%$$

$$= \quad 104.17\%$$

The capacity ratio shows that more hours have been worked than were budgeted.

Activity ratio

$$\text{Activity ratio} \quad = \quad \frac{\text{Standard hours for actual production}}{\text{Budgeted hours}} \times 100\%$$

$$= \quad \frac{4,500 \text{ units} \times 2 \text{ hours}}{4,800 \text{ units} \times 2 \text{ hours}} \times 100\%$$

$$= \quad \frac{9,000}{9,600} \times 100\%$$

$$= \quad 93.75\%$$

This shows that actual output was only 93.75% of the budgeted output.

This performance could also be calculated as a production volume ratio:

$$\textbf{Production volume ratio} \quad = \quad \frac{\text{Actual output}}{\text{Budgeted output}} \times 100\%$$

$$= \quad \frac{4,500 \text{ units}}{4,800 \text{ units}} \times 100\%$$

$$= \quad 93.75\%$$

Relationship between the control ratios

The three control ratios are related to each other as follows:

Efficiency ratio	×	Capacity ratio	=	Activity ratio

This means that we can explain the activity ratio by referring to the other two ratios.

The relationship also shows that the volume of output actually achieved in a period, compared with the budgeted output, depends on a combination of efficiency (= output in the hours worked) and the number of hours worked (= capacity).

HOW IT WORKS

Using the figures for Factory C, remember that the three control ratios were calculated as:

Efficiency ratio	90%
Capacity ratio	104.17%
Activity ratio	93.75%

These are related as follows:

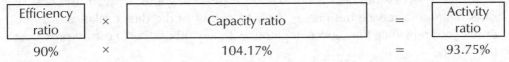

Efficiency ratio	×	Capacity ratio	=	Activity ratio
90%	×	104.17%	=	93.75%

The activity ratio shows production was only 93.75% of the budgeted level. We can now explain that this was due to the significantly lower level of efficiency than budgeted for, despite the work force working for more hours than budgeted.

Task 2

A manufacturing organisation had a budgeted output planned for the month of October of 288,000 units. 268,000 units were in fact produced. The standard production time for each unit is 3 hours.

What is the activity ratio for the month?

☐ %

PROFITABILITY MEASURES

The aim of most businesses is to make a profit, therefore management will be interested in profitability performance measures. The profitability measures could also be described as efficiency indicators, as they are measuring the efficiency with which the business has used its assets to earn profits.

Gross profit margin

The GROSS PROFIT of a business is the sales for the period less the cost of those sales. In a manufacturing business, the cost of sales figure is the manufacturing cost of goods sold. In a retail business, the cost of sales is the purchase cost of the goods that were sold during the period. The cost of sales is calculated as follows:

Cost of sales	£
Opening inventory	X
Add: Purchases/Production cost	X
	X
Less closing inventory	(X)
= Cost of sales	X

For a service organisation, sales for the period is usually the amount of revenue that is billed to customers for the services provided. However, the cost of sales figure for a service business is not based on physical goods. Instead, the cost of sales figure in a service business is likely to consist of the direct salaries of those employees providing the service, together with any other direct costs of providing the service.

The GROSS PROFIT MARGIN for a period is the gross profit as a percentage of sales.

$$\text{Gross profit margin} = \frac{\text{Gross profit}}{\text{Sales}} \times 100\%$$

This ratio shows the amount of gross profit that has been made for every £1 of sales revenue.

Operating profit margin

The OPERATING PROFIT of a business is the gross profit less the selling, distribution and administration costs. This is also the same as the profit before any interest payable or any tax.

The OPERATING PROFIT MARGIN is the operating profit as a percentage of sales revenue for the period:

$$\text{Operating profit margin} = \frac{\text{Operating profit}}{\text{Sales}} \times 100\%$$

This ratio shows the amount of operating profit (= profit from operations, after deducting all operating costs) for every £1 of sales revenue.

Net profit margin

The NET PROFIT of a business is the profit shown in the statement of profit or loss (income statement) after deduction of all expenses, including interest and tax for the period. The NET PROFIT MARGIN is calculated by showing the net profit as a percentage of the sales figure for the period:

$$\text{Net profit margin} = \frac{\text{Net profit}}{\text{Sales}} \times 100\%$$

Expenses

It is also sometimes useful to express individual items of expense as a percentage of the sales figure, in order to determine how these expenses have changed. This is done by the following calculation:

$$\text{Expense percentage} = \frac{\text{Expense}}{\text{Sales}} \times 100\%$$

For example, we may want to measure labour costs as a percentage of sales revenue, especially when management think that labour costs may be excessive.

If a ratio of an expense to sales revenue is monitored to see how the ratio changes over time, it may be important to allow for changes in sales and production levels. It is also important to be aware of the difference between variable expenses and fixed elements in the expense. If sales and production are increasing then we would also expect to see:

- Similar increases in variable expenses therefore the expense as a percentage of sales revenue should remain fairly constant.

- Fixed expenses should be reasonably constant from one period to the next, so an increase in the volume of production and sales should result in a fall in the expense as a percentage of sales revenue.

HOW IT WORKS

The statement of profit or loss for Hampton Manufacturing for the year ending 30 September is given below:

Hampton Manufacturing – statement of profit or loss for the year ended 30 September

	£	£
Revenue*		1,350,400
Cost of sales		
Opening inventory	144,300	
Purchases	49,200	
	993,500	
Less closing inventory	156,300	
		837,200
Gross profit		513,200
Less expenses		
Selling and distribution costs	168,400	
Administration expenses	105,600	
		274,000
Operating profit		239,200

***Note.** That the term 'revenue' in the statement of profit or loss is just the technical accounting name for sales.

What is the gross profit margin, the operating profit margin and the expense/sales percentage for each category of expense?

Gross profit margin $= \dfrac{£513,200}{£1,350,400} \times 100\%$

$= 38.0\%$

Operating profit margin $= \dfrac{\text{Operating profit}}{\text{Sales}} \times 100\%$

$= \dfrac{£239,200}{£1,350,400} \times 100\%$

$= 17.7\%$

Selling costs percentage $= \dfrac{\text{Selling cost}}{\text{Sales}} \times 100\%$

$= \dfrac{£168,400}{£1,350,400} \times 100\%$

$= 12.5\%$

Administration costs percentage $= \dfrac{\text{Administration cost}}{\text{Sales}} \times 100\%$

$= \dfrac{£105,600}{£1,350,400} \times 100\%$

$= 7.8\%$

If the expenses are compared over a number of time periods in which sales volumes are rising, we would probably expect to see:

(a) The ratio of selling costs to sales to remain fairly stable, because a large proportion of selling costs are likely to be variable costs.

(b) The ratio of administration costs to sales to fall, because most administration costs are probably fixed costs.

Comparison of gross profit margin and operating profit margin

It has already been noted that when performance indicators are calculated it is normally for the purpose of comparison with previous periods, with the budget, or with similar performance figures for a rival organisation or for the industry average.

If the gross profit margin is monitored and compared over time, any changes or differences are likely to be caused by:

- Changes in the selling price of the goods
- Changes in the mix of the goods sold
- Changes in the production costs or the price of the goods
- A combination of these factors

Any change in the operating profit margin will be explained in part by changes in the gross profit margin. If the operating profit does not move in line with the gross profit margin, then this will be due to changes in the expenses as a percentage of sales percentages (which may be due to the expenses being either variable or fixed).

Task 3

A business has a gross profit of £58,700 and net profit of £22,500 for the month of November, after deducting interest of £2,500 and tax of £4,750. The sales for the month were £133,400.

What is the gross profit margin, the operating profit margin and the net profit margin?

Gross profit margin ☐ %

Operating profit margin ☐ %

Net profit margin ☐ %

Improvement in gross profit margin

If the gross profit margin for a business can be increased by raising selling prices or reducing the cost of sales, then the overall profitability of the business can be increased.

HOW IT WORKS

Hampton Manufacturing has a gross profit margin of 38% on sales of £1,350,000. However other firms in the same line of business achieve a gross profit margin of 40%. If Hampton were to improve its gross profit margin to 40%, it would make additional profit for the year.

	£
Current gross profit	513,200
Gross profit @ 40% margin (£1,350,400 × 40%)	540,160
Additional profit from increasing the gross profit margin	26,960

Based on the current year's sales level, if the gross profit margin can be increased by 2 percentage points, profit can be increased by almost £27,000.

Note that one way in which the gross profit margin can be increased is by an increase in selling price. An increase in price has no effect on any costs, either variable or fixed. The gross profit margin will therefore be higher, and this will result in higher total profit provided that sales volume is maintained. However from a commercial point of view, an increase in selling price may make the company's products much less competitive. So raising selling prices is not always a sensible way of trying to increase profit.

Another way of increasing total profit is to increase the sales volume. If the cost of sales are all variable costs, an increase in sales volume will have no effect on the gross profit margin, but total gross profit will increase. This should also lead to an increase in operating profit and net profit. Higher sales volume is likely to result in a higher operating profit ratio and a higher net profit ratio because many expenses are fixed.

Return on capital employed

Ratios of profit to sales do not take into consideration the amount of investment that is required to achieve the profit for a business. An important measure of profitability is the ratio of profit to the amount of capital invested.

The RETURN ON CAPITAL EMPLOYED (ROCE) is sometimes known as the primary ratio and is of great importance to a business. As well as being useful to compare the relative profitability of different businesses, ROCE is also an indicator of investment efficiency as it looks at how well a business has invested the capital available to it.

It is calculated as:

$$\text{Return on capital employed (ROCE)} = \frac{\text{Profit}}{\text{Capital employed}} \times 100\%$$

As such it is relating the profit that has been earned for the period (from the statement of profit or loss) to the capital from the statement of financial position to determine what return has been made on the owners' investment in the business.

ROCE can be measured in different ways. Both the return element (the profit), and the capital can be calculated in different ways and it is important to ensure that the figure for return that is used is consistent with the figure for capital employed that is used.

(a) Return may be net profit or operating profit (profit before interest and taxation). It is not likely to be gross profit.

(b) Capital employed may be total assets minus current liabilities, or total assets minus total liabilities. Assets may be measured by their accounting value or by their current market value (realisable value).

HOW IT WORKS

Given below is the full statement of profit or loss for Hampton Manufacturing for the year ending 30 September 20X1 and the statement of financial position at that date.

Hampton Manufacturing: statement of profit or loss for the year ended 30 September 20X1

	£	£
Revenue		1,350,400
Cost of sales		
Opening inventory	144,300	
Purchases	849,200	
	993,500	
Less closing inventory	156,300	
		37,200
Gross profit		513,200
Less expenses		
Selling and distribution costs	168,400	
Administration expenses	105,600	
		274,000
Operating profit		239,200
Interest payable		50,000
Profit after interest payable		189,200
Tax		56,000
Profit after tax		133,200

Statement of financial position as at 30 September 20X1

	£	£
Non-current assets		2,428,300
Current assets:		
Inventory	156,300	
Receivables	225,000	
Bank	10,200	
	391,500	
Payables	(169,800)	
Net current assets		221,700
		2,650,000
Less long term loan		400,000
		2,250,000
Capital		1,500,000
Reserves		200,000
Retained earnings		550,000
		2,250,000

What is the return on capital employed?

Method 1

The most common method of calculating ROCE is to compare the operating profit (profit before interest and tax) with the total long-term capital provided by all the providers of long-term funds (= capital). This is not only the shareholders, whose funds are the capital plus all reserves including the retained earnings, but also any long term capital within the business such as long term loans.

When ROCE is measured in this way, we are looking at the ability of the business to make operating profits with the total amount of the long-term capital invested.

The total of shareholder capital and long-term liabilities is the same as the total assets of the business minus the current liabilities. So the figure for capital employed can be calculated in one of two ways:

From the capital side of the statement of financial position:

	£
Capital	1,500,000
Reserves	200,000
Retained earnings	550,000
Long term loan	400,000
Capital employed = shareholder capital plus long term debt	2,650,000

From the assets side of the statement of financial position:

	£
Non-current assets	2,428,300
Current assets	391,500
Less current liabilities	(169,800)
Capital employed = total assets minus current liabilities	2,650,000

As you can see the same figure for capital employed is reached with each method.

Return on Capital Employed is the operating profit as a percentage of this capital employed, and in our example this is:

$$\text{ROCE} = \frac{\text{Operating profit}}{\text{Share and loan capital} + \text{reserves} = \text{capital employed}}$$

$$= \frac{239,200}{2,650,000} \times 100\%$$

$$= 9.0\%$$

It is **recommended** that you use this method of calculation in your assessment if it asks for **Return on Capital Employed**.

Method 2

An alternative method of calculating return on capital is to use just the capital relating to the shareholders – share capital, reserves and the retained earnings. (This is the same as total assets minus total liabilities). This is then compared with the profit that is attributable to the shareholders, which is the profit after interest (and tax).

Technically this ratio is known as the RETURN ON SHAREHOLDERS' FUNDS or the RETURN ON NET ASSETS (RONA) as it shows the profit that has been generated from the net assets of the business.

$$\text{Return on shareholders' funds/Return on Net Assets} = \frac{\text{Profit after tax}}{\text{Shareholders' funds}} \times 100\%$$

$$= \frac{£133,200}{£2,250,000} \times 100\%$$

$$= 5.9\%$$

It is **recommended** that you use this method of calculation in the assessment if it asks for **Return on Net Assets**.

Task 4

A business has made an operating profit of £365,800 for the year. The statement of financial position shows that shareholders' funds total £1,700,000 and that there is a long term loan outstanding of £600,000, on which annual interest is paid at 12%.

What is the return on capital employed using each of the methods above?

Method 1 (ROCE) [_____] %

Method 2 (RONA) [_____] %

RESOURCE UTILISATION

Performance measures relating to RESOURCE UTILISATION show how efficiently (and effectively) an organisation is using the various resources at its disposal.

We will start with measures that consider the overall assets and liabilities of the business and then consider the more detailed elements of the working capital of the business.

Asset turnover

ASSET TURNOVER is a performance indicator which compares the sales revenue of the business to the capital employed. The measure is calculated as follows:

$$\text{Asset turnover} = \frac{\text{Revenue}}{\text{Capital employed}}$$

Remember that total capital from the statement of financial position is equal to the assets of the organisation less the current liabilities, or alternatively shareholders' funds + long term loans.

You will note that asset turnover is an absolute figure and not a percentage. What this figure is showing is the amount of sales revenue that is being earned by every £1 of capital or every £1 of investment in assets and liabilities.

It may be expressed as 'x times'. For example, if annual sales are £2,000,000 and capital employed is £1,000,000, the asset turnover is 2 times. What this means is that the business has achieved sales of £2 for every £1 of capital invested.

Asset turnover and return on capital employed

Asset turnover is an important indicator in its own right, as it shows how effectively the assets and liabilities of the business have been used to create

revenue during the period. It is also an important figure as it is one of the elements that makes up ROCE, as can be seen below:

| ROCE | = | Asset turnover | × | Operating profit margin |

If we look at how each of these figures is calculated you will see how this works:

$$\frac{\text{Operating profit}}{\text{Capital employed}} = \frac{\text{Revenue}}{\text{Capital employed}} \times \frac{\text{Operating profit}}{\text{Revenue}}$$

The importance of this relationship is that we can explain any change in ROCE by changes in asset turnover and changes in the operating profit margin.

HOW IT WORKS

Given below is a summary of these three performance indicators for Jason Enterprises for the last two years, 20X5 and 20X6:

	20X6	20X5
Operating profit margin	13%	15%
Asset turnover	1.40	1.44
Return on capital employed	18.2%	21.6%

The return on capital employed has fallen significantly from one year to the next, from 21.6% down to 18.2%. By looking at the component elements of ROCE, we can see that the reduction is due to a combination of a decrease in the operating profit margin of 2% (from 15% to 13%) and a fall in asset turnover from 1.44 to 1.40, so that the business was achieving fewer sales per £1 invested in 20X6.

Non-current asset turnover

Another indicator of how well a business is using its resources is a measure of how much revenue is earned from the non-current assets of the business. A business invests in capital equipment and other non-current assets in order to create business. Management should therefore want non-current assets to achieve a high level of sales per £1 invested in capital assets.

NON-CURRENT ASSET TURNOVER, like asset turnover, is measured as an absolute figure rather than as percentage. It shows the amount of revenue earned for each £1 invested in non-current assets:

$$\text{Non-current asset turnover} = \frac{\text{Revenue}}{\text{Net book value of non} - \text{current assets}}$$

It is similar to the asset turnover ratio, except that it measures revenue per £1 of capital assets invested rather than sales revenue per £1 of total capital invested.

HOW IT WORKS

We will now return to the statement of financial position of Hampton Manufacturing:

Hampton Manufacturing – statement of financial position as at 30 September 20X1

	£	£
Non-current assets		2,428,300
Current assets:		
Inventory	156,300	
Receivables	225,000	
Bank	10,200	
	391,500	
Payables	(169,800)	
Net current assets		221,700
		2,650,000
Less long term loan		400,000
		2,250,000
Capital		1,500,000
Reserves		200,000
Retained earnings		550,000
		2,250,000

Sales revenue for the year was £1,350,400, the operating profit margin was 17.7% and ROCE was 9.0%.

We can now calculate the asset turnover and non-current asset turnover and show how the ROCE is made up.

$$\text{Asset turnover} = \frac{\text{Revenue}}{\text{Capital employed}}$$

$$= \frac{£1,350,400}{£2,650,000}$$

$$= 0.51 \text{ times}$$

This tells us that for every £1 invested in the capital of the business, 51 pence of sales revenue has been earned in the year.

We can now relate the ROCE to the net profit margin and asset turnover:

ROCE		Asset turnover		Operating profit margin
9.0%	=	0.51	×	17.7%

Finally we can calculate the non-current asset turnover:

$$\text{Non-current asset turnover} = \frac{\text{Revenue}}{\text{Net book value of non-current assets}}$$

$$= \frac{£1,350,400}{£2,428,300}$$

$$= 0.56$$

For every £1 invested in the non-current assets, 56 pence of sales revenue was achieved. This ratio can be used to compare performance with previous years or with the non-current asset turnover of a similar/competitor organisation.

Working backwards through a ratio

In the computer based test you may be given some information about a ratio and from this information you may be expected to work backwards to calculate a figure from the statement of profit or loss or the statement of financial position.

This type of problem requires you to find a balancing figure.

HOW IT WORKS

A business has an asset turnover of 2 times and capital employed of £450,000. What is the annual revenue of the business?

$$\text{Asset turnover} = \frac{\text{Revenue}}{\text{Capital employed}}$$

$$2 = \frac{\text{Revenue}}{£450,000}$$

$$\text{Annual revenue} = 2 \times £450,000 = £900,000$$

Task 5

An accountancy firm has asset turnover of 1.2 in the month of June and the capital of the firm totals £350,000.

What is the revenue for the month?

£ [   ]

WORKING CAPITAL RATIOS

Another aspect of asset utilisation is the efficiency of management of working capital, and we will now consider the WORKING CAPITAL of the business in more detail.

Working capital is the total of the current assets of a business less its current liabilities. Performance measurement relating to working capital considers:

(a) Liquidity.

(b) The management of the cash cycle or working capital cycle: this aspect of performance measurement considers the management of inventory, trade receivables and trade payables.

The main component elements of working capital are inventory, trade receivables, cash and trade payables. These are constantly changing as the diagram below illustrates:

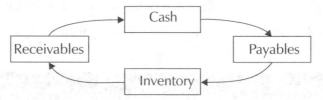

- Inventory is used to produce goods (or services) for sale, and when the goods are sold, they become receivables.

- Inventory is purchased on credit which means we have trade payables.

- Receivables are eventually turned into cash when customers pay what they owe.

- Cash is used to pay the trade payables.

A business must have enough cash to pay what it owes, and we should normally expect that trade payables will be paid from the cash that is earned from sales revenue.

Liquidity

The LIQUIDITY of a business is the extent to which it is able to make payments to trade payables out of the cash that comes from the business cycle. The business cycle is the cycle of turning inventory into sales and receivables and turning receivables into cash.

Liquidity is a measure of how safe the business is in terms of the availability of cash. Even if a business is profitable, it must still have enough cash to be able to pay its trade payables when they fall due.

Two ratios can be used to measure the liquidity of a business:

(a) The current ratio

(b) The quick ratio or acid test ratio

The current ratio

The CURRENT RATIO is the ratio of total current assets to total current liabilities:

$$\text{Current ratio} = \frac{\text{Current assets}}{\text{Current liabilities}}$$

This can be expressed as a ratio, for example 2.4 : 1 or as a number only, 2.4. In the assessment you should present your answer as a single number. It shows how many times the current liabilities of a business are covered by its current assets.

It is often suggested that a current ratio of 2 (current assets are twice current liabilities) is 'safe'. However although this can be used as a benchmark figure, care should be taken with the type of business that you are dealing with. For example, supermarkets tend to have much lower current ratios than this, as they have few, if any, receivables, rapid inventory movements and large amounts of payables. In fact, supermarkets often sell goods out of inventory for cash before they even have to pay their suppliers.

Management should have an idea of the 'safe' level for the current ratio for their business, and should monitor changes in the current ratio to check that it is not becoming dangerously low.

When it is low, there is a risk that the business may be unable to pay its payables on time.

Quick ratio

A problem with using the current ratio as a measure of liquidity is that for some types of business the inventory, although a current asset, is not a particularly liquid asset. For inventory to be turned into cash, it must first be processed or manufactured, then it must be sold and turned into receivables and only finally will it become cash when the customers pay. A wine-making business, for example, may hold on to wine for several years until it has matured sufficiently for sale.

Due to the lack of liquidity of inventory, another liquidity ratio, the QUICK RATIO (sometimes known as the acid test ratio), may be calculated. This is similar to the current ratio, except that it excludes inventory from current assets.

$$\text{Quick ratio} = \frac{\text{Current assets} - \text{inventory}}{\text{Current liabilities}}$$

Like the current ratio, this can be expressed either as a ratio or a single number (0.75:1 or 0.75) but it should be expressed as a single number for the purpose of the assessment.

It is often suggested that a quick ratio of at least 1:1 is 'safe' because if the trade payables of a business do not exceed its receivables plus cash, it should have sufficient liquidity to meet payments to trade payables when they are due. A ratio of 1:1 can certainly be used as a benchmark figure for the quick ratio. However, again, the type of business must be considered, and what is 'safe' for one type of business may not be safe for another.

Working capital turnover ratios

We shall now look at another aspect of working capital management. This is the speed with which a business can complete the continuous cycle from making a payment to suppliers for trade payables, to making sales with the goods purchased from suppliers and to receiving cash from customers in order to pay suppliers. There are three main elements in this 'working capital cycle' or 'cash cycle' of operations:

(a) Inventory, and the length of time a business takes to use the inventory that it buys

(b) Trade receivables, and the time taken by customers to pay for goods that they have bought

(c) Trade payables, and the length of credit period that the business takes from its suppliers before paying them for materials it has purchased

An efficient business should use the inventory that it buys as quickly as it can. It should try to obtain payment from customers in reasonable time, and should certainly not allow customers to take longer credit than has been agreed. It should also try to negotiate a reasonable period of credit from its suppliers, and should not pay for purchases before it has to.

Inventory and inventory turnover

It is useful for management to understand how long inventories are being held before they are used or sold. In some businesses inventory must be sold – or 'turned over' – quickly, for example if the inventory consists of perishable foods. However in other businesses inventory may be held for some considerable period before it is sold (eg in the construction industry).

A business needs to control how long inventory is being held, as capital is tied up in the inventory while it is waiting to be sold. Therefore an INVENTORY DAYS ratio (also known as the inventory holding period) can be calculated to measure and monitor the length of time that inventory is held in the business.

$$\text{Inventory days} = \frac{\text{Average inventory}}{\text{Cost of sales}} \times 365 \text{ days}$$

This will indicate the number of days on average that inventory is being held before it is used or sold. Note that 'average inventory' is used here. This is calculated as:

$$\text{Average inventory} = \frac{\text{Opening inventory + closing inventory}}{2}$$

In some tests you may not have information about opening inventory, in which case the closing inventory figure should be used in the calculation instead of average inventory. However if the opening inventory figure is available, then use average inventory in your calculation.

Rather than being expressed in terms of the number of days for which inventory is held, inventory turnover can also be expressed as the number of times a year that the inventory is turned over:

$$\text{Inventory turnover} = \frac{\text{Cost of sales}}{\text{Average/closing inventory}}$$

A high inventory turnover figure calculated on this basis indicates that inventory is moving in and out of the business quickly, whereas a low figure indicates that inventory is in the business for some time before it is sold.

Receivables' collection period

The RECEIVABLES' COLLECTION PERIOD, also known as receivables' days, is a measure that shows how long it is taking on average for customers of the business to pay for the goods or services they buy.

$$\text{Receivables' collection period} = \frac{\text{Trade receivables}}{\text{Credit sales}} \times 365 \text{ days}$$

There are a number of potential problems with this calculation. First a separate figure for credit sales may not be available, in which case total sales must be used. However if the total sales include a large proportion of cash sales this will distort the picture shown.

A further problem may be with the use of year end receivables. The receivables at the end of the year may not be representative of the average amounts of receivables during the year. Therefore if possible, use the average of opening and closing receivables. However in tests it is rare for this information to be available and it is normally necessary to use the year-end amount.

The receivables collection period can be measured and monitored over time in order to assess how well receivables are being managed. For example, if the average collection period is getting longer, this may be a sign of inefficiency in the accounts department.

The receivables collection period can also be compared with the credit terms agreed with customers. For example if a business arranges with all its customers that invoices must be paid within 60 days, we would not want the average collection period (receivables days) to be much more than this figure – at worst! In addition a business should try, if possible to match its receivables and payables days, so that it is not giving more credit to customers than it is receiving from suppliers.

Payables' payment period

Management may also wish to know how long the business is taking to pay its credit suppliers and so how much credit it is taking. This is calculated by the PAYABLES' PAYMENT PERIOD, or payables' days.

$$\text{Payables' payment period} = \frac{\text{Trade payables}}{\text{Credit purchases}} \times 365 \text{ days}$$

As with sales, we may not have a separate figure for credit purchases. If this is the case then a figure for total purchases should be used instead. When a figure for total purchases is not available, the cost of sales should be used. If the average of opening and closing payables is available, this is again a better figure than just the closing figure. However normally only the closing statement of financial position figure will be available, so you should use the closing payables figure.

The payables' payment period can be measured and monitored over time to check whether there is a trend in payment times. The payment period should also be compared to the receivables' collection period. As stated earlier, a business should try not to allow the payments period to be much shorter than the collections period, because this can put a strain on cash flow. For example if customers are taking 75 days on average to pay, then we would not wish to have a payables' payment period of just 15 days, because this would mean that money is being paid out of the business much more rapidly than it is being received.

HOW IT WORKS

Given below are the statement of profit or loss and statement of financial position for Hampton Manufacturing again:

Hampton Manufacturing – statement of profit or loss for the year ended 30 September 20X1

	£	£
Revenue		1,350,400
Cost of sales		
Opening inventory	144,300	
Purchases	849,200	
	993,500	
Less closing inventory	156,300	
		837,200
Gross profit		513,200
Less expenses		
Selling and distribution costs	168,400	
Administration expenses	105,600	
		274,000
Operating profit		239,200
Interest payable		50,000
Profit after interest payable		189,200
Tax		56,000
Profit after tax		133,200

Statement of financial position as at 30 September 20X1

	£	£
Non-current assets		2,428,300
Current assets:		
Inventory	156,300	
Receivables	225,000	
Bank	10,200	
	391,500	
Payables	(169,800)	
Net current assets		221,700
		2,650,000
Less long term loan		400,000
		2,250,000
Capital		1,500,000
Reserves		200,000
Retained earnings		550,000
		2,250,000

We will now calculate all the working capital ratios.

$$\text{Current ratio} = \frac{\text{Current assets}}{\text{Current liabilities}}$$

$$= \frac{£391,500}{£169,800}$$

$$= 2.3$$

$$\text{Quick ratio} = \frac{\text{Current assets} - \text{inventory}}{\text{Current liabilities}}$$

$$= \frac{£391,500 - £156,300}{£169,800}$$

$$= 1.4$$

$$\text{Average inventory} = \frac{£144,300 + £156,300}{2}$$

$$= £150,300$$

$$\text{Inventory days} = \frac{\text{Average inventory}}{\text{Cost of sales}} \times 365$$

$$= \frac{£150,300}{£837,200} \times 365$$

$$= 66 \text{ days}$$

$$\text{Inventory turnover (times)} = \frac{\text{Cost of sales}}{\text{Average inventory}}$$

$$= \frac{£837,200}{£150,300}$$

$$= 5.6 \text{ times}$$

$$\text{Receivables' collection period} = \frac{\text{Trade receivables}}{\text{Credit sales}} \times 365$$

$$= \frac{£225,000}{£1,350,400} \times 365$$

$$= 61 \text{ days}$$

$$\text{Payables' payment period} = \frac{\text{Trade payables}}{\text{Credit purchases}} \times 365$$

$$= \frac{£169,800}{£849,200} \times 365$$

$$= 73 \text{ days}$$

Task 6

A business has opening inventory of £13,500 and closing inventory of £17,000. Purchases during the year were £99,000.

What is the average inventory turnover period or 'inventory days'?

☐ days

Improvement in working capital management

As we saw at the start of this section, the components of working capital are constantly changing but inventory, trade receivables and trade payables will all eventually become cash receipts or cash payments.

We have seen how performance indicators for individual elements of working capital – inventory, receivables and payables – can be calculated. These performance measurements can be 'improved' by reducing inventory days and the receivables collection period, and by increasing the length of the payment period for payables.

If the management of working capital can be improved, by shortening inventory days or receivables' collection period, or by extending the payables' payment period, then this will mean that the business will have additional cash available. It will receive cash from sales sooner and will make payments to suppliers later.

HOW IT WORKS

The performance indicators for Hampton Manufacturing show the following:

Inventory days	66 days
Receivables' collection period	61 days
Payables' payment period	73 days

The industry average figures for working capital are:

Inventory days	50 days
Receivables' collection period	48 days
Payables' payment period	80 days

If Hampton were to improve its working capital practices in order to be in line with the industry average figures, what effect would this have on the cash balance?

Reduction in inventory days (66 days – 50 days) = 16 days

235

The value of 16 days of inventory is:

$$\frac{\text{Cost of sales}}{365} \times 16 = \frac{837,200}{365} \times 16$$
$$= £36,699$$

Reduction in receivables' collection period (61 days – 48 days) = 13 days

The value of 13 days of receivables is:

$$\frac{\text{Credit sales}}{365} \times 13 = \frac{1,350,400}{365} \times 13$$
$$= £48,096$$

Increase in payables' payment period (80 days – 73 days) = 7 days

The value of 7 days of payables is:

$$\frac{\text{Credit purchases}}{365} \times 7 = \frac{849,200}{365} \times 7$$
$$= £16,286$$

If all three improvements were made there would be an improvement in the cash balance of £101,081 (£36,699 + 48,096 + 16,286).

Months not days

In the assessment you may be asked to calculate inventory holding period, receivables' collection period or payables' payment period in months rather than in days. In these situations simply substitute 12 months for 365 days in the formulae and the answer will automatically be expressed in months.

HOW IT WORKS

A business has payables of £24,000 and purchases during the year were £101,000. What is the payables' payment period in months?

$$\text{Payables' payment period} = \frac{\text{Payables}}{\text{Purchases}} \times 12$$
$$= \frac{£24,000}{£101,000} \times 12$$
$$= 2.9 \text{ months}$$

GEARING

Many companies are financed by a combination of shareholders' capital and debt such as loans from banks. Loans are shown separately in a company's statement of financial position.

When loans are taken out this produces additional commitments for a company:

- The company needs to be able to pay the annual interest on the loan.

- The company needs to be able to pay off the loan when repayment of the borrowed capital falls due.

These additional commitments mean that companies with significant amounts of loan capital may be considered more risky than companies without any long term loans or with smaller amounts of loan capital. For this reason management should monitor the amount of debt in their capital structure. There are two main performance indicators that measure the effect of long-term debt capital such as loans on the financial position of a company.

Interest cover

INTEREST COVER is a measure of whether the company can make the interest payments on its debt capital out of annual profits. It is measured as:

$$\text{Interest cover} = \frac{\text{Profit before interest charges}}{\text{Interest charges}}$$

This gives an indication of how safe the annual interest payments are in terms of the profit that the company is making.

We should always expect profit before interest to be more than the interest costs, otherwise the company would be making a loss.

However, we should also expect the interest cover to be at least a 'safe' minimum amount, so that there will be no problem if there is a fall in sales revenues and profit, or if interest rates on bank loans go up.

Gearing ratio

The GEARING RATIO is a measure of the amount of loan capital (= debt capital on which interest is paid) that a company has compared to its equity sources of finance (shareholder funds). The gearing ratio can be measured in one of two ways:

Method 1   Gearing ratio   = Total debt/Equity × 100

This is sometimes known as the debt: equity ratio

Method 2   Gearing ratio   = Total debt/(Total debt + Equity) × 100

Whichever method is used:

- Total debt includes both long term and short term debt.

- Equity refers to the share capital and reserves of the company (shareholders' funds).

In the assessment, both computer marked and human marked tasks will allow both calculations.

HOW IT WORKS

Returning to Hampton Manufacturing:

Hampton Manufacturing – statement of profit or loss for the year ended 30 September 20X1

	£	£
Revenue		1,350,400
Cost of sales		
Opening inventory	144,300	
Purchases	849,200	
	993,500	
Less closing inventory	156,300	
		837,200
Gross profit		513,200
Less expenses		
Selling and distribution expenses	168,400	
Administration expenses	105,600	
		274,000
Operating profit		239,200
Interest payable		50,000
Profit after interest payable		189,200
Tax		56,000
Profit after tax		133,200

Statement of financial position as at 30 September 20X1

	£	£
Non-current assets		2,428,300
Current assets:		
Inventory	156,300	
Receivables	225,000	
Bank	10,200	
	391,500	
Payables	(169,800)	
Net current assets		221,700
		2,650,000
Less long term loan		400,000
		2,250,000
Capital		1,500,000
Reserves		200,000
Retained earnings		550,000
		2,250,000

$$\text{Interest cover} = \frac{\text{Profit before interest charges}}{\text{Interest charges}}$$

$$\text{Interest cover} = \frac{£239,200}{£50,000}$$

$$= 4.78$$

This indicates that the interest payments due for the year are just over one fifth of the profits made during the year. This would tend to indicate that the interest payments are quite safe unless there is a large fall in sales and profits.

The gearing ratio can be measured in one of two ways:

Method 1 Gearing ratio = Long term loan finance/Shareholders' funds × 100

$$\text{Gearing ratio} = \frac{£400,000}{£2,250,000} \times 100\%$$

$$= 17.8\%$$

Method 2 Gearing ratio = Long term loan finance/(Shareholders' funds + long term finance) × 100%

$$\text{Gearing ratio} = \frac{£400,000}{£2,250,000 + £400,000} \times 100\%$$

$$= 15.1\%$$

Whichever method is used, this indicates that the gearing ratio of the company is quite low. Compared to either the shareholders' funds or the total capital the amount of loan capital is relatively low. Also in the case of Hampton, there is only a long term loan and no short term debt (debt on which interest is paid).

RATIO ANALYSIS

As well as being able to calculate the performance indicators described in this chapter, you will also need to be able to interpret them and comment intelligently on them. The performance indicators that you calculate may be:

- Monitored over time to see whether performance is getting better or worse

- Compared with target or budgeted levels of performance, or with another similar organisation, or with industry average figures

Interpreting the performance indicators

In the next example we will bring together many of the performance indicators covered in this chapter and not only calculate them but also comment on their significance to explain what they reveal about the business.

HOW IT WORKS

Jamboree Ltd is a manufacturing organisation which produces a range of small plastic tricycles for children. You are given below summarised statements of profit or loss for the years ended 31 October 20X7 and 31 October 20X8 and summarised statements of financial position at those dates.

Summarised statements of profit or loss (income statements)

	Y/e 31 Oct 20X8 £'000	Y/e 31 Oct 20X7 £'000
Revenue	420	320
Cost of sales	256	180
Gross profit	164	140
Expenses	100	89
Operating profit	64	51
Interest payable	10	10
Profit before tax	54	41
Tax	16	12
Profit after tax	38	29

Summarised statements of financial position

	31 Oct 20X8		31 Oct 20X7	
	£'000	£'000	£'000	£'000
Non-current assets		394		369
Current assets:				
Inventory	50		30	
Receivables	69		44	
Cash	2		12	
	121		86	
Payables	52		30	
Net current assets		69		56
		463		425
Long term loan		100		100
		363		325
Capital		250		250
Retained earnings		113		75
		363		325

You are required to calculate the following ratios and then to comment on the performance of the company over the last two years in the light of these ratios:

(a) Gross profit margin
(b) Operating profit margin
(c) Expenses to sales
(d) Return on capital employed
(e) Asset turnover
(f) Non-current asset turnover
(g) Current ratio
(h) Quick ratio
(i) Inventory days
(j) Receivables' collection period
(k) Payables' payment period
(l) Interest cover
(m) Gearing ratio (total debt/equity)

Calculate the ratios first and tabulate them so that they are easy to compare.

		20X8	20X7
(a)	Gross profit margin		
	164/420 × 100	39.0%	
	140/320 × 100		43.8%
(b)	Operating profit margin		
	64/420 × 100	15.2%	
	51/320 × 100		15.9%
(c)	Expenses to sales		
	100/420 × 100	23.8%	
	89/320 × 100		27.8%
(d)	Return on capital employed		
	64/463 × 100	13.8%	
	51/425 × 100		12.0%
(e)	Asset turnover		
	420/463	0.91	
	320/425		0.75
(f)	Non-current asset turnover		
	420/394	1.07	
	320/369		0.87
(g)	Current ratio		
	121/52	2.3	
	86/30		2.9
(h)	Quick ratio	20X8	20X7
	71/52	1.4	
	56/30		1.9
(i)	Inventory days		
	50/256 × 365	71 days	
	30/180 × 365		61 days
(j)	Receivables' collection period		
	69/420 × 365	60 days	
	44/320 × 365		50 days
(k)	Payables' payment period		
	52/256 × 365	74 days	
	30/180 × 365		61 days
(l)	Interest cover		
	64/10	6.4	
	51/10		5.1
(m)	Gearing ratio (total debt/equity)		
	100/363	27.5%	
	100/325		30.8%

Now consider the whole picture – look at the change in each ratio between one year and the next and decide why it might have changed and how all the changes in the ratios may relate to each other piece together. The main points to make about this example are given below – you may find it useful to consider profitability, resource utilisation and working capital in separate sections of

analysis. Remember that as well as summarising the movement you need to try and explain why it might have happened.

Profitability

- Revenue has increased by 31% ($\frac{(420-320)}{320} \times 100\%$)

- Gross profit margin has decreased – this may be due to a reduction in selling prices in order to increase sales volume (and sales revenue in this example) and market share.

- Operating profit margin has decreased slightly but not as much as the gross profit margin, because the percentage of expenses to sales revenue has decreased. This may be due to the fact that some of the expenses are fixed costs that have therefore not increased with the increase in sales revenue.

- Return on capital employed has increased despite the fall in profit margins, due to a significant improvement in asset turnover and non-current asset turnover.

Resource utilisation

- Asset turnover has increased significantly as has non-current asset turnover.

- There has obviously been investment in non-current assets during 20X8 as the non-current asset total has increased despite this year's depreciation having been charged.

- Therefore the increase in asset and non-current asset turnover may be due to efficiencies as a result of the new non-current assets.

Working capital

- Both the current ratio and the quick ratio have fallen, but they are still at 'healthy' levels – the main reasons for the fall in the ratios are the reduction in cash and the significant increase in payables.

- Investment in inventory has increased with inventory now being held for 71 days rather than 61 days – there is no obvious reason for this although it could be due to the company stocking a wider range of tricycles.

- The receivables' collection period has also increased by 10 days to 60 days, which may be due to offering longer credit periods to attract new customers.

- The payables' payment period has increased by 13 days to 74 days which may be due to the lack of cash, evidenced by the significantly reduced level of cash at the year-end.

Gearing

Gearing is relatively low and interest cover quite high. Therefore the company looks quite safe in this area and has not borrowed excessively.

Task 7

A business had a gross profit margin of 38.7% for the year ending 30 June 20X7 and a gross profit margin of 35.2% for the year ending 30 June 20X8.

Suggest reasons for the change in gross profit margin.

LIMITATIONS OF RATIO ANALYSIS

The point has been made throughout this chapter that care must be taken when using ratios in order to draw conclusions about an organisation. There are several reasons for treating ratios with caution. These limitations of ratio analysis are now summarised below:

Comparing like with like – If ratios are to be compared then they must be calculated in the same way, using comparable figures. When comparing ratios over time in an organisation, if there has been a change in accounting policies over the period then this may have an impact on the ratios. When comparing ratios for two different companies it is likely that the companies will have different accounting policies and adjustments should be made to bring their accounting policies in line before calculating and comparing the ratios.

Inflation – If ratios are being compared over time on the basis of historical cost accounting figures then adjustments must be made using an appropriate index in order to restate all the figures in terms of one particular price level.

Representative figures – In many cases we use year-end figures from a statement of financial position in order to calculate ratios. These year-end figures may not be representative of the average value for the year.

Accounting adjustments – When year-end figures are used to calculate ratios, just one significant accounting adjustment or transaction before the year end can alter the position shown by the statement of financial position and the resulting

BPP
LEARNING MEDIA

ratios. For example if a large cash payment is made to a major supplier just before the year end, this would significantly reduce the payables' payment period.

Age of non-current assets – If we are comparing one company to another using ratio analysis, the figures may not be entirely comparable unless the non-current assets are of similar age (and their depreciation policies are similar).

Key performance indicators and the behaviour of managers – The way in which managers are assessed on their performance can have a major influence on the decisions that they make. If key performance indicators such as ROCE are used to assess a manager then there is the possibility of a lack of goal congruence in decision making. For example a new piece of machinery may benefit the business as a whole as it will reduce costs and improve quality but the manager in charge of that department may be reluctant to invest if it will reduce the department's ROCE on which he/she is assessed.

THE BALANCED SCORECARD

So far in this chapter we have considered a variety of performance indicators, mainly financial but some non-financial, which can be used to provide information to management to help them to set performance targets for the business and monitor performance.

The BALANCED SCORECARD is a framework that can be used to determine a number of different performance indicators that are important to a business. The balanced scorecard approach is to recognise that there is not just one perspective of performance – financial performance – but four different perspectives of a business, all of which must be monitored.

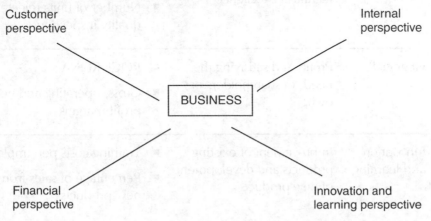

The non-financial aspects of performance may not have an immediate effect on profits and return, but in the long run they may be crucially important if the business is to maintain its competitiveness and financial success.

- The financial perspective is concerned with achieving the financial objectives of the business, in both the short term and over the longer term.

- The customer perspective is concerned with giving satisfaction to customers and meeting customer needs. If a business fails to do this, it will not succeed in the longer term.

- The internal perspective is concerned with operational performance and the efficient and effective management of resources.

- The innovation and learning perspective is concerned with the need both to innovate continually in order to survive and also to ensure that the work force improves in quality through learning and experience.

We will now consider the types of performance indicator that may be calculated to measure these four perspectives.

Perspective	Concerned with:	Possible performance indicators
Customer	Customer satisfaction and loyalty therefore quality, delivery, after-sales service	■ Number of repeat orders ■ Average delivery period ■ Number of complaints
Internal	Internal processes and technical excellence	■ Value added ■ Number of units rejected in quality inspections
Financial	Profits and satisfying the needs of shareholders or owners	■ ROCE/RONA ■ Gross, operating and net profit margins
Innovation and learning	Improvement of existing products and development of new products	■ Training costs per employee ■ Percentage of sales from new products

HOW IT WORKS

Lampoon Productions has in the past produced just one fairly successful product. Recently, however, a new version of this product has been launched. Development work continues to add a related product to the product range. Given below are some details of the activities during the month of November.

Units produced	—	Existing product	25,000
	—	New product	5,000
Cost of units produced	—	Existing product	£375,000
	—	New product	£70,000
Sales revenue	—	Existing product	£550,000
	—	New product	£125,000
Hours worked	—	Existing product	5,000
	—	New product	1,250
Development costs			£47,000

Suggest and calculate performance indicators that could be used for each of the four perspectives in the balanced scorecard.

Customer

- Percentage of sales represented by new products

$$= \frac{£125,000}{£550,000 + £125,000} \times 100$$

$$= 18.5\%$$

Internal

- Productivity — Existing product $= \dfrac{25,000 \text{ units}}{5,000 \text{ hours}}$

  $= 5$ units per hour

  — New product $= \dfrac{5,000 \text{ units}}{1,250 \text{ hours}}$

  $= 4$ units per hour

- Unit cost — Existing product $= \dfrac{£375,000}{25,000 \text{ units}}$

  $= £15$ per unit

  — New product $= \dfrac{£70,000}{5,000 \text{ units}}$

  $= £14$ per unit

Financial

- Gross profit   –   Existing product $= \dfrac{£550,000 - 375,000}{£550,000}$

                                       $= 32\%$

                 –   New product $= \dfrac{£125,000 - 70,000}{£125,000}$

                                         $= 44\%$

Innovation and learning

- Development costs as % of sales $= \dfrac{£47,000}{£675,000}$

                                                      $= 7\%$

SERVICE ORGANISATIONS

So far in this chapter we have concentrated on performance indicators for manufacturing organisations. Performance indicators are also calculated for organisations that provide a service rather than a manufactured product. There are many different types of service business, such as accountancy firms, a transport provider, a hotel, or a college of education.

Many of the performance indicators described previously in this chapter are relevant to service industries, although they may need to be expressed slightly differently. For example, whereas we may measure the cost per unit in a manufacturing industry, we may measure the cost per chargeable hour in an accountancy firm or the cost per passenger mile in a transport provider.

Productivity measurements for a service organisation should also be adapted to suit the characteristics of the business. For example in an accountancy firm productivity may be measured as the percentage of chargeable hours to total hours; in a college of education the number of students enrolled per lecturer; in a transport company the number of passengers transported per month.

Commercial service organisations should expect to make a profit and therefore most of the **financial performance indicators** will be relevant to service organisations.

It should be noted, however, that often the main revenue-generating assets of a service business are its employees. As the 'worth' of employees is not shown on the statement of financial position, measures such as ROCE, asset turnover and non-current asset turnover are perhaps not as relevant or significant for some businesses in the service sector.

A major difference between manufacturing and service organisations is that the service organisations will probably be more interested in **non-financial**

performance indicators, because employees in a service business come face-to-face much more with customers and customers are often concerned about issues such as service quality and satisfaction. For example, an accountancy firm will monitor the number of clients that leave the firm for another firm, a transport provider will be concerned about delays on routes, a college of education will take particular note of the students' assessments of the lecturers.

Service organisations are sometimes the scenario in an assessment for a number of tasks. Use the information in the scenario and the techniques that you have learnt in this chapter to adapt performance indicators to the requirements of the organisation being considered. However the AAT have made it clear that if the formula for performance indicator is not obvious then it will be given.

'WHAT IF' ANALYSIS

Throughout the chapter we have covered a variety of performance indicators. In an assessment, in addition to calculating and comparing performance indicators you may be required to conduct **'WHAT IF' ANALYSIS**, which is a technique that assesses the impact of potential changes before they actually occur.

- Forecast performance indicators based on the assumptions you are given.

- Re-calculate performance indicators to take account of changes to a business, for example, the purchase of new machinery.

- Use performance indicators to evaluate and recommend the best course of action in a given situation.

- Show what the results of the business would have looked like if certain performance targets (benchmarks) had been achieved.

CHAPTER OVERVIEW

- Performance indicators can be calculated to summarise productivity, profitability and resource utilisation – some of the performance indicators are financial measures and some are non-financial measures

- Productivity can be measured as units produced per hour or units produced per employee. Productivity can also be measured by considering the value added per employee

- A further method of measuring productivity is to use the three control ratios – efficiency, capacity and activity ratios

- The gross profit margin measures the profitability of the trading element of a business and the operating and net profit margins give a measure of profitability after deduction of expenses

- The return on capital employed relates the operating profit to the amount of capital invested in the business to give an overall return to the providers of that capital – the return on capital employed is made up of the asset turnover multiplied by the operating profit margin

- Return on net assets (also known as return on shareholders' funds) is a similar measure to ROCE and assesses the efficiency with which shareholders' funds have been used by the business to generate profits.

- Measures of resource utilisation include asset turnover and non-current asset turnover, which show the amount of revenue earned for each £1 investment

- The liquidity of a business is its ability to make payments to payables when these are due. Liquidity can be monitored by means of the current ratio and the quick ratio. Individual elements of working capital can be controlled by monitoring and managing inventory days, the receivables' collection period and the payables' payment period

- The gearing level (amount of debt finance) can be measured using the gearing ratio and the interest cover ratio. Gearing considers the ability of a business to service its debt

- Performance indicators must also be interpreted. In order to do this comparative figures (or benchmarks) are required

- The balanced scorecard is an approach to monitoring performance indicators which recognises that there are four distinct perspectives to the achievement of business objectives – the customer perspective, internal perspective, financial perspective and innovation and learning perspective

- Service organisations also use performance indicators but these may be slightly different from those for manufacturing or retail organisations, due to the different nature of the service organisation

- 'What if' analysis involves forecasting performance indicators or results given certain assumptions about a business or re-calculating these to take account of given changes to the business in order to assess the impact of different courses of action

Keywords

Performance indicators – ways of summarising elements of performance using a formula

Benchmarking – comparison of actual figures to a pre-determined target or industry best practice (a 'benchmark' for performance)

Productivity – a measure of how efficiently employees are working

Value added – sales value less the cost of materials and bought in services

Control ratios – the productivity measures of efficiency, capacity and activity

Efficiency ratio – a measure of how efficiently the employees have worked compared to standard efficiency

Capacity ratio – a measure comparing actual hours worked with budgeted hours

Activity ratio – an indicator of how the actual output compares to budgeted output

Gross profit – sales value minus cost of sales

Gross profit margin – gross profit as a percentage of sales

Operating profit – profit after deduction of cost of sales, selling, administration and distribution expenses (= profit before interest and tax)

Operating profit margin – operating profit as a percentage of sales

Net profit – operating profit minus interest and tax

Net profit margin – net profit as a percentage of sales

Return on capital employed – operating profit as a percentage of total capital (shareholders' capital plus debt capital)

Return on net assets/ Return on shareholders' funds – net profit as a percentage of net assets (shareholders' funds)

Resource utilisation – how productively and effectively an organisation uses its resources

Asset turnover – the amount of sales revenue earned for each £1 invested in the capital of the business

Non-current asset turnover – the amount of sales revenue earned for each £1 invested in non-current assets

Working capital – current assets less current liabilities

Liquidity – how much cash the business has or can access within a fairly short time

Current ratio – ratio of current assets to current liabilities

Quick ratio – ratio of current assets less inventory to current liabilities

Inventory days – number of days inventory is held (on average)

Inventory turnover –the number of times a year inventory is turned over

Receivables' collection period – the number of days it takes customers to pay (on average)

Payables' payment period – the number of days before suppliers are paid (on average)

Interest cover – the number of times that the annual interest charge is covered by the annual profit before interest

Gearing ratio – is a measure of the percentage of total debt (long and short term loan capital) in the capital structure

Balanced scorecard – a framework for performance indicators which recognises that there are four perspectives of a business (customer, internal, financial and innovation & learning)

'What if' analysis – a technique that is used to assess the impact of potential changes before they are actually made

TEST YOUR LEARNING

Test 1

Given below are the production figures for a factory for the last four months.

	August	September	October	November
Output in units	257,300	251,400	262,300	258,600
Budgeted output	250,000	255,000	260,000	260,000
Hours worked	24,400	24,600	26,700	25,600

The standard time for each unit of production is 6 minutes.

Complete the table below showing the performance indicators for each of the four months:

	Aug	Sept	Oct	Nov
Productivity per labour hour				
Efficiency ratio				
Capacity ratio				
Activity ratio				

Test 2

Given below are the production figures for a factory for the last three months.

	April	May	June
Production costs	£418,300	£424,500	£430,500
Production wages	£83,700	£86,000	£86,300
Output in units	121,700	123,500	128,000
Hours worked	11,200	11,500	11,500
Budgeted output	120,000	125,000	125,000
Sales revenue	£625,000	£634,000	£656,000
Number of employees	81	83	83

Production costs are made up of the materials for production and the bought in services required in the month. It is estimated that 11 units should be produced each hour.

Complete the table to calculate the following performance indicators for each of the last three months and for the three months in total:

(a) (i) Productivity per labour hour
    (ii) Efficiency ratio
    (iii) Capacity ratio
    (iv) Activity ratio
    (v) Value added per employee

	April	May	June	Total
Productivity per labour hour				
Efficiency ratio				
Capacity ratio				
Activity ratio				
Value added per employee				

(b) The labour rate is £7.50 per hour. Production for July will be the same as in June. If productivity can be increased to 11.5 units per hour, what is the cost saving in production wages?

£ _____

Test 3

A travel firm employs five sales representatives. Sales of holidays are seasonal and you are provided with the following figures for the last year:

	July – Sept	Oct – Dec	Jan – March	April – June
Holidays sold	6,200	4,100	7,700	5,900
Total costs	£113,200	£115,400	£125,500	£120,400

(a) For each quarter of the year complete the following table to calculate:

(i) The productivity per sales representative

(ii) The cost per holiday sold

	July – Sept	Oct – Dec	Jan – Mar	Apr – June	
Productivity					
Cost per holiday					

(b) Comment upon why you think the cost per holiday sold fluctuates so much.

Test 4

Given below is a summary of a business's performance for the last six months:

	Jan £000	Feb £000	Mar £000	April £000	May £000	June £000
Revenue	400	480	450	510	560	540
Cost of sales	210	270	260	320	340	330
Expenses	140	144	141	136	157	152
Interest	–	–	–	3	3	3
Shareholders' funds	240	290	319	353	406	434
Loan	–	–	–	40	40	40

For each month of the year, complete the table to calculate the following performance indicators:

(a) Gross profit margin
(b) Operating profit margin
(c) Percentage of expenses to revenue
(d) Return on capital employed
(e) Asset turnover

Comment on what the performance measures indicate about the business activities for the last six months.

	Jan	Feb	Mar	April	May	June
Gross profit margin						
Net profit margin						
% expenses to revenue						
Return on capital employed						
Asset turnover						

Test 5

Given below is a summary of the performance of a business for the last three years:

	20X6	20X7	20X8
	£000	£000	£000
Revenue	820	850	900
Cost of sales	440	445	500
Expenses	290	305	315
Interest	—	3	3
Capital and reserves	500	560	620
Long term loan	—	50	50
Non-current assets	385	453	498
Receivables	85	112	128
Inventory	50	55	67
Payables	30	34	41
Bank balance	10	24	18

For each of the three years complete the table to calculate the following performance measures and comment on what the measures indicate about the performance of the business over the period:

(a) Gross profit margin
(b) Operating profit margin
(c) Return on capital employed
(d) Asset turnover
(e) Non-current asset turnover
(f) Current ratio
(g) Quick ratio
(h) Receivables' collection period
(i) Inventory days
(j) Payables' payment period
(k) Interest cover
(l) Gearing ratio

	20X6	20X7	20X8
Gross profit margin			
Operating profit margin			
Return on capital employed			
Asset turnover			
Non-current asset turnover			
Current ratio			
Quick ratio			
Receivables' collection period			
Inventory days			
Payables' payment period			
Interest cover			
Gearing ratio			

Test 6

A retail business has three small department stores in Flimwell, Hartfield and Groombridge. The figures for the first six months of 20X8 are given below:

	Flimwell	Hartfield	Groombridge
Financial details	£	£	£
Revenue	540,000	370,000	480,000
Opening inventory	51,000	45,000	30,000
Closing inventory	56,000	50,000	32,000
Purchases	210,000	165,000	192,000
Expenses	270,000	175,000	225,000
Net Assets	550,000	410,000	510,000
Payables	25,800	27,500	30,500

Non-financial details			
Floor area	2,400 sq m	1,700 sq m	2,000 sq m
Employees	28	13	26
Hours worked	30,500	14,100	28,300

(a) Complete the table to calculate the following performance indicators for each store:

   (i)   Gross profit margin
   (ii)   Operating profit margin
   (iii) Return on net assets
   (iv) Net asset turnover
   (v)   Inventory days
   (vi) Payables' payment period
   (vii) Sales per square metre of floor area
   (viii) Sales per employee
   (ix) Sales per hour worked

	Flimwell	Hartfield	Groombridge
Gross profit margin			
Operating profit margin			
Return on net assets			
Net asset turnover			
Inventory days			
Payables' payment period			
Sales per sq m			
Sales per employee			
Sales per hour worked			

(b) Use the performance indicators calculated in (a) to write a report to the sales director of the chain comparing the performances of the three stores for the six month period. In the report explain the effect on the cash balance if the payables payment period in Flimwell were increased to that of Hartfield.

Test 7

(a) A business operates on a gross profit margin of 44% and sales for the period were £106,500. What is the gross profit?

£ [   ]

(b) A business operates on a gross profit margin of 37.5% and the gross profit made in the period was £105,000. What was the figure for revenue for the period?

£ [   ]

(c) A business had revenue of £256,000 in a month, with a gross profit margin of 41% and an operating profit margin of 13.5%. What were the expenses for the month?

£ ⎡_____⎤

(d) A business has a return on capital employed of 12.8% and made an operating profit for the period of £50,000. What is the capital employed?

£ ⎡_____⎤

(e) A business has an operating profit percentage of 10% and a return on capital employed of 15%. What is the asset turnover of the business?

⎡_____⎤ times

(f) A business has opening inventory and closing inventory of £118,000 and £104,000 respectively and made purchases during the year totalling £465,000. How many times did inventory turn over during the year?

⎡_____⎤ times

(g) A business has a receivables' collection period of 64 days and the closing receivables figure is £64,000. What is the figure for revenue for the year?

£ ⎡_____⎤

Test 8

Given below is the summarised statement of profit or loss (income statement) and statement of financial position of a manufacturing company for the year ended 30 September 20X8:

Statement of profit or loss (income statement)

	£'000	£'000
Revenue		372
Opening inventory of finished goods	19	
Materials	28	
Labour	40	
Production overheads	14	
	101	
Closing inventory of finished goods	21	
Cost of sales		80
Gross profit		292
Administration costs	184	
Interest payable	6	
Training costs	9	
Research costs	25	
		224
		68

Statement of financial position

	£'000	£'000
Non-current assets		232
Current assets:		
Inventory of finished goods	21	
Receivables	62	
Cash	9	
	92	
Payables	24	
Net current assets		68
		300
Long term loan		(100)
		200
Capital and reserves		200

You are to complete the table to calculate the following
indicators and for each one to identify which balanc
perspective is being measured.

(a) Operating profit margin
(b) Return on capital employed
(c) Inventory days
(d) Asset turnover
(e) Research costs as a percentage of production costs
(f) Training costs as a percentage of the labour cost

		Balanced scorecard perspective
Operating profit margin		
Return on capital employed		
Inventory days		
Asset turnover		
Research costs as % of production costs		
Training costs as a % of labour cost		

BPP
LEARNING MEDIA

chapter 8:
COST MANAGEMENT

WHAT IS QUALITY?

So far in this Text we have been considering performance mainly from a financial perspective and productivity perspective. There is a view that the success of a business also depends on its ability to provide quality. This means quality in the product that is made or the service that is provided, but also quality in operational procedures.

Businesses that show concern for quality may be described as customer-centred. However, it is also argued that the most successful businesses are those that recognise the importance of quality and quality management. The great success of Japanese industry from the 1950s onwards, for example, was based largely on the concept of Total Quality Management.

Quality and value

QUALITY can be described as the 'degree of excellence of the product or service' or 'how well the product or service serves its purpose'.

Quality is judged by the customer. A product or service has quality only if it satisfies the customer. To do this the product or service must have two main elements:

- It must be fit for the purpose for which it has been acquired
- It must represent value for money to the customer.

This does not mean that products or services need to be made more expensive by using better materials or more highly skilled staff. Provided that the product or service does what it is meant to do and is viewed as value for money by the customer, then this product or service will have quality. For example, high quality in a car does not have to mean producing an expensive car. A customer may think that a low-priced but economical car is excellent value for money and meets his or her need for a small car to drive in a city.

HOW IT WORKS

Let us consider travelling by aeroplane from London to Zurich. The basic requirements of this service to a customer are:

- The customer reaches the destination safely.
- The flight departs and arrives on time.

Provided that these requirements are met, then the service will be fit for its purpose.

The price that the customer will pay for the flight however will depend upon the customer's perspective of value. One customer may choose a low cost 'no frills' flight which includes no food or refreshment and probably less leg-room in the seats. This will represent value to that customer.

Alternatively another customer may choose a first class seat on a scheduled flight as their perception of value is the luxury of the first class lounge, additional space, more comfortable seats and the provision of refreshments.

Both services have quality if they serve their purpose and are perceived as value for money by the customer.

Enhancement of value

Value is important in judging whether a product or service has quality, so it is important to consider what the customer expects from the product or service.

Many industries are now highly competitive, with many businesses providing the same type of goods or services and competing for customers. In these situations, value can be enhanced by considering what the customer requires and adapting the product or service to improve the perceived value of the product or service.

HOW IT WORKS

If we consider the banking system, there are many High Street banks and building societies that provide the same basic services of current and deposit accounts, cheque books and debit cards. In order to compete for customers, many of these banks have attempted to enhance the value of the service that they provide, by offering additional services that are thought to enhance the value of the basic service to the customer, with no additional cost to the customer. Therefore many banks now try to compete by offering services such as telephone banking, internet banking and text messaging banking.

COSTS OF QUALITY

One approach to the management of quality is to measure and manage quality costs. The aim should be to achieve a desirable standard of quality for the least cost.

The COSTS OF QUALITY are the costs of ensuring and assuring quality and also any losses incurred when quality is not achieved.

There are four main areas of quality related costs and for computer based assessments these are terms that you need to be able to define. The four types of quality costs are:

- Prevention costs
- Appraisal costs
- Internal failure costs
- External failure costs

Prevention costs

PREVENTION COSTS are the costs incurred prior to, or during, production in order to prevent or reduce defects in products or mistakes in services. In other words, they are the costs of preventing quality failures.

Prevention costs can include any of the following:

- Improvements in product design or specification to reduce the proportion of defective products
- Improvements in systems and procedures that are designed to reduce mistakes in the provision of services
- Design, development and maintenance of quality control equipment
- Administration of quality control
- Provision of training for quality control: training staff so that they make fewer mistakes

Appraisal costs

APPRAISAL COSTS are the costs incurred in initially monitoring how the product or service conforms to quality requirements. They are the costs associated with assessing the level of quality achieved. Typically, appraisal costs are associated with costs of inspection and testing.

These costs include:

- Design, development and maintenance of inspection equipment
- Inspection of goods and raw materials received from suppliers
- Inspection of production processes and work in progress
- Inspection or performance testing of finished goods
- Appraisal of the quality of services provided
- Sample testing of finished production, perhaps to the point of destruction

Internal failure costs

INTERNAL FAILURE COSTS are the costs arising from inadequate quality before the goods or services are sold to the customer. Therefore they are costs arising within the organisation due to the failure to achieve the required level of quality. A large part of internal failure costs are associated with the cost of correcting faults that are found in products and correcting procedural errors in service provision – but before the goods or service are delivered to the customer. They are the cost of correcting faults that customers do not learn about.

Internal failure costs include:

- Cost of investigation and analysis of failed units

- Re-work costs for items that fail inspection tests

- Re-inspection costs

- Cost of defective units scrapped or lost contribution from selling defective items at a lower price than normal

- Losses due to faults in raw materials purchased

- Costs of reviewing product design or specification after finding defective units

- Costs of production delays

External failure costs

EXTERNAL FAILURE COSTS are costs arising from inadequate quality discovered after the goods or services have been sold to the customer.

These costs include:

- Costs of running a customer service department

- Costs of dealing with customer complaints

- Product liability costs

- Costs of replacing or repairing goods returned from customers

- Loss of future custom from dissatisfied customers: this may be the biggest quality cost of all, but is the most difficult to measure reliably

Managing quality costs

Managing quality costs can be difficult. In order to reduce some quality costs, it may be necessary to increase others. For example:

- To reduce external failure costs, it may be necessary to increase spending on appraisal costs and internal failure costs, to reduce the number of defective items sold to customers.

- To reduce internal and external failure costs, it may be necessary to spend much more on prevention costs, such as costs of better product design and staff training.

267

Task 1

Categorise the following examples in terms of the four different types of quality costs:

(a) Improvements in product design or specification to reduce defective products

(b) Loss of future custom from dissatisfied customers

(c) Lost contribution on defective units scrapped or sold at a lower price than normal

(d) Sample testing of finished production

HOW IT WORKS

Smithson Ltd is a manufacturer of small electrical items of kitchen equipment such as toasters, food processors and microwave ovens.

A number of events that occurred recently are given below.

(a) One line of microwave ovens has had to be recalled due to a few isolated incidents where the oven has caught fire. It is highly likely that the company may have to pay damages to the customers involved in the fires. It is unlikely that any of the owners of the recalled products will buy Smithson goods again.

(b) The company engineers have designed a new motor for one of the food processors which should ensure far fewer breakdowns and a longer life of the machine.

(c) It has been discovered that the external surface of one of the toasters, which has been made with a new material from a new supplier, gets scratched in the production process and all of these toasters can only be sold at a lower price as seconds.

(d) The company has introduced more detailed inspection procedures for microwave ovens following the recall incident.

(e) The company produces a range of different food mixers and it has been discovered that one particular line fails more often than others and the cause is to be investigated and put right.

We will now analyse each of these events and determine what effects they are likely to have on the various categories of quality costs – prevention, appraisal, internal failure and external failure.

(a) **Recall of microwaves**

Prevention costs – these will increase as the fault must be eliminated which may require redesign of the product

Appraisal costs – these will probably increase as this microwave will require closer monitoring in future to ensure that the problem has been eliminated

Internal failure costs – these will increase due to investigation of the failure, repairs to any ovens in inventory which may cause disruption to the production process and re-inspection costs

External failure costs – the costs of repairing the microwaves, any damages claims received from customers and the loss of these customers for future sales

(b) **Design of new motor**

Prevention costs – these would be the cost of the design and its implementation

Internal failure costs – these should be reduced as the product is more reliable

External failure costs – these should be reduced as the product is more reliable and has a longer lifespan

(c) **Scratched toasters**

Prevention costs – new design or finding a new supplier

Internal failure costs – the lost contribution from having to sell the toasters at a lower price

(d) **Inspection procedures for microwaves**

Appraisal costs – these will increase with the costs of inspection procedures

Internal failure costs – these should reduce as the benefits of the inspection are felt

External failure costs – these should reduce as fewer defective products will be sold to customers

(e) **Food mixers**

Prevention costs – these will be incurred in the re-design of the product once the cause has been identified

Internal failure costs – these will increase due to investigation of the problem

External failure costs – these should reduce as fewer defective products are sold to customers

Task 2

A car manufacturer recalls a particular make of car due to the fact that the handbrake fails if the car door is slammed shut.

Complete the table to show what effect will this have on the different categories of quality cost.

Cost of quality	Effect
Prevention costs	
Appraisal costs	
Internal costs	
External costs	

Measuring the costs of quality

Having analysed quality costs into their constituent elements, we now need to consider how to measure these costs within a cost accounting system.

Normally the cost accounting system of an organisation must be adapted in order to record the costs of quality.

For example, in a traditional cost accounting system there is an allowance for 'normal losses' in the cost of production. Therefore the costs of wasted materials, scrapping of defective products and reworking of products with faults are all included in the production cost of finished output and they are not separately identifiable or highlighted for management attention. Similarly costs of inspections are included in production overheads without being separately identified.

Therefore if the costs of quality are to be measured, the cost accounting system must be amended so that the costs of quality can be separately identified, recorded and reported to management.

Explicit and implicit costs of quality

The costs of quality that can be quantified from the cost accounting records are known as EXPLICIT QUALITY COSTS. However, there are other types of cost which are not recorded in the accounting records and which can only be estimated – these are known as IMPLICIT QUALITY COSTS.

Implicit costs include:

- The opportunity cost of lost sales to existing customers who have bought a defective product and so will not purchase from the organisation again.

- Loss of goodwill or reputation due to factors such as the widespread recall of one of an organisation's products, affecting potential customers.

- Costs of disruption to production due to reworking of faulty products – these costs will be included in normal production costs and will not be separately recorded.

- Costs incurred due to the practice of holding higher levels of inventory of raw materials in order to allow faulty materials to be replaced without disruption to production.

HOW IT WORKS

Given below is a summary of the costs of quality identified earlier for Smithson Ltd. Now we will decide which are explicit costs and which are implicit costs.

	Explicit	Implicit
(a) Recall of microwaves		
Prevention costs – Redesign costs	x	
Appraisal costs – Inspection costs	x	
Internal failure costs –		
Investigation of the failure	x	
Disruption of production process from reworking		x
Re-inspection costs	x	
External failure costs –		
Cost of repairs to the microwaves	x	
Damages claims		x
Loss of customers		x
(b) Design of new motor		
Prevention costs –		
Cost of the design/implementation	x	
Internal failure costs – Reduced due to design		x
External failure costs – Reduced due to design		x

	Explicit	Implicit
(c) **Scratched toasters**		
Prevention costs –		
New design		✗
Finding a new supplier		✗
Internal failure costs – Lost contribution		✗
(d) **Inspection procedures for microwaves**		
Appraisal costs – Costs of inspection procedures	✗	
Internal failure costs – Reduced due to inspections		✗
External failure costs – Reduced as fewer defective products will be sold		✗
(e) **Food mixers**		
Prevention costs – Re-design of the product	✗	
Internal failure costs – Investigation of the problem	✗	
External failure costs –		
Reduced as fewer defective products are sold to customers		✗

This analysis of the costs of quality highlights a few areas:

- The explicit costs should all be available from the cost accounting records.

- Some of the implicit costs can also be estimated, such as the amount of likely claims for damages from customers of the microwaves.

- Other implicit costs may not be possible to estimate such as the lost customers for microwave ovens or the disruption to the production process from repairs and reworking.

- Some of the implicit elements are not costs but reductions of quality costs such as the reduction of external quality costs as less defective products are sold – it will not often be possible to put a value to these.

Task 3

Give two examples of explicit quality costs and two examples of implicit quality costs.

Explicit quality costs

    (1)

    (2)

Implicit quality costs

    (1)

    (2)

Calculating the costs of quality

As we have just seen, in practice measuring quality costs is a complicated business. However in tests the situation will be simplified and you may be required to identify and total the costs of quality.

HOW IT WORKS

Scooby Products estimates that two out of every 1,000 of its products that are sold are defective in some way. When the goods are returned they are replaced free of charge. It is estimated that every customer who buys a faulty product will return it and will not buy Scooby Products' goods again. Each unit costs £30 to manufacture and is sold at a price of £40.

Due to quality inspections it is also estimated that 10,000 defective units a year are discovered before they are sold and these can then be sold as 'seconds' at a price of £25. The quality inspections cost £450,000 each year.

The unit sales of the product are 20 million each year.

We will analyse and calculate the explicit costs of quality:

If unit sales are 20 million and two out of every 1,000 units sold are defective then the number of defective units is 20,000,000/1,000 × 2 = 40,000 units.

	£
Appraisal costs – inspection costs	450,000
Internal failure costs – lost contribution on seconds	
(10,000 units × (£40 – £25))	150,000
External failure costs – cost of replacement products	
(40,000 × £30)	1,200,000
	1,800,000

There is also the implicit cost of the loss of 40,000 customers each year who will not buy Scooby Products' items again.

Task 4

A manufacturing business estimates that it has to sell 3,000 defective units of its product at a 'seconds' price of £12 per unit. The normal selling price is £25 per unit and the inspection procedure that identifies these defective units costs £20,000.

What is the total cost of quality and what type of quality costs has the business incurred?

£ [ ]

Type of quality costs [ ]

PERFORMANCE INDICATORS FOR QUALITY

In just the same way that performance indicators are produced to summarise the production operations for a business, so too can performance indicators be produced to assess the quality of an organisation's products or services. Most of these performance indicators are measures of customer satisfaction.

If we start by thinking about performance indicators for the quality of physical goods these can be a mixture of financial and non-financial performance indicators.

Financial indicators

Financial indicators to assess customer satisfaction with a product and therefore the quality of the product may include the following:

- Cost per customer of the customer service department
- Cost per customer of after-sales service
- The sales value of returned goods as a percentage of total sales value
- Unit cost of returned goods
- Unit cost of repair of returned goods
- Cost of reworking defective goods as a percentage of total production cost

Non-financial indicators

- Number of goods returned

- Number of goods returned as a percentage of the number of goods sold

- Number of warranty claims as a percentage of total units sold

- Number of customer complaints as a percentage of total number of sales orders

Quality control and inspections

At this stage a distinction should be drawn between quality control (prevention – before the event) and quality inspections (detection – after the event). Quality control is about prevention of defective products or mistakes in provision of a service. Quality inspections are to do with detection and identification of defective products or mistakes in the provision of a service. Ideally an organisation would plan to have zero defects. However, the costs of quality assurance needed to prevent all errors and guarantee zero defects may be so high as to be prohibitive, and so some defects may be tolerated because it would cost too much to eliminate them.

Quality inspections

When a manufacturing business carries out quality inspections, this is often done by taking a sample of the production output and testing this for defective products. The inspection process is not applied to 100% of output. Quality inspections normally take place at three points in the production process:

- Receiving inspections when raw materials and components are received from suppliers

- Production floor or process inspections for work in progress (work during the course of manufacture)

- Final inspection of finished goods

From these inspections, and using the sample results, further performance indicators can be established such as:

- Percentage of defective materials compared to total materials
- Number of anticipated defective units
- Percentage of defective units to total of units produced

Measuring quality of services

Deciding on performance indicators for the quality of manufactured goods is much more straightforward than finding performance indicators for the quality of services.

Measuring the quality of a service again involves measuring customer satisfaction, therefore the first stage is to ensure that the organisation knows what the customer expects from the service.

Some performance indicators for quality of a service may be qualitative, such as surveys of customer opinion. A further method of assessing the quality of a service may be by inspection, either by an internal or an external body, such as government inspections of schools.

There can also be quantitative, although normally non-financial, performance indicators for a service, such as average waiting times for hospital operations or the percentage of train journeys that did not run on time.

Task 5

What type of quality performance indicators might a taxi firm consider?

TOTAL QUALITY MANAGEMENT

TOTAL QUALITY MANAGEMENT (TQM) is a quality management system in an organisation that involves all activities of the organisation not just the production activities. The philosophy behind Total Quality Management must be applied to all the activities of the business – design, production, marketing, administration, purchasing, sales and even the finance function.

TQM can be defined as 'a continuous improvement in quality, productivity and effectiveness obtained by establishing management responsibility for processes as well as output. In this system every process has an identified process owner and every person in an entity operates within a process and contributes to its improvement' (Chartered Institute of Management Accountant's (CIMA) *Official Terminology*).

Principles of TQM

As we have seen, defective products or mistakes in production or provision of a service are costly. These costs include:

- Materials wastage
- Idle time
- Reworking costs
- Production disruption costs
- Re-inspection costs
- Costs of dealing with complaints
- Costs of replacing faulty goods
- Costs of loss of customer goodwill

TQM is based on several different but consistent principles, because it was developed as a concept by a number of different people and different companies. Its origins are attributed to Toyota, the Japanese car manufacturer.

- One principle of TQM is continuous improvement. An organisation should continually look for ways of improving performance. These improvements will all be small improvements, but the cumulative effect of many small improvements over time will be substantial. An organisation should never stop looking for and finding more improvements that can be made.

- Another principle is GETTING IT RIGHT FIRST TIME . Faults and errors should not happen. If these are eliminated, internal and external failure costs will not exist. Costs of prevention are less than the costs of correction.

TQM seeks to ensure that the goods produced or the services supplied are of the highest quality.

Training

In order for TQM to work in all areas of an organisation, training and motivation of staff is vital in order for each individual to have the attitude of constantly seeking improvement in what they do. All staff within the organisation must be taught that they have customers. These may be external customers of the business or internal customers in the form of colleagues in the business that use an individual's work. Each individual should endeavour to ensure that they get it right first time and therefore that their excellent work is passed on in the chain.

Quality circles

Another concept in TQM is that every employee is involved with quality and anyone with an idea should be allowed to put this forward. This is often done by forming discussion groups of employees within the organisation, known as QUALITY CIRCLES.

Quality circles normally consist of about ten employees with a range of skills, roles and seniority who meet regularly to discuss problems of quality and quality control and to perhaps suggest ways of improving processes and output. This means that there is input from all levels within the organisation and from different disciplines such as marketing, design, engineering, information technology and office administration as well as production.

TARGET COSTING

We shall now turn to another aspect of performance.

When a company is designing a new product, it may have a good idea of how much customers will pay for it. This should be the target selling price. The company will also know how much profit margin it will want from the new product. If it knows the target selling price and the required profit margin, it can identify a target cost for the new product.

The TARGET COST is determined by taking the fixed target selling price and deducting the required profit margin. Be careful in tasks to see whether you are given a required profit margin (profit as a percentage of sales price) or a required mark-up (cost as a percentage of sales price) when determining target costs.

Once determined, this target cost is then presented to the product designers for them to achieve. The product will not be put into commercial production unless and until the target cost is achieved. Often it may be necessary to change the product design in order to reduce costs. One technique that may be used for target costing is value analysis.

Task 6

A car manufacturer wants to calculate a target cost for a new car, the price of which will be set at £27,950. The company requires an 8% profit margin.

The target cost is £ [   ]

There may be some costs that a business is unable to influence or reduce (particularly in the short term), for example certain fixed overheads. Such costs must be deducted from the target cost to ascertain the maximum amount that is then available to the business to spend on other costs for example, materials/labour.

Task 7

A manufacturer, operating in a competitive market, can sell its product at £25 per unit. It wishes to make a profit margin of 40%. Each unit of product requires 0.5 hours of labour at £6/hour and incurs other overheads at a rate of £8/labour hour. The product requires 2kg of material per unit. What is the maximum that the manufacturer can afford to pay for each kg of material?

Maximum £ per kg [   ]

Value analysis

The aim behind VALUE ANALYSIS is to reduce the cost of a product or service without any reduction in the value to the customer. Value analysis is where every aspect of a product or service is analysed to determine whether it provides value to the customer and whether the same value can be provided in any other way at a lower cost.

Value engineering

Technically, value analysis is applied to products or services already being produced or provided. If this process takes place during the design stage of a new product or in the planning stage of a service then it is known as VALUE ENGINEERING.

Specialists in design, engineering, work methods and technology, amongst others, will be involved in this process. When designing a product or planning a service each element of the product or service must be considered to determine whether it adds value to the product or service for the consumer and then to ensure that this is included in the product or service at the lowest possible cost.

There is usually much greater scope for reducing costs through value engineering at the new product design stage than there is for reducing costs through value analysis of existing products.

Cost reduction

The aim of value analysis is cost reduction; however, care must be taken to ensure that short term cost reduction does not affect long term profitability. For example, costs could be reduced by cutting back on staff training. However, this could lead to inefficiencies, wastage, low morale or high labour turnover.

The aim should be long term cost reduction by improving productivity and the efficiency with which all of the resources of the organisation are used.

Assessment of cost reductions

A variety of methods can be used to assess whether cost reductions are possible including:

- Work study
- Organisation and method study
- Variety reduction

Work study

Work study can be used in manufacturing processes to determine factors such as:

- The most efficient layout of the factory and the stores function
- The most efficient usage of materials, labour and machinery to reduce wastage and idle time
- The most efficient work methods and procedures

Organisation and method study

This is similar to work study but it is used in the administrative functions of the business in order to improve office procedures and determine factors such as:

- Maximising the benefits from computerisation
- Determining the most efficient office layout, work flows and communications
- Elimination of unnecessary or duplicated office procedures
- Minimising the amount of paperwork

Variety reduction

The aim of variety reduction is to reduce either the number of products produced, or the number of different types of components used, in order to reduce costs.

By reducing the range of products that are produced and concentrating on just a small number of products, this can increase economies of scale of production, but this must be balanced with value to the customer. If consumers require a wide range of choices of a product then such cost cutting will not be of benefit due to lost sales and goodwill.

Often a more effective way of cutting costs is to standardise the components used in the products. If the same basic components are used in many different products, then cost savings can be made through bulk buying from suppliers and holding a smaller range of inventories.

Benefits of value analysis

If value analysis and cost reduction procedures are successfully carried out in an organisation this can have a number of benefits for both the organisation and the customer:

- Reduced costs for the organisation and potentially reduced prices for the customer with no loss of value
- Continuous improvement in the design and manufacture of products

- Improvement of customer service due to the use of standard components
- Design of products and services with customer value always considered

Value analysis and value engineering can help an organisation to reduce costs while still maintaining the quality of the product or service that it provides.

PRODUCT LIFE CYCLE

The final aspect of cost and performance that will be described in this chapter is product life cycle costs.

Most products have a limited PRODUCT LIFE CYCLE. A product life cycle consists of different phases or stages in the commercial life of the product. At each stage sales volumes, costs and profitability are different.

A product life cycle can often be divided into five separate consecutive stages:

- Development
- Launch (or introduction)
- Growth
- Maturity
- Decline

Development and launch stages

These are the stages when the product is developed for the first time and introduced initially to the market.

During this period of the product's life there are large outgoings in terms of development expenditure, the purchase of non-current assets necessary for production, building up inventory levels and advertising and promotion expenses. Costs are incurred but no revenue (during the development stage) or only a limited amount of revenue (during the launch or introduction stage) is generated.

Launch/introduction stage

The product is introduced to the market. It is likely that even after the launch sales will be quite low and the product will be making a loss at this stage. Further amounts are spent on advertising to make potential customers aware of the product.

Growth stage

If the launch of the product is successful then during the growth stage there will be a fairly rapid increase in sales and a move to profitability. The costs incurred during the development and launch stages may be recovered. The growth in sales will not continue indefinitely, and new competitors enter the market, attracted by the success and profitability of the product.

Maturity stage

In the maturity stage of the product life cycle, the growth in total demand for the product will slow down and annual sales volumes will become more constant. New competitors may not enter the market, but existing competition prevents excessive profits for any organisation in the market. In many cases this is the stage where the product is modified or improved, in order to sustain demand, and this may then result in a small and temporary surge in sales.

Decline stage

At some point in its life cycle, the product will reach the end of its sale life. The market will have bought enough of the product and it will reach saturation point where sales will decline. This is the point where the business should consider no longer producing the product.

For some products, the life cycle may be very long and the product may not ever reach a decline phase. However, when products are seen as a brand or particular design, the life cycle can be very short. For example, the life cycle for women's dresses may be very long, but the life cycle for a particular fashion style may be extremely short.

The level of sales and profits earned over a life cycle can be illustrated diagrammatically as follows.

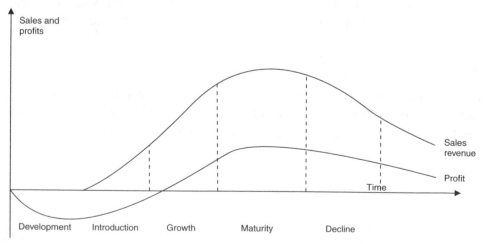

The horizontal axis measures the duration of the life cycle, which can last from, say, 18 months to several hundred years. Children's crazes or fad products have very short lives while some products, such as binoculars (invented in the eighteenth century) can last a very long time.

Market considerations

It is also important to consider the overall market for a particular product. Is the market a new, emerging market for a new product, an established market for a long-standing product or a declining market for a product which is no longer of great interest to consumers?

For example no matter how technologically advanced a VHS video recorder is, DVD players meant that demand for video recorders went into terminal decline and now downloading films from the internet has put the DVD player into decline.

Life cycle costing

Under traditional costing methods the costs of a product are only recorded and analysed once production of the product has begun. However, a product's life cycle costs are incurred from its design stage through development to market launch, production and sales, and finally to its eventual withdrawal from the market. It is recognised that in reality a large proportion of the costs of a product are incurred before production has started in the early stages of the product life cycle.

Life cycle costing recognises all of these pre-production costs of the product such as:

- Design costs
- Prototyping
- Programming
- Process design
- Equipment acquisition

Traditional cost accumulation systems are based on the financial accounting year and tend to dissect a product's life cycle into a series of 12-month periods. This means that traditional cost accounting systems do not accumulate costs over a product's entire life cycle and do not therefore assess a product's profitability over its entire life. Instead they measure costs on a periodic basis and write off the costs in the period when they are incurred.

The aim of life cycle costing is to accumulate all the costs of the product over the whole of its life cycle in order to ensure that all costs are covered by sales revenue from the product and that the product is profitable taking its entire life cycle into consideration. It may be necessary to use the discounted cash flow techniques that we considered earlier in this Text (to calculate net present values) when calculating life cycle costs.

Task 8

A manufacturer is developing a new high-technology product which is expected to sell rapidly once launched. However, the product will have a very short life cycle, as competitors develop new innovations and this product becomes obsolete.

The development of the product will require purchase of specialist equipment for £100,000 in December 20X4. This equipment will have scrap value of £20,000 in December 20X8.

Development staff costs of £200,000 will be incurred in 20X5. Assume these costs occur at the end of the year.

In December 20X5, the company will pay a PR agency £30,000 to begin designing and delivering an advertising campaign. Sales of the product are then expected as follows, with profit margin of 40%. Assume sales are received and the costs of production are incurred at the end of each year.

	Sales (£)
20X6	800,000
20X7	2,000,000
20X8	200,000

The company will cease making and selling the product by December 20X8.

(a) Calculate the total life cycle costs and total profit over the life cycle of this product, ignoring the time value of money.

(b) Calculate the net present value of the project at December 20X4, assuming the company's cost of capital is 10% so the discount factors are:

Year	Discount factor @ 10%
0	1.000
1	0.909
2	0.826
3	0.751
4	0.683

(c) Using your answers, advise the company whether it should undertake this project.

CHAPTER OVERVIEW

- Quality of a product or service is what is perceived from the customer's perspective – is the product/service fit for its purpose and value for money?

- An aspect of a product has value if the customer perceives it as being worth paying money for

- Quality costs can be analysed into four types – prevention costs, appraisal costs, internal failure costs and external failure costs

- In order to measure the costs of quality the cost accounting system may have to be modified in order to record the relevant figures. Costs that can be taken from the cost accounting records are explicit costs of quality but there may also be other implicit costs of quality which cannot be found from the accounting records

- An organisation can monitor its quality levels and costs of quality with a variety of financial and non-financial performance indicators. For an organisation which provides a service some of the performance indicators will tend to be qualitative rather than quantitative

- Total Quality Management is an ethos. It is based on principles such as continuous improvement and 'getting it right first time'

- Target costing involves setting a target for the cost of a product or service by deducting the desired profit margin from the market selling price. The target cost represents the maximum amount of cost that the organisation can incur and still make the desired level of profit

- Value analysis is a method of analysing the constituent elements of a product or service in order to try to reduce the cost with no loss in value to the customer. This method of analysis applied to new product design is known as value engineering

- Most products have a limited life cycle which involves the stages of development and launch, growth, maturity and decline. The position of the product within its life cycle will affect sales and profitability patterns and be an important factor in cost management

- The aim of life cycle costing is to ensure that all the costs of a product (including development costs) are accumulated over the whole of its life cycle, with or without discounting, in order to ensure that all costs are covered by revenue from the product

Keywords

Quality – the degree of excellence of a product/service and how well it serves its purpose

Getting it right first time –a basic concept behind Total Quality Management.

Costs of quality – costs of ensuring quality and costs incurred when quality is not achieved

Prevention costs – costs incurred to investigate, prevent and reduce defects or mistakes

Appraisal costs – costs associated with inspection and assessing the level of quality achieved

Internal failure costs – costs arising within the organisation due to the failure to achieve quality, eg re-working of defective units

External failure costs – costs arising from inadequate quality discovered after the goods/services have been sold to customers, eg cost of repairs under warranty or guarantee

Explicit costs – costs that can be found within the accounting records

Implicit costs – costs not recorded in the accounting records

Total quality management – a philosophy of management based on achieving continuous improvement in quality, productivity and effectiveness

Quality circles – groups of employees who meet regularly to discuss quality issues

Target cost – the desired cost of a product which the designers must achieve, based on deducting the desirable profit margin from the target selling price

Value analysis – analysis of every aspect of existing products/services in order to reduce the cost with no reduction in value to the customer

Value engineering – value analysis in the design stage of a product or planning stage of a service

Product life cycle – model to show different sales and profitability patterns at different stages of a product's life

Life cycle costing – accumulation of all costs of a product over its life cycle including pre-production costs

TEST YOUR LEARNING

Test 1

For each of the following, state which type of cost of quality it is (prevention, appraisal, internal failure or external failure):

		Type of cost of quality
(a)	Products scrapped due to faulty raw materials	
(b)	Training for quality control staff	
(c)	Costs of customer after sales service department	
(d)	Lost contribution on defective products sold as seconds	
(e)	Costs of inspection of raw materials	
(f)	Maintenance of quality control equipment	
(g)	Cost of replacing faulty products returned by customers	
(h)	Costs of production delays due to re-working defective products discovered in quality inspection	
(i)	Claims from customers relating to defective products	
(j)	Performance testing of finished goods	

Test 2

A business estimates that one in 3,000 of its products are found to be faulty after sale. Of these it is estimated that 60% are returned by customers and can be repaired at a cost of £20 per product. It is felt that the customers who do not return the products will not buy the company's products again and the cost of advertising for replacement customers is £40,000 per annum.

Total sales of the product are 5,000,000 units each year.

Complete the table to list all of the costs of quality and the amount of that cost where possible. State into which category of cost of quality each cost falls.

Cost of quality	Amount £	Category of cost

Test 3

A manufacturing organisation carries out quality inspections on product A. In the last year 2,000 defective units were discovered and had to be sold as seconds at a price of £45, compared with the normal selling price of £80. The costs of the quality inspections totalled £60,000 for the year.

Sales of product A are 1 million units each year and it is estimated that a further 1 in every 1,000 sales will be defective. Of these it is expected that 75% will be returned by customers and will be replaced at no cost to the customer. The cost of producing a unit of product A is £50. The customers who do not return their products are unlikely to buy the company's products again.

Complete the table to list all of the costs of quality incurred by the business and the amount of each cost if possible. State which type of cost of quality each cost is and whether it is an explicit cost or an implicit cost.

Cost of quality	Amount £	Category of cost	Explicit or implicit

Test 4

A manufacturing business has the following details for the period just ended:

Total sales	£1,500,000
Cost of customer after sales service department	£280,000
Total sales returns (sales value)	£120,000
Costs of repairs of returned products	£40,000
Number of after sales service customers	60,000
Total units sold	50,000 units
Number of units returned	4,000
Number of customer complaints	3,000

Complete the table calculating the performance indicators for quality from the information provided.

Cost per after sales service customer	
Sales returns as a % of sales	
Repair cost per returned units	
Complaints as a % of unit sales	

Test 5

Explain what is meant by Total Quality Management.

Test 6

Explain the stages of a product life cycle including the likely effect of each stage on sales quantity and profitability.

ANSWERS TO CHAPTER TASKS

CHAPTER 1   Costs

1   **Fixed cost per unit:**

Production level	Budgeted fixed cost per unit £
20,000 units	5.00
40,000 units	2.50
80,000 units	1.25

Working

Production level			Cost £
20,000 units	£100,000/20,000	=	£5.00 per unit
40,000 units	£100,000/40,000	=	£2.50 per unit
80,000 units	£100,000/80,000	=	£1.25 per unit

2   The **relevant range** is the span of activity over which certain cost behaviour holds true.

3

Cost	Behaviour
Stores department costs which include £5,000 of insurance premium and an average of £100 cost per materials receipt or issue	Semi-variable
Machinery depreciation based upon machine hours used	Variable
Salary costs of lecturers in a training college where one lecturer is required for every 200 students enrolled	Stepped
Buildings insurance for a building housing the stores, the factory and the canteen	Fixed
Wages of production workers who are paid per unit produced, with a guaranteed weekly minimum wage of £250	Fixed, then semi-variable

4

Sales	Monthly salary £
4 sales	880
8 sales	960
15 sales	1,100

Working

Sales			Monthly salary £
4 sales	£800 + (4 × £20)	=	£880
8 sales	£800 + (8 × £20)	=	£960
15 sales	£800 + (15 × £20)	=	£1,100

5

The variable rate of production costs is

£6 per unit

The fixed amount of production costs is

£23,000

Workings

	Activity level – units	Cost – £
Highest	28,000	191,000
Lowest	20,000	143,000
Increase	8,000	48,000
Variable rate = £48,000/8,000	=	£6 per unit
Fixed amount using highest level:		
Variable cost 28,000 units × £6		£168,000
Total cost		£191,000
Fixed cost		£23,000

CHAPTER 2   Methods of costing

1

Costing method	Cost per unit £
Absorption costing	15.00
Marginal costing	10.00

Workings

Cost per unit – absorption costing

	£
Direct materials	12,000
Direct labour	15,000
Variable overheads	23,000
Fixed overheads	25,000
Total cost	75,000
Cost per unit	= £75,000/5,000
	= £15 per unit

Cost per unit – marginal costing

	£
Direct materials	12,000
Direct labour	15,000
Variable overheads	23,000
Total cost	50,000
Cost per unit	= £50,000/5,000
	= £10 per unit

2

	£
Absorption cost profit	504,000
Change in inventory: Decrease in inventory	
2,500 – 1,500 = 1,000 units × fixed cost per unit £2	2,000
Marginal cost profit	506,000

3 There has been a reduction in inventory levels during the month.

	£	£
Absorption cost profit (balancing figure)		2,000
Fall in inventory values, absorption costing	(60,000 – 24,000)	36,000
Fall in inventory values, marginal costing	(40,000 – 16,000)	(24,000)
Marginal cost profit		14,000

4 (a) The overhead absorption rate based on direct labour hours is £0.90 per direct labour hour.

   (b) The **over**-absorption of £**2,500** should be **added to** profit.

   Workings

   (a) Overhead absorption rate $= \dfrac{£54,000}{60,000h}$ (budgeted direct labour hours)

   $= £0.90$ per direct labour hour

   (b)

	£
Actual overheads	47,000
Absorbed overheads (55,000h × £0.90 per h)	49,500
Over-absorption	2,500

   The amount over-absorbed will be an addition to profit.

5 Overhead absorption rate per direct labour hour =

   Budgeted overhead expenditure/Budgeted direct labour hours

   $= £2,000,000/200,000$ hours

   £10 per direct labour hour.

	£	£
Profit before adjustment		270,000
Actual overheads	2,150,000	
Overheads absorbed (190,000 × £10)	1,900,000	
Under-absorbed		(250,000)
Actual profit		20,000

6 The absorption rate is £3,000,000/250,000 hours = £12 per direct labour hour.

   (a)

	£
Fixed overhead incurred	2,930,000
Fixed overhead absorbed (220,000 hours × £12.00)	2,640,000
Overhead under-absorbed	290,000

(b)

	£
Budgeted fixed overhead	3,000,000
Actual fixed overhead	2,930,000
Fixed overhead expenditure variance	70,000
	Favourable

As the actual fixed overhead is less than the budgeted figure, this is a 'favourable variance' that contributes to over-absorption of fixed overheads.

(c)

Actual level of activity (direct labour hours)	220,000 hrs
Budgeted level of activity	250,000 hrs
Difference: actual hours less than budgeted hours	30,000 hrs
× Absorption rate per direct labour hour	× £12
Fixed overhead level of activity variance in £	£360,000 Adverse

The variance is 'adverse' because less hours were worked than budgeted, and this has the effect of causing under-absorption of fixed overheads.

	£
Fixed overhead expenditure variance	70,000 Favourable
Fixed overhead level of activity variance	360,000 Adverse
Under-absorbed fixed overhead	290,000

7

(a)

Overhead included in Product A	£5,000
Overhead included in Product B	£26,000

Workings

Cost per inspection	=	£74,000/370
	=	£200 per inspection
Overhead included in A's cost	=	£200 × 25
	=	£5,000
Overhead included in B's cost	=	£200 × 130
	=	£26,000

(b)

Product A overhead cost per unit	£0.50
Product B overhead cost per unit	£2.00

Product A	£5,000/10,000 units	=	£0.50
Product B	£26,000/13,000 units	=	£2.00

CHAPTER 3   Decision making

1   Break-even point $\quad = \quad \dfrac{£360,000}{£28 - £19}$

$\qquad\qquad\qquad\qquad\quad = \quad$ 40,000 units

2   Target profit output $\quad = \quad \dfrac{£250,000 + £150,000}{£80 - £60}$

$\qquad\qquad\qquad\qquad\quad = \quad$ 20,000 units

3   Break-even point $\quad = \quad \dfrac{£480,000}{£32 - £24}$

$\qquad\qquad\qquad\qquad\quad = \quad$ 60,000 units

$\qquad$ Margin of safety $\quad = \quad \dfrac{£75,000 - 60,000}{75,000} \times 100$

$\qquad\qquad\qquad\qquad\quad = \quad$ 20%

4   Contribution/Sales ratio $\quad = \quad \dfrac{£36 - £27}{£36} \times 100$

$\qquad\qquad\qquad\qquad\quad = \quad$ 25%

$\qquad$ Break-even point $\quad = \quad \dfrac{£360,000}{0.25}$

$\qquad\qquad\qquad\qquad\quad = \quad$ £1,440,000

5   Contribution/Sales ratio = $(18 - 12)/18 = 0.3333$ or 33.33%

Target contribution = £1,000,000 + £500,000 = £1,500,000

Sales revenue required to achieve target profit = £1,500,000/33.33% = £4,500,000

6

(a)

Product	Units produced
R	1,000
S	4,000
P	2,000
Q	3,750

Workings

	P	Q	R	S
Contribution per kg	£4.00	£3.75	£9.00	£7.00
Ranking	3	4	1	2

Production plan

	Units produced	Kgs used
R	1,000	1,000
S	4,000	8,000
P	2,000	6,000
Q (balance = 15000/4)	3,750	15,000
		30,000

(b) The profit earned from this production plan will be £115,250

Workings

Profit	**£**
P (2,000 × £12)	24,000
Q (3,750 × £15)	56,250
R (1,000 × £9)	9,000
S (4,000 × £14)	56,000
Contribution	145,250
Less fixed costs	30,000
Profit	115,250

7 The correct answer is product A only

	A	B	C
	£	£	£
Direct materials	1.60	2.00	0.80
Direct labour	3.20	3.60	1.60
Direct overheads	0.80	1.20	0.40
Variable cost of production	5.60	6.80	2.80
External price	5.50	8.40	4.00

On the basis of costs alone only product A should be purchased externally as it is cheaper to buy than to make.

8

Year	0	1	2	3	4
Cash flow	-400,000	-45,000	-45,000	-45,000	105,000
Discount factor	1.000	0.952	0.907	0.864	0.823
Present value	-400,000	-42,840	-40,815	-38,880	86,415
Net present cost	-436,120				

CHAPTER 4   Statistical methods

1 A cyclical variation in a time series is due to the long term fluctuations of the economy as a whole. A seasonal variation is a regular variation in the results due to the nature of the business, and will repeat itself within a short-term period, eg a week, quarter, year.

2

Month	Actual £	Three month moving average £
March	226,504	
April	251,600	238,768
May	238,200	245,800
June	247,600	242,100
July	240,500	250,300
August	262,800	

3

	Actual £	Four year moving average £	Centred moving average = trend £
20X1	226,700		
20X2	236,500		
		236,500	
20X3	240,300		238,175
		239,850	
20X4	242,500		240,988
		242,125	
20X5	240,100		243,038
		243,950	
20X6	245,600		244,663
		245,375	
20X7	247,600		
20X8	248,200		

4

Month	Cost £
January	228,800
February	217,830
March	205,700

Workings

January	£205,600 + 23,200	=	£228,800
February	£208,600 + 9,230	=	£217,830
March	£209,200 − 3,500	=	£205,700

5

		Profit £	Index
20X7	Quarter 1	86,700	100.0
	Quarter 2	88,200	101.7
	Quarter 3	93,400	107.7
	Quarter 4	90,500	104.4
20X8	Quarter 1	83,200	96.0
	Quarter 2	81,400	93.9
	Quarter 3	83,200	96.0
	Quarter 4	85,000	98.0

Workings

20X7	Quarter 1	86,700	100.0
	Quarter 2	88,200/86,700 × 100	101.7
	Quarter 3	93,400/86,700 × 100	107.7
	Quarter 4	90,500/86,700 × 100	104.4
20X8	Quarter 1	83,200/86,700 × 100	96.0
	Quarter 2	81,400/86,700 × 100	93.9
	Quarter 3	83,200/86,700 × 100	96.0
	Quarter 4	85,000/86,700 × 100	98.0

6

		Costs £	RPI	Restated costs £
20X7	June	133,100	171.1	133,100
	July	133,800	170.5	134,271
	Aug	133,600	170.8	133,835
	Sept	134,600	171.7	134,130
	Oct	135,800	171.6	135,404
	Nov	135,100	172.1	134,315
	Dec	135,600	172.1	134,812
20X8	Jan	134,700	171.1	134,700
	Feb	135,900	172.0	135,189
	Mar	136,200	172.2	135,330
	April	136,500	173.1	134,923
	May	136,700	174.2	134,267

Workings

		£	£
20X7	June	133,100 × 171.1/171.1	133,100
	July	133,800 × 171.1/170.5	134,271
	Aug	133,600 × 171.1/170.8	133,835
	Sept	134,600 × 171.1/171.7	134,130
	Oct	135,800 × 171.1/171.6	135,404
	Nov	135,100 × 171.1/172.1	134,315
	Dec	135,600 × 171.1/172.1	134,812
20X8	Jan	134,700 × 171.1/171.1	134,700
	Feb	135,900 × 171.1/172.0	135,189
	Mar	136,200 × 171.1/172.2	135,330
	Apr	136,500 × 171.1/173.1	134,923
	May	136,700 × 171.1/174.2	134,267

7

		Costs £	RPI	Restated costs £
20X7	June	133,100	171.1	135,512
	July	133,800	170.5	136,704
	Aug	133,600	170.8	136,259
	Sept	134,600	171.7	136,560
	Oct	135,800	171.6	137,858
	Nov	135,100	172.1	136,749
	Dec	135,600	172.1	137,255
20X8	Jan	134,700	171.1	137,141
	Feb	135,900	172.0	137,638
	Mar	136,200	172.2	137,782
	April	136,500	173.1	137,367
	May	136,700	174.2	136,700

Workings

Adjusted figures

		£	£
20X7	June	$133,100 \times 174.2/171.1$	135,512
	July	$133,800 \times 174.2/170.5$	136,704
	Aug	$133,600 \times 174.2/170.8$	136,259
	Sept	$134,600 \times 174.2/171.7$	136,560
	Oct	$135,800 \times 174.2/171.6$	137,858
	Nov	$135,100 \times 174.2/172.1$	136,749
	Dec	$135,600 \times 174.2/172.1$	137,255
20X8	Jan	$134,700 \times 174.2/171.1$	137,141
	Feb	$135,900 \times 174.2/172.0$	137,638
	Mar	$136,200 \times 174.2/172.2$	137,782
	Apr	$136,500 \times 174.2/173.1$	137,367
	May	$136,700 \times 174.2/174.2$	136,700

8 It is generally assumed that the level of sales will depend on the advertising undertaken, so:

- Dependent variable – sales volume
- Independent variable – advertising costs

9   Production costs   =   63,000 + (3.2 × 44,000)

            =   £203,800

10 y = 4.8 + 1.2 x

The first two years account for x = 1 to x = 24

Thus the x values in which we are interested are x = 25, 26, 27

Month 1   x = 25:   y = 4.8 + 1.2(25) = 34.8   ie £34,800

Month 2   x = 26:   y = 4.8 + 1.2(26) = 36.0   ie £36,000

Month 3   x = 27:   y = 4.8 + 1.2(27) = 37.2   ie £37,200

CHAPTER 5   Standard costing

1   If ideal standards are used to calculate variances, then the result will be adverse variances. This will tend to mean that these adverse variances become the norm and are accepted without questioning. Ideal standards will also tend to demotivate managers and employees, as they cannot hope to meet the standards.

2   (a)   Total materials cost variance

	£
24,000 units should have cost (× 12 × £20.50)	5,904,000
But did cost	6,240,000
	336,000 (A)

(b)   Materials price variance

312,000 litres should have cost (× £20.50)	6,396,000
But did cost	6,240,000
	156,000 (F)

(c)   Materials usage variance

24,000 units should have used (× 12 litres)	288,000
But did use 312,000 × £20.50	312,000
Materials usage variance in litres	24,000 (A)
× Standard price per litre	× £20.50
Materials usage variance in £	£492,000 (A)

3   (a)   Materials price variance £5,000 favourable

(b)   Materials usage variance £2,000 adverse

Workings

(a)

8,000kg should have cost (× £10.00)	80,000
But did cost	75,000
Materials price variance	5,000 (F)

(b)

	kg
1,500 units should have used (× 5 kg)	7,500
But did use	7,700
Materials usage variance in kg	200 (A)
× Standard price per kg	× £10
Materials usage variance in £	£2,000 (A)

4 (a) Total direct labour cost variance

	£
12,000 units should have cost (× 4 × £6.50)	312,000
But did cost	306,000
	6,000 (F)

(b) Labour rate variance

45,000 hours should cost (× £6.50)	292,500
But did cost	306,000
Labour rate variance	13,500 (A)

(c) Labour efficiency variance

	Hours
12,000 units should have taken (× 4 hours)	48,000
But did take	45,000
Labour efficiency variance in hours	3,000 (F)
× Standard rate per hour	× £6.50
Labour efficiency variance in £	£19,500 (F)

5 (a) Total fixed overhead variance

	£
Fixed overhead incurred	24,500
Fixed overhead absorbed (standard fixed cost): 2,500 × £10.00	25,000
Total fixed overhead cost variance	500 (F)

(b) Fixed overhead expenditure variance

Budgeted fixed overhead	26,000
Actual fixed overhead	24,500
	1,500 (F)

(c)   Fixed overhead volume variance

	Units
Actual production in units	2,500
Budgeted production in units	2,600
Volume variance in units	100 (A)
Standard fixed cost per unit	×£10
Fixed overhead volume variance	£1,000 (A)

6   (a)   Budgeted direct labour hours   =   2,600 × 2

=   5,200 hours

(b)   Fixed overhead efficiency variance

	£
2,500 units should take (× 2hrs)	5,000 hrs
But did take	5,500 hrs
	500 (A)
× Standard fixed overhead rate per hour	×£5
Fixed overhead efficiency variance	£2,500 (A)

(c)   Fixed overhead capacity variance

Budgeted hours of work	5,200 hrs
Actual hours of work	5,500 hrs
Capacity variance in hours	300 hrs (F)
× Standard fixed overhead rate per hour	× £5
Fixed overhead capacity variance in £	£1,500 (F)

7   If the starting point for the reconciliation is the standard cost of the actual production and there is a favourable variance this means that the actual cost was less than the standard cost and therefore the favourable variance is deducted.

8   The correct answer is £5.04.

	£
Actual hours should have cost (x standard rate per hour) 10,400 x £5	52,000
Add adverse labour rate variance	416
Actual hours did cost	52,416
÷ Actual hours worked	10,400 hrs
Actual rate per hour	£5.04

Alternatively:

Rate variance per hour worked = $\dfrac{£416}{10,400}$ = £0.04 Adverse

Actual rate per hour = £(5.00 + 0.04) = £5.04

You should have been able to eliminate £4.95 and £4.96 because they are both below the standard rate per hour. If the rate variance is adverse then the actual rate must be above standard.

£5.05 is incorrect because it results from basing the calculations on standard hours rather than actual hours.

9   **The quantity used is** 57,650 **kgs.**

Workings

Let the quantity of material X used = Y

5,750 units should have used (× 10kgs)	57,500 kgs
but did use	Y kgs
Usage variance in kgs	(57,500 –Y) kgs
× standard price per kg	× £10
Usage variance in £	£1,500 (A)

$$10(57,500 - Y) = -1,500$$

$$57,500 - Y = -150$$

$$Y = 57,650 \text{ kgs}$$

Alternatively:

Standard material cost of actual production	575,000
5,750 x 10kgs x £10	
Usage variance (adverse)	£1,500
So actual material used should have cost (at standard price per kg)	£576,500
÷ Standard price per kg	÷ £10
Actual material used	57,650 kg

10   The correct answer is

Debit   Material usage variance account

Credit   Work-in-progress control account

CHAPTER 6   Standard costing – further aspects

1   Use of a lower grade of labour than anticipated.

2   The favourable labour rate variance could be due to the manager responsible for hiring labour taking on a lower grade of worker, hence the lower rate of pay per hour.

The less skilled workers may have taken longer to do the job and been more inefficient in their usage of material, causing the adverse labour efficiency and materials usage variances.

An independent investigation would need to be carried out into the grade of labour hired and the normal hourly rate for such labour. Other independent factors that may have caused material wastage (e.g. poor quality material) or labour inefficiency (machine breakdowns) should also be investigated.

Note: since this is the first period for the new contract it is possible that the manager responsible for hiring workers has provided valid information and that the other variances are caused by the fact that the standards set were inaccurate or that there was some learning process involved

3   (a)   The total materials price variance was **£3,080 adverse**

(b)   The non-controllable variance due to the price increase was **£3,680 adverse**

The controllable variance due to other factors was **£600 favourable**

Workings

Total materials price variance

	£
4,600 kg should have cost (× £8.20)	37,720
But did cost	40,800
	3,080 (A)

Non-controllable variance due to the price increase

Standard price of actual quantity	
4,600 kg × £8.20	37,720
Adjusted price for actual quantity	
4,600 kg × £9.00	41,400
	3,680 (A)

Controllable variance due to other causes

	£
Adjusted price for actual quantity	
4,600 kg × £9.00	41,400
Actual quantity at actual price	40,800
	600 (F)

4 (a) The total materials price variance was **£7,700 adverse**

   (b) The non-controllable variance due to the seasonal price change was **£9,270 adverse**

   The controllable variance due to other factors was **£1,570 favourable**

Workings

Total materials price variance

	£
10,300 kg should have cost (× £6.00)	61,800
Actual quantity at actual price	69,500
	7,700 (A)

Non-controllable variance due to seasonal price

Standard price of actual quantity	
10,300 kg × £6.00	61,800
Adjusted price for actual quantity	
10,300 kg × (£6.00 + £0.90)	71,070
	9,270 (A)

Controllable variance due to other factors

Adjusted price for actual quantity	
10,300 kg × (£6.00 + £0.90)	71,070
Actual quantity at actual price	69,500
	1,570 (F)

5 (a) The total labour efficiency variance was **£37,200 adverse**

   (b) The non-controllable variance due to early production problems was **£65,100 adverse**

   The controllable variance due to other causes was **£27,900 favourable**

Workings

Total labour efficiency variance

	Hours
12,000 units should have taken (× 3.5 hrs)	42,000
But did take	48,000
Efficiency variance in hours	6,000 (A)
× Standard rate per hour	× £6.20
Labour efficiency variance in £	37,200 (A)

Non-controllable variance due to early production problems

Standard hours for actual quantity at standard rate	
12,000 × 3.5 × £6.20	260,400
Adjusted hours for actual quantity at standard rate	
12,000 × (3.5 × 1.25) × £6.20	325,500
	65,100 (A)

Controllable variance due to other causes

	£
Adjusted hours for actual quantity at standard rate	
12,000 × (3.5 × 1.25) × £6.20	325,500
Actual hours at standard rate	
48,000 × £6.20	297,600
	27,900 (F)

6   (a)   The total labour rate variance was **£2,500 adverse**

      (b)   The non-controllable variance due to the labour rate increase was **£13,125 adverse**

         The controllable variance due to other causes was **£10,625 favourable**

Total labour rate variance

	£
21,000 hours should have taken (× £7.50)	157,500
But did take	160,000
	2,500 (A)

Non-controllable variance due to rate increase

Standard rate for actual hours	
21,000 × £7.50	157,500
Adjusted price for actual hours	
21,000 × £7.50 × 130/120	170,625
	13,125 (A)

Controllable variance due to other causes

Adjusted price for actual hours	
21,000 × (£7.50 × 130/120)	170,625
Actual hours at actual rate	160,000
	10,625 (F)

CHAPTER 7   Performance indicators

1

	Current quarter	Previous quarter
Productivity		
216/26	8.3 per executive	
188/22		8.5 per executive

2   Activity ratio $= \dfrac{\text{Standard hours for actual production}}{\text{Budgeted hours}} \times 100$

$= \dfrac{268,000 \times 3}{288,000 \times 3} \times 100$

$= 93.1\%$

3   Gross profit margin $= \dfrac{£58,700}{£133,400} \times 100$

$= 44.0\%$

Operating profit $=$ Profit before interest and tax

$=$ 22,500 + 2,500 + 4,750

$=$ 29,750

Operating profit margin $= \dfrac{£29,750}{£133,400} \times 100$

$= 22.3\%$

Net profit margin $= \dfrac{£22,500}{£133,400} \times 100$

$= 16.9\%$

4   ROCE $= \dfrac{£365,800}{£1,700,000 + £600,000} \times 100 = 15.9\%$ (Method 1)

or

RONA $= \dfrac{£365,800 - (12\% \times £600,000)}{£1,700,000} \times 100 = 17.3\%$ (Method 2)

5   Asset turnover, 1.2 $= \dfrac{\text{Revenue}}{£350,000}$

Revenue $=$ 1.2 × £350,000 $=$ £420,000

6   Average inventory $= \dfrac{£13,500 + £17,000}{2}$ $=$ £15,250

Cost of sales $=$ £13,500 + 99,000 – 17,000 $=$ £95,500

Inventory days $\quad = \quad \dfrac{£15,250}{£95,500} \times 365$

$\qquad\qquad\qquad = \quad 58$ days

7   Possible reasons for a decrease in gross profit margin include:

■   Decrease in selling price
■   Increase in purchases or production costs
■   Large write off of inventories

CHAPTER 8   Cost management

1   (a)   Improvements in product design or specification to reduce defective products = prevention cost

(b)   Loss of future custom from dissatisfied customers = external failure cost

(c)   Lost contribution on defective units scrapped or sold at a lower price than normal = internal failure cost

(d)   Sample testing of finished production = appraisal cost

2

Cost of quality	Effect
Prevention costs	Increase as product design must be modified to eliminate the problem in future
Appraisal costs	There may be none, although could increase if this product line has to be more closely monitored in future
Internal costs	Increase due to investigation of problem, review of product design, repairs and re-inspection
External costs	Increase due to cost of repairs, any claims relating to the failure and loss of customer goodwill

3   Explicit quality costs

■   Costs of quality inspections
■   Costs of repairs to faulty products returned
■   Costs of replacing faulty products
■   Costs of design review to ensure quality

Implicit quality costs –

- Loss of customer goodwill
- Disruption of production process due to repairs/reworking
- Potential claims from customers

(**Note.** Only two examples of each were required)

4

	£
Inspection costs – Appraisal cost	20,000
Lost contribution on seconds – Internal failure cost	
3,000 units × (£25 – £12)	39,000
Total quality cost	59,000

5 Quality performance indicators for a taxi firm:

- Percentage of taxis arriving on time compared to total taxi journeys
- Percentage of repeat customers compared to total customers
- Survey results of customer satisfaction
- Number of customer complaints

6 The target cost is £25,714

Working

Profit required = 8% × £27,950 = £2,236

Target cost = £ 27,950 – £2,236 = £25,714

7 **Maximum £ per kg = £4**

		£
Selling price		25.00
40% margin		10.00
Target cost		15.00
Less		
Labour	0.5 hrs @£6/hr	(3.00)
Overheads	0.5 hrs @£8/hr	(4.00)
Available for 2kg material		8.00
Maximum price per kg		£4.00

8   (a)   The profit over the life cycle of the product is £890,000.

       Workings

	£
Sales (800,000 + 2,000,000 + 200,000)	3,000,000
Cost of sales (balancing figure)	(1,800,000)
Profit = 40% x sales =	1,200,000
Loss on specialist equipment (100,000 – 20,000)	(80,000)
Development staff costs	(200,000)
PR agency costs	(30,000)
Profit	890,000

    (b)   The net present value of the project is £624,350

       Workings

Time (end of year)	Cash inflows/(outflows)	Discount factor @ 10%	PV
0 (20X4)	(100,000)	1.000	(100,000)
1 (20X5)	(200,000 + 30,000) = (230,000)	0.909	(209,070)
2 (20X6)	800,000 x 40% = 320,000	0.826	264,320
3 (20X7)	2,000,000 x 40% = 800,000	0.751	600,800
4 (20X8)	20,000 + 200,000 x 40% = 100,000	0.683	68,300
Total net present value			624,350

    (c)   A profit is generated over the product's life cycle, and the net present value of the project is also positive, and so this project should be undertaken.

TEST YOUR LEARNING
– ANSWERS

CHAPTER 1   Costs

1

True   ✓

10,000 units   Cost per unit £43,600/10,000   =   £4.36

12,000 units   Cost per unit £52,320/12,000   =   £4.36

As the cost per unit is the same at each level of production this would appear to be a purely variable cost.

2

Activity level	Total fixed cost £	Fixed cost per unit £
3,000 units	64,000	21.33
10,000 units	64,000	6.40
16,000 units	64,000	4.00

Working

3,000 units   £64,000/3,000 = £21.33

10,000 units   £64,000/10,000 = £6.40

16,000 units   £64,000/16,000 = £4.00

3   The marginal cost per month is

£52,500

The full production cost per month is

£70,000

Workings

	Production cost £
Direct material costs (£5 × 3,500)	17,500
Direct labour costs (£10 × 3,500)	35,000
Marginal cost	52,500
Rent	10,000
Supervisor cost	7,500
Full production cost	70,000

4 (a) The variable element of the production cost is

£3 per unit

The fixed element of the production cost is

£169,000

(b)

Level of production	Production cost £
120,000 units	529,000
150,000 units	619,000

Workings

(a)

		£
Highest level	126,000	547,000
Lowest level	101,000	472,000
Increase	25,000	75,000

$$\text{Variable rate} = \frac{£75,000}{25,000} = £3 \text{ per unit}$$

Using highest level:

	£
Variable cost 126,000 × £3	378,000
Fixed costs (balancing figure)	169,000
Total cost	547,000

(b)   (i)

120,000 units		£
Variable cost 120,000 × £3		360,000
Fixed cost		169,000
Total forecast cost		529,000

(ii)

150,000 units		£
Variable cost 150,000 × £3		450,000
Fixed cost		169,000
Total forecast cost		619,000

(c)   The estimate of costs for 120,000 units is likely to be more accurate than that for 150,000 units. This is due to the fact that 120,000 is within the range of activity levels used to calculate the variable costs and fixed costs (interpolation) whereas 150,000 units is outside that range (extrapolation). We cannot be sure that the costs will still behave in the same manner at an activity level of 150,000 units.

CHAPTER 2   Methods of costing

1   (a)   The correct answer is £20.00

(b)   The correct answer is £15.00

Workings

$$\text{Department P1} = \frac{£50,000}{2,500\,h}$$
$$= £20 \text{ per direct labour hour}$$

$$\text{Department P2} = \frac{£60,000}{4,000\,h}$$
$$= £15 \text{ per machine hour}$$

2

	Amount of under-/over- absorption £	Under- or over- absorption	Add or subtract in statement of profit or loss (income statement)
An overhead absorption rate of £3 per unit, based on expected production levels of 500 units. Actual overheads turn out to be £1,600, and actual production is 650 units.	350.00	Over-	Add
The budget is set at 1,000 units, with £9,000 overheads recovered on the basis of 600 direct labour hours. At the end of the period, overheads amounted to £8,600, production achieved was only 950 units and 590 direct labour hours had been worked.	250.00	Over-	Add

Workings

(a)

	£
Actual overheads	1,600
Absorbed overheads (650 units @ £3 per unit)	1,950
Over-absorption	350

The over-absorption of £350 would be added to profit in the statement of profit or loss (income statement).

(b)

	£
Actual overheads	8,600
Absorbed overheads (590h × £15* per h)	8,850
Over-absorption	250

$$* \text{ Overhead absorption rate} = \frac{£9,000}{600 \text{ direct labour hours}}$$

$$= £15 \text{ per direct labour hour}$$

The over-absorption of £250 would be added to profit in the statement or profit or loss (income statement).

3 (a)

Department	Overhead absorption rate
X	£2.60 per machine hour
Y	£3.17 per direct labour hour

Workings

$$X = \frac{£260,000}{100,000}$$

= £2.60 per machine hour

as X is a highly mechanised department most of the overhead will relate to the machinery therefore machine hours have been used to absorb the overhead.

$$Y = \frac{£380,000}{120,000}$$

= £3.17 per direct labour hour

as Y is a highly labour intensive department most of the overhead will relate to the hours that are worked by the labour force therefore labour hours are used to absorb the overhead.

(b) The overhead to be included in the cost of product A is £25.68

Working

Product A – department X overhead	£2.60 × 5	= £13.00
Product A – department Y overhead	£3.17 × 4	= £12.68
		£25.68

4 In an absorption costing system all fixed production overheads are absorbed into the cost of the products and are included in unit cost. In a marginal costing system the fixed production overheads are written off in the statement or profit or loss (income statement) as a period cost.

5

Method of costing	Budgeted cost £
Absorption costing	59.70
Marginal costing	57.11

Workings

Absorption costing – unit cost

	£
Direct materials	12.50
Direct labour assembly (4 × £8.40)	33.60
Finishing (1 × £6.60)	6.60
Assembly overheads (£336,000/60,000)	5.60
Finishing overheads (£84,000/60,000)	1.40
	59.70

Marginal costing – unit cost

		£
Direct materials		12.50
Direct labour assembly	(4 × £8.40)	33.60
Finishing	(1 × £6.60)	6.60
Assembly overheads	$\dfrac{£336,000 \times 60\%}{60,000}$	3.36
Finishing overheads	$\dfrac{£84,000 \times 75\%}{60,000}$	1.05
		57.11

6   Unit cost

	£
Direct materials	12.00
Direct labour	8.00
Variable overhead (£237,000/15,000)	15.80
Marginal costing unit cost	35.80
Fixed overhead (£390,000/15,000)	26.00
Absorption costing unit cost	61.80

(a) (i) **Absorption costing – statement of profit or loss (income statement)**

	November		December	
	£	£	£	£
Sales				
(12,500/18,000 × £75)		937,500		1,350,000
Less cost of sales				
Opening inventory				
(2,000 × £61.80)	123,600			
(4,500 × £61.80)			278,100	
Production costs				
(15,000 × £61.80)	927,000		927,000	
	1,050,600		1,205,100	
Less closing inventory				
(4,500 × £61.80)	278,100			
(1,500 × £61.80)			92,700	
		772,500		1,112,400
Profit		165,000		237,600

(ii) **Marginal costing – statement of profit or loss (income statement)**

	November		December	
	£	£	£	£
Sales				
(12,500/18,000 × £75)		937,500		1,350,000
Less cost of sales				
Opening inventory				
(2,000 × £35.80)	71,600			
(4,500 × £35.80)			161,100	
Production costs				
(15,000 × £35.80)	537,000		537,000	
	608,600		698,100	
Less closing inventory				
(4,500 × £35.80)	161,100			
(1,500 × £35.80)			53,700	
		447,500		644,400
Contribution		490,000		705,600
Less fixed overheads		390,000		390,000
Profit		100,000		315,600

(b)

	November £	December £
Absorption costing profit	165,000	237,600
Inventory changes	(65,000)	78,000
Marginal costing profit	100,000	315,600

Workings

	November £	December £
Increase in inventory × fixed cost per unit ((4,500 – 2,000) × £26)	(65,000)	
Decrease in inventory × fixed cost per unit ((4,500 – 1,500) × £26)		78,000

7

Product	Budgeted cost per unit £	Budgeted overhead per unit £
LM	9.78	3.68
NP	27.41	20.81

Workings

Stores cost	=	$\dfrac{£140,000}{320}$
	=	£437.50 per materials requisition
Production set-up costs	=	$\dfrac{£280,000}{280}$
	=	£1,000 per set-up
Quality control costs	=	$\dfrac{£180,000}{90}$
	=	£2,000 per inspection

Product costs

		LM £	NP £
Direct materials	50,000 × £2.60	130,000	
	20,000 × £3.90		78,000
Direct labour	50,000 × £3.50	175,000	
	20,000 × £2.70		54,000
Stores costs	100 × £437.50	43,750	
	220 × £437.50		96,250
Production set-up costs	80 × £1,000	80,000	
	200 × £1,000		200,000
Quality control costs	30 × £2,000	60,000	
	60 × £2,000		120,000
Total cost		488,750	548,250
Cost per unit		$\dfrac{488,750}{50,000}$	$\dfrac{548,250}{20,000}$
		= £9.78	= £27.41

Analysis of total unit cost

Direct costs	(2.60 + 3.50)	6.10	
	(3.90 + 2.70)		6.60
Overheads	$\dfrac{(43,750 + 80,000 + 60,000)}{50,000}$	3.68	
	$\dfrac{(96,250 + 200,000 + 120,000)}{20,000}$	9.78	20.81 27.41

CHAPTER 3   Decision making

1   As activity levels increase, the total fixed costs will be split amongst more units, and the amount of fixed costs absorbed into the cost of a unit will get smaller. With no change in selling cost or variable cost, the total unit cost will decrease.

2   The break-even point is **30,000** units

The margin of safety is **21%**

Workings

$$\text{Break-even point} = \frac{£360,000}{£57 - £45}$$

$$= 30,000 \text{ units}$$

$$\text{Margin of safety} = \frac{38,000 - 30,000}{38,000}$$

$$= 21\%$$

3 The correct answer is 201,429 units

$$\text{Target profit sales} = \frac{£910,000 + £500,000}{£24 - £17}$$

$$= 201,429 \text{ units}$$

4 The sales revenue required in order to make a profit of £200,000 is **£1,500,000**

Workings

$$\text{Profit volume ratio} = \frac{£(40-32)}{£40} \times 100$$

$$= 20\%$$

$$\text{Target profit sales revenue} = \frac{£100,000 + £200,000}{0.20}$$

$$= £1,500,000$$

Alternatively: Units required to make £200,000 profit = £300,000/8 = 37,500 units

Total revenue required = 37,500 × £40 = £1,500,000

5 (a) The limiting factor of production resources is materials/labour hours/**machine hours**.

Working

Resource requirements for maximum demand

	R	S	T	Total
Materials	80,000 kg	120,000 kg	25,000 kg	225,000 kg
Labour hours	20,000 hours	80,000 hours	5,000 hours	105,000 hours
Machine hours	60,000 hours	80,000 hours	15,000 hours	155,000 hours

Therefore the machine hours available are the limiting factor.

(b)

Product	Units produced
S	20,000
T	5,000
R	4,166

Workings

Contribution per machine hour

	R	S	T
Contribution	£6	£12	£6
Machine hours	6	4	3
Contribution/machine hour	£1.00	£3.00	£2.00
Ranking	3	1	2

Production plan

Product	Units produced	Machine hours used
S	20,000	80,000
T	5,000	15,000
R (balance 25,000/6 = 4,166.67 = 4,166 complete units))	4,166	24,996
		119,996

(c) The profit that will be earned under this production plan is £244,996

Workings

Product contribution:	£
R (4,166 × £6)	24,996
S (20,000 × £12)	240,000
T (5,000 × £6)	30,000
Total contribution	294,996
Less fixed costs	(50,000)
Profit	244,996

6 The correct answer is Neither X nor Y

	X	Y
	£	£
Direct materials	2.50	3.00
Direct labour	8.00	6.00
Variable cost of production	10.50	9.00
External price	11.00	10.00

On the basis of costs alone neither product should be purchased externally as they are cheaper to make.

7

Year	Cash flows £	Discount factor at 7%	Present value £
0	(340,000)	1.000	(340,000)
1	80,000	0.935	74,800
2	70,000	0.873	61,110
3	90,000	0.816	73,440
4	120,000	0.763	91,560
5	60,000	0.713	42,780
Net present value			3,690

Remember that depreciation is not a cash flow and is therefore excluded from the net present value calculations.

8

(a)

Year	Cash flows £	Discount factor at 11%	Present value £
0	(90,000)	1.000	(90,000)
1	23,000	0.901	20,723
2	31,000	0.812	25,172
3	40,000	0.731	29,240
4	18,000	0.659	11,862
Net present value			(3,003)

(b) As the investment in the new plant and machinery has a negative net present value at the cost of capital of 11%, the investment should not take place.

CHAPTER 4   Statistical methods

1

	Actual	Three month moving average
	£	£
July	397,500	
August	403,800	400,300
September	399,600	402,900
October	405,300	403,667
November	406,100	406,633
December	408,500	407,500
January	407,900	408,933
February	410,400	411,433
March	416,000	413,167
April	413,100	415,533
May	417,500	417,467
June	421,800	

2

		Actual	Four quarter moving average	Centred moving average = TREND	Seasonal variations
		£	£	£	£
20X5	Quarter 1	383,600			
	Quarter 2	387,600			
			365,400		
	Quarter 3	361,800		365,688	-3,888
			365,975		
	Quarter 4	328,600		366,575	-37,975
			367,175		
20X6	Quarter 1	385,900		366,013	+19,887
			364,850		
	Quarter 2	392,400		366,125	+26,275
			367,400		
	Quarter 3	352,500		368,225	-15,725
			369,050		
	Quarter 4	338,800		371,288	-32,488
			373,525		
20X7	Quarter 1	392,500		375,575	+16,925
			377,625		
	Quarter 2	410,300		378,325	+31,975
			379,025		
	Quarter 3	368,900		379,750	-10,850
			380,475		
	Quarter 4	344,400		382,388	-37,988
			384,300		
20X8	Quarter 1	398,300			
	Quarter 2	425,600			

Working

Seasonal variations:

	Quarter 1 £	Quarter 2 £	Quarter 3 £	Quarter 4 £
20X5	–	–	–3,888	–37,975
20X6	+19,887	+26,275	–15,725	–32,488
20X7	+16,925	+31,975	–10,850	–37,988
	+36,812	+58,250	–30,463	–108,451
Average	+18,406	+29,125	–10,154	–36,150

Total of seasonal variations

18,406 + 29,125 – 10,154 – 36,152	=	1,227	
Adjustment required	=	1,227/4	
	=	307	

	Quarter 1 £	Quarter 2 £	Quarter 3 £	Quarter 4 £
Unadjusted	+18,406	+29,125	–10,154	–36,150
Adjustment	–307	–307	–306	–307
Seasonal variation	+18,099	+28,818	–10,460	–36,457

3

	Cost £	Index
January	59,700	100.0
February	62,300	104.4
March	56,900	95.3
April	60,400	101.2
May	62,400	104.5
June	66,700	111.7

Workings

January	59,700/59,700 = 100.0
February	62,300/59,700 = 104.4
March	56,900/59,700 = 95.3
April	60,400/59,700 = 101.2
May	62,400/59,700 = 104.5
June	66,700/59,700 = 111.7

4 (a)

	Wages cost £	RPI	Adjusted cost £
January	126,700	171.1	126,848
February	129,700	172.0	129,172
March	130,400	172.2	129,718
April	131,600	173.0	130,307
May	130,500	172.1	129,893
June	131,600	171.3	131,600

Workings

	Wages cost £	Adjusted cost £
January	126,700 × 171.3/171.1	126,848
February	129,700 × 171.3/172.0	129,172
March	130,400 × 171.3/172.2	129,718
April	131,600 × 171.3/173.0	130,307
May	130,500 × 171.3/172.1	129,893
June	131,600 × 171.3/171.3	131,600

(b)

	Adjusted cost £	Working	Index
January	126,848	126,848/126,848	100.0
February	129,172	129,172/126,848	101.8
March	129,718	129,718/126,848	102.3
April	130,307	130,307/126,848	102.7
May	129,893	129,893/126,848	102.4
June	131,600	131,600/126,848	103.7

5 $y = 5{,}000 + 10\,b$

Production cost of 1,400 units = £19,000

Workings

£15,000 = a + (1,000 × b)

£25,000 = a + (2,000 × b)

£(25,000 – 15,000) = (a + (2,000 × b)) – (a + (1,000 × b))

£10,000 = a + 2,000b – a – 1,000b

£10,000 = 1,000 × b

b = £10,000/1,000 = £10

£15,000 = a + (1,000 × 10)

a = £15,000 – £10,000

a = £5,000

so the regression line is y = 5,000 + 10 b

Production cost of 1,400 units = 5,000 + (10 × 1,400) = £19,000

6

	Production Units	Costs £
January	5,400	17,320
February	5,600	17,480
March	5,700	17,560
April	6,000	17,800
May	5,500	17,400
June	6,100	17,880

Workings

Stores costs:

January	13,000 + (0.8 × 5,400)	17,320
February	13,000 + (0.8 × 5,600)	17,480
March	13,000 + (0.8 × 5,700)	17,560
April	13,000 + (0.8 × 6,000)	17,800
May	13,000 + (0.8 × 5,500)	17,400
June	13,000 + (0.8 × 6,100)	17,880

7

	Value of x	Trend	Seasonal variation	Forecast sales
Quarter 1 20X9	13	2,785	– 200	2,585
Quarter 2 20X9	14	2,830	+ 500	3,330
Quarter 3 20X9	15	2,875	+ 350	3,225
Quarter 4 20X9	16	2,920	– 650	2,270

Workings

Value of x for Quarter 1, 20X9

Quarter 1 20X6 = 1

Add 3 years of 4 quarters = $\dfrac{12}{13}$

Trend for Quarter 1, 20X9: 2,200 + (45 × 13) = 2,785

Trend for Quarter 2, 20X9: 2,200 + (45 × 14) = 2,830

Trend for Quarter 3, 20X9: 2,200 + (45 × 15) = 2,875

Trend for Quarter 4, 20X9: 2,200 + (45 × 16) = 2,920

CHAPTER 5   Standard costing

1   The information for the amount of labour time for each cost unit would come from payroll records such as time sheets or from physical observations such as time and motion studies. Factors that should be taken into account include:

- The level of skill or training of the labour grade to be used on the product

- Any anticipated changes on the grade of labour used on the product

- Any anticipated changes in work methods or productivity levels

- The effect of any bonus scheme on productivity

The hourly rate for the direct labour can be found from payroll records but the following factors should be considered:

- Anticipated pay rises
- Anticipated changes in grade of labour
- Effect of any bonus scheme on the labour rate
- Whether any anticipated overtime is built into the hourly rate.

2   The information for the amount of material required for each unit of a product can be found from the original product specification – the amount originally considered necessary for each unit. Factors that should be taken into account include:

- The level of skill of the labour to be used on the product

- Any anticipated changes to the quality of material sourced

- Any anticipated changes in work methods/equipment used to work the material.

This figure may however be amended over time as the actual amount used in production is monitored.

The basic price of the material can be found from suppliers' quotations or invoices. However when setting the standard, the following should also be taken into account:

- General inflation rates

- Any foreseen increases in the price of this particular material

- Any seasonality in the price

- Any discounts available for bulk purchases

- Any anticipated scarcity of the material which may mean paying a higher price

3   Ideal standards are set on the basis of perfect working conditions. No allowance is made for normal wastage or inefficiencies. Target standards are standards that are set on the basis of normal working conditions by building in some element to reflect normal wastage or inefficiencies. Target standards are capable of being met by efficient operations. Basic standards are the original historical standards based upon the original expectations of cost for the product.

4   (a)   Total materials cost variance

	£
Standard cost of actual production	
1,800 units should have cost ($\times$ 7 kg $\times$ £6.00)	75,600
But did cost	70,800
	4,800 (F)

(b)   Materials price variance

	£
12,000 kg should have cost ($\times$ £6.00)	72,000
But did cost	70,800
	1,200 (F)

(c) Materials usage variance

1,800 units should have used (× 7 kg)	12,600
But did use	12,000
Variance in kg	600 (F)
× standard price per kg	× £6
Material usage variance in £	£3,600 (F)

5 (a) Total labour cost variance

	£
Standard cost of actual production	
15,400 units should have cost (× 2.5 hours × £6.80)	261,800
But did cost	265,200
	3,400 (A)

(b) Labour rate variance

Actual hours at standard rate	
41,000 hrs should cost (× £6.80)	278,800
But did cost	265,200
	13,600 (F)

(c) Labour efficiency variance

Standard hours for actual production at standard rate	
15,400 units should have taken (× 2.5 hrs)	38,500
But did take	41,000
	2,500 (A)
× standard rate per hour	× £6.80
	£17,000 (A)

6 (a) Budgeted fixed overhead = 7,000 units × £7.50 per unit = £52,500.

(b) Fixed overhead expenditure variance

	£
Budgeted fixed overhead	52,500
Actual fixed overhead expenditure	56,000
Fixed overhead expenditure variance	3,500 (A)

(c) Fixed overhead volume variance

	Units
Budgeted output	7,000
Actual output	6,400
Volume variance in units	600 (A)
Standard fixed overhead cost per unit	£7.50
Fixed overhead volume variance in £	4,500 Adv

(d) Fixed overhead efficiency variance

6,400 units should take (× 3hrs)	19,200 hrs
But did take	20,000 hrs
Efficiency variance in hours	800 hrs (A)
× Standard absorption rate per hour	× £2.50
Fixed overhead efficiency variance	£2,000 Adv

(e) Fixed overhead capacity variance

Budgeted hours of work (7,000 × 3hrs)	21,000 hrs
Actual hours of work	20,000 hrs
Capacity variance in hours	1,000 hrs (A)
× Standard absorption rate per hour	× £2.50
Capacity variance in £	2,500 (A)

7 (a) Materials price variance

	£
7,500kg should have cost (× £3.60)	27,000
But did cost	25,900
	1,100 (F)

Materials usage variance

	£
1,750 units should have used (× 4.2kg)	7,350 kg
But did use	7,500 kg
Materials usage variance in kg	150 kg (A)
× Standard price per kg	× £3.60
Materials usage variance in £	540 (A)

(b) Labour rate variance

2,580 hrs should have cost (× £7.80)	20,124
But did cost	20,600
	476 (A)

Labour efficiency variance

1,750 units should have taken (× 1.5 hrs)	2,625 hrs
But did take	2,580 hrs
Efficiency variance in hrs	45 hrs (F)
× Standard rate per hour	× £7.80
Labour efficiency variance in £	351 (F)

(c) Fixed overhead expenditure variance

Budgeted fixed overhead 1,800 × £4.20	7,560
Actual fixed overhead	8,100
Fixed overhead expenditure variance	540 (A)

Fixed overhead efficiency variance

Efficiency variance in hours (same as labour efficiency	45 hrs (F)
× Standard fixed overhead absorption rate per hour	£2.80
Fixed overhead efficiency variance in £	£126 (F)

Fixed overhead capacity variance

Budgeted hours of work (1,800 × 1.5)	2,700 hrs
Actual hours of work	2,580 hrs
Capacity variance in hours	120 hrs (A)
× Standard fixed overhead absorption rate per hour	× £2.80
Capacity variance in £	£336 (A)

(d) Standard cost of actual production

Direct materials 1,750 × 4.2 × £3.60	26,460
Direct labour 1,750 × 1.5 × £7.80	20,475
Fixed overhead 1,750 × £4.20	7,350
Total cost 1,750 × £31.02	54,285

Operating statement – Absorption costing

	Favourable variances	Adverse variances		£
Standard cost of production				54,285
Variances:				
Materials price	1,100			
Materials usage		540		
Labour rate		476		
Labour efficiency	351			
Fixed overhead expenditure		540		
Fixed overhead efficiency	126			
Fixed overhead capacity		336		
	1,577	1,892		315 (A)
Actual cost of production				54,600

8 (a) Total direct materials cost variance

		£
Standard cost of actual production		
2,400 × 12 × £4.80		138,240
Actual cost of actual production		145,000
		6,760 (A)

Materials price variance

	£
Actual quantity should have cost	
29,600 × £4.80	142,080
But did cost	145,000
	2,920 (A)dv

Materials usage variance

Actual production should have used (2,400 x 12)	28,800kgs
But did use	29,600kgs
Materials usage variance in kg	800kgs (A)
× Standard price per kg	£4.80
Materials usage variance in £	3,840 (A)

(b) Total direct labour variance

	£
Standard labour cost of actual production	
2,400 × 3 × £8.00	57,600
Actual labour cost of actual production	56,200
	1,400 (F)

Labour rate variance

Actual hours should have cost	
6,900 × £8.00	55,200
But did cost	56,200
Labour rate variance	1,000 (A)

Labour efficiency variance

	Hours
Actual production should have taken	
2,400 × 3 × £8.00	7,200
But did take	6,900
Labour efficiency variance in hours	300 hrs (F)
× Standard rate per hour	£8
Labour efficiency variance in £	2,400 (F)

(c) Fixed overhead expenditure variance

Actual fixed overhead	92,000
Budgeted fixed overhead	95,000
	3,000 (F)

(d)   Standard cost of production

	£
Direct materials 2,400 × 12 × £4.80	138,240
Direct labour 2,400 × 3 × £8.00	57,600
Standard variable cost (2400 × 81.60)	195,840

			£
Standard variable cost of actual production			195,840
Budgeted fixed overhead			95,000
Variances	**Favourable variances**	**Adverse variances**	
Materials price		2,920	
Materials usage		3,840	
Labour rate		1,000	
Labour efficiency	2,400		
Fixed overhead expenditure	3,000		
	5,400	7,760	2,360 (A)
Total actual cost			293,200

9   Material usage variance, variable overhead efficiency variance and idle time variance. The material price variance is recorded in the stores control account. The labour rate variance is recorded in the wages control account.

CHAPTER 6   Standard costing – further aspects

1   REPORT

To:	Managing Director
From:	Accountant
Date:	xx.xx.xx
Subject:	November production cost variances

The November production cost is 5% more than the standard cost for the actual production, due to a number of fairly significant adverse variances.

The main cause appears to have been the labour that was used in production for the month which was a more junior grade than normal due to staff shortages. Although this has given a favourable labour rate variance, it has also caused adverse labour efficiency and materials usage variances due to inefficiencies and wastage from the staff. This inefficiency in labour hours has also led to the fixed overhead efficiency adverse variance.

For future months we should either ensure that we have enough of the normal grade of labour for production of this product or train the junior staff in the production process.

There is also an adverse materials price variance which has been due to an increase in the price of our materials. As it is believed that this is a permanent price increase by all suppliers, we should consider altering the direct materials standard cost to reflect this, otherwise each month we will have adverse materials price variances.

The factory now has an additional rent cost which has presumably caused the adverse fixed overhead expenditure variance. If the additional inventory requirement and hence the additional rent is a permanent change then this should be built into the budgeted fixed overhead figure.

Due to the labour inefficiency, more hours have been worked than were budgeted for, leading to the favourable capacity variance. This indicates that the factory has more capacity than we have been making use of which, if the inefficiencies are sorted out, could be used to increase monthly production if required.

2

Scenario	Possible effects
A business replaces machinery with new equipment	▪ Favourable materials usage variance, if new machinery leads to less waste ▪ Alternatively, adverse materials usage variance, if workers have to adapt to using new machinery ▪ Adverse fixed overheads expenditure variance (higher depreciation charged, although overheads may decrease leading to favourable variance if more power-efficient) ▪ Favourable labour efficiency if workers can work faster (and so favourable overhead efficiency variance)
A company has supply issues with a raw material	▪ Adverse materials price variance ▪ Possible adverse materials usage variance, if can only source inferior material ▪ Adverse labour efficiency variance (idle time) if no material for production ▪ Possible adverse labour rate efficiency, if must use overtime to catch up, when material does become available

3 (a) The total materials price variance was **£4,900 adverse**

(b) The non-controllable variance due to the price increase was **£5,600 adverse**

The controllable variance due to other factors was **£700 favourable**

Workings

Total materials price variance

	£
14,000 litres should have cost × £2.40	33,600
But did cost	38,500
	4,900 (A)

Non-controllable variance due to price increase

	£
Standard price of actual quantity used	
14,000 × £2.40	33,600
Adjusted price for actual quantity	
14,000 × £2.80	39,200
	5,600 (A)

Controllable variance due to other causes

	£
Adjusted price for actual quantity	
14,000 × £2.80	39,200
Actual quantity at actual price	38,500
	700 (F)

4 (a) The total materials price variance is **£3,200 favourable**

(b) The non-controllable variance due to the seasonal variation is **£4,920 favourable**

The controllable variance due to other factors is **£1,720 adverse**

Workings

Total materials price variance

	£
12,300 kg should have cost × £8.00	98,400
But did cost	95,200
	3,200 (F)

Non-controllable variance due to seasonal variation

	£
Standard price for actual quantity used	
12,300 × £8.00	98,400
Adjusted price for actual quantity	
12,300 × (£8.00 – £0.40)	93,480
	4,920 (F)

Controllable variance due to other factors

	£
Adjusted price for actual quantity	
12,300 × (£8.00 – £0.40)	93,480
Actual quantity at actual price	95,200
	1,720 (A)

5 (a) The total labour efficiency variance was **£36,720 adverse**

(b) The non-controllable variance due to the learning process was **£32,640 adverse**

The controllable variance due to other factors was **£4,080 adverse**

Workings

Total labour efficiency variance

2,400 units should take (× 9 hrs)	21,600 hrs
But did take	27,000 hrs
Efficiency variance in hrs	5,400 hrs
	× £6.80
	£36,720 (A)

Non-controllable variance due to learning process

Standard hours for actual production at standard rate 2,400 × 9 × £6.80	146,880
Adjusted hours for actual production at standard rate 2,400 × 11 × £6.80	179,520
	32,640 (A)

Controllable variance due to other causes

Adjusted hours for actual production at standard cost 2,400 × 11 × £6.80	179,520
Actual hours at standard rate	183,600
	4,080 (A)

6 (a) The total materials price variance was **£20,000 adverse**

(b) The non-controllable variance due to price changes was **£40,000 adverse**

The controllable variance due to other factors was **£20,000 favourable**

Workings

Total materials price variance

	£
100,000kg should have cost (× £6.50)	650,000
But did cost	670,000
	20,000 (A)

Non-controllable variance due to price change

Standard price for actual quantity used 100,000 × £6.50	650,000
Adjusted price for actual quantity 100,000 × (£6.50 × 138/130)	690,000
	40,000 (A)

Controllable variance due to other causes

Adjusted price for actual quantity	
100,000 × (£6.50 × 138/130)	690,000
Actual quantity at actual price	670,000
	20,000 (F)

CHAPTER 7   Performance indicators

1

	Aug	Sept	Oct	Nov
Productivity per labour hour	10.5 units	10.2 units	9.8 units	10.1 units
Efficiency ratio	105.5%	102.2%	98.2%	101.0%
Capacity ratio	97.6%	96.5%	102.7%	98.5%
Activity ratio	102.9%	98.6%	100.9%	99.5%

Workings

		August	September	October	November
(a)	Productivity per labour hour	$\dfrac{257,300}{24,400}$	$\dfrac{251,400}{24,600}$	$\dfrac{262,300}{26,700}$	$\dfrac{258,600}{25,600}$
		= 10.5 units	= 10.2 units	= 9.8 units	= 10.1 units
(b)	Standard hours for actual	$\dfrac{257,300}{10}$	$\dfrac{251,400}{10}$	$\dfrac{262,300}{10}$	$\dfrac{258,600}{10}$
		= 25,730	= 25,140	= 26,230	= 25,860
	Efficiency ratio	$\dfrac{25,730}{24,400}\times100$	$\dfrac{25,140}{24,600}\times100$	$\dfrac{26,230}{26,700}\times100$	$\dfrac{25,860}{25,600}\times100$
		= 105.5%	= 102.2%	= 98.2%	= 101.0%
(c)	Budgeted hours	$\dfrac{250,000}{10}$	$\dfrac{255,000}{10}$	$\dfrac{260,000}{10}$	$\dfrac{260,000}{10}$
		= 25,000	= 25,500	= 26,000	= 26,000
	Capacity ratio	$\dfrac{24,400}{25,000}\times100$	$\dfrac{24,600}{25,500}\times100$	$\dfrac{26,700}{26,000}\times100$	$\dfrac{25,600}{26,000}\times100$
		= 97.6%	= 96.5%	= 102.7%	= 98.5%
(d)	Activity ratio	$\dfrac{25,730}{25,000}\times100$	$\dfrac{25,140}{25,500}\times100$	$\dfrac{26,230}{26,000}\times100$	$\dfrac{25,860}{26,000}\times100$
		= 102.9%	= 98.6%	= 100.9%	= 99.5%

2

	April	May	June	Total
Productivity per labour hour	10.9 units	10.7 units	11.1 units	10.9 units
Efficiency ratio	98.8%	97.6%	101.2%	99.2%
Capacity ratio	102.7%	101.2%	101.2%	101.7%
Activity ratio	101.4%	98.8%	102.4%	100.9%
Value added per employee	£2,552	£2,524	£2,717	£2,598

Workings

(a)

		April	May	June	Total

(i) Productivity per labour hour

$$\frac{121,700}{11,200} \quad \frac{123,500}{11,500} \quad \frac{128,000}{11,500} \quad \frac{373,200}{34,200}$$

$$= 10.9 \text{ units} \quad = 10.7 \text{ units} \quad = 11.1 \text{ units} \quad = 10.9 \text{ units}$$

(ii) Standard hours for actual production

$$\frac{121,700}{11} \quad \frac{123,500}{11} \quad \frac{128,000}{11} \quad \frac{373,200}{11}$$

$$= 11,064 \quad = 11,227 \quad = 11,636 \quad = 33,927$$

Efficiency ratio

$$\frac{11,064}{11,200}\times100 \quad \frac{11,227}{11,500}\times100 \quad \frac{11,636}{11,500}\times100 \quad \frac{33,927}{34,200}\times100$$

$$=98.8\% \quad =97.6\% \quad =101.2\% \quad =99.2\%$$

(iii) Budgeted hours

$$\frac{120,000}{11} \quad \frac{125,000}{11} \quad \frac{125,000}{11} \quad \frac{370,000}{11}$$

$$= 10,909 \quad = 11,364 \quad = 11,363 \quad = 33,636$$

Capacity ratio

$$\frac{11,200}{10,909}\times100 \quad \frac{11,500}{11,364}\times100 \quad \frac{11,500}{11,363}\times100 \quad \frac{34,200}{33,636}\times100$$

$$= 102.7\% \quad = 101.2\% \quad = 101.2\% \quad = 101.7\%$$

(iv) Activity ratio

$$\frac{11,064}{10,909}\times100 \quad \frac{11,227}{11,364}\times100 \quad \frac{11,636}{11,363}\times100 \quad \frac{33,927}{33,636}\times100$$

$$= 101.4\% \quad = 98.8\% \quad = 102.4\% \quad = 100.9\%$$

(v)   Value added

£625,000 – £418,300	£206,700			
£634,000 – £424,500		£209,500		
£656,000 – £430,500			£225,500	£641,700

Value added per employee	$\dfrac{206,700}{81}$	$\dfrac{209,500}{83}$	$\dfrac{225,500}{83}$	$\dfrac{641,700}{247}$
	= £2,552	= £2,524	= £2,717	= £2,598

The value added per employee for the total three months could also have been calculated as the value added over the three month period divided by the 82 employees, the average for the three months, giving £641,700/82 = £7,826.

(b)   £2,767.50

Hours at increased productivity level	=	$\dfrac{128,000 \text{ units}}{11.5}$
	=	11,131 hours
June hours		11,500
Saving in hours		369

Cost saving 369 @ £7.50 = £2,767.50

3   (a)

	July – Sept	Oct – Dec	Jan – Mar	Apr – June	
Productivity	1,240	820	1,540	1,180	
Cost per holiday	£18.26	£28.15	£16.30	£20.41	

Workings

		July – Sept	Oct – Dec	Jan – Mar	Apr – June
(i)	Productivity	$\dfrac{6,200}{5}$	$\dfrac{4,100}{5}$	$\dfrac{7,700}{5}$	$\dfrac{5,900}{5}$
		= 1,240	= 820	= 1,540	= 1,180
(ii)	Cost per holiday	$\dfrac{113,200}{6,200}$	$\dfrac{115,400}{4,100}$	$\dfrac{125,500}{7,700}$	$\dfrac{120,400}{5,900}$
		= £18.26	= £28.15	= £16.30	= £20.41

(b) The cost per holiday booking fluctuates from £16.30 to £28.15 depending upon the quarter in question. This is due to the fact that the large majority of the costs appear to be fixed costs with similar total costs each quarter. However, as the output (the holiday bookings) change, these fixed costs will remain the same and will simply be spread over more or fewer holiday bookings depending upon the quarter. For example in October to December the costs are similar to those of the other quarters but they are only being spread over 4,100 holiday bookings.

4

	Jan	Feb	Mar	April	May	June
Gross profit margin	47.5%	43.8%	42.2%	37.3%	39.3%	38.9%
Net profit margin	12.5%	13.8%	10.9%	10.6%	11.3%	10.7%
% expenses to revenue	35.0%	30.0%	31.3%	26.7%	28.0%	28.1%
Return on capital employed	20.8%	22.8%	15.4%	15.3%	15.5%	13.4%
Asset turnover	1.67	1.66	1.41	1.30	1.26	1.14

Workings

		Jan	Feb	Mar	Apr	May	June
(a)	Gross profit margin	$\frac{190}{400}$	$\frac{210}{480}$	$\frac{190}{450}$	$\frac{190}{510}$	$\frac{220}{560}$	$\frac{210}{540}$
		47.5%	43.8%	42.2%	37.3%	39.3%	38.9%
(b)	Operating profit margin	$\frac{50}{400}$	$\frac{66}{480}$	$\frac{49}{450}$	$\frac{54}{510}$	$\frac{63}{560}$	$\frac{58}{540}$
		12.5%	13.8%	10.9%	10.6%	11.3%	10.7%
(c)	Expenses to revenue	$\frac{140}{400}$	$\frac{144}{480}$	$\frac{141}{450}$	$\frac{136}{510}$	$\frac{157}{560}$	$\frac{152}{540}$
		35.0%	30.0%	31.3%	26.7%	28.0%	28.1%
(d)	Return on capital employed	$\frac{50}{240}$	$\frac{66}{290}$	$\frac{49}{319}$	$\frac{54}{393}$	$\frac{63}{446}$	$\frac{58}{474}$
		20.8%	22.8%	15.4%	13.7%	14.1%	12.2%
(e)	Asset turnover	$\frac{400}{240}$	$\frac{480}{290}$	$\frac{450}{319}$	$\frac{510}{393}$	$\frac{560}{446}$	$\frac{540}{474}$
		1.67	1.66	1.41	1.30	1.26	1.14

There has been a rapid rise in revenue of 35% over the six-month period which has been partly funded by additional loan capital in April. This increase in revenue however has not yet been matched by increases in profits.

The gross profit margin has reduced over the period and at its lowest was almost 10% below the margin for January. The operating profit margin has been steadily decreasing but not as dramatically as the gross profit margin due to the fact that expenses appear to be being well controlled. The decrease in the expenses to sales percentage indicates that many of the expenses are fixed and are therefore not rising in line with the increase in turnover.

Return on capital employed has also declined over the period partly due to the decrease in operating profit margin but also due to a significantly worsening asset turnover. This may be due to the fact that the new assets that have been funded by the loan have not yet become fully functional and we will see an improvement in asset turnover when the benefit of these new assets starts to be seen.

5

	20X6	20X7	20X8
Gross profit margin	46.3%	47.6%	44.4%
Operating profit margin	11.0%	11.8%	9.4%
Return on capital employed	18.0%	16.4%	12.7%
Asset turnover	1.64	1.39	1.34
Non-current asset turnover	2.13	1.88	1.81
Current ratio	4.8:1	5.6:1	5.2:1
Quick ratio	3.2: 1	4.0:1	3.6:1
Receivables' collection period	38 days	48 days	52 days
Inventory days	41 days	45 days	49 days
Payables' payment period	25 days	28 days	30 days
Interest cover	N/a	33.3	28.3
Gearing ratio	N/a	8.9%	8.1%

Workings

		20X6	20X7	20X8
(a)	Gross profit margin	$\frac{380}{820} \times 100$	$\frac{405}{850} \times 100$	$\frac{400}{900} \times 100$
		46.3%	47.6%	44.4%
(b)	Operating profit margin	$\frac{90}{820} \times 100$	$\frac{100}{850} \times 100$	$\frac{85}{900} \times 100$
		11.0%	11.8%	9.4%
(c)	Return on capital employed	$\frac{90}{500} \times 100$	$\frac{100}{610} \times 100$	$\frac{85}{670} \times 100$
		18.0%	16.4%	12.7%
(d)	Asset turnover	$\frac{820}{500}$	$\frac{850}{610}$	$\frac{900}{670}$
		1.64	1.39	1.34
(e)	Non-current asset turnover	$\frac{820}{385}$	$\frac{850}{453}$	$\frac{900}{498}$
		2.13	1.88	1.81
(f)	Current ratio	$\frac{145}{30}$	$\frac{191}{34}$	$\frac{213}{41}$
		4.8	5.6	5.2
(g)	Quick ratio	$\frac{95}{30}$	$\frac{136}{34}$	$\frac{146}{41}$
		3.2	4.0	3.6
(h)	Receivables' collection period	$\frac{85}{820} \times 365$	$\frac{112}{850} \times 365$	$\frac{128}{900} \times 365$
		38 days	48 days	52 days
(i)	Inventory days	$\frac{50}{440} \times 365$	$\frac{55}{445} \times 365$	$\frac{67}{500} \times 365$
		41 days	45 days	49 days
(j)	Payables' payment period	$\frac{30}{440} \times 365$	$\frac{34}{445} \times 365$	$\frac{41}{500} \times 365$
		25 days	28 days	30 days
(k)	Interest cover	n/a	100/3	85/3
			= 33.3	= 28.3
(l)	Gearing ratio	n/a	50/560 × 100	50/620 × 100
			=8.9%	=8.1%

PROFITABILITY

Between 20X6 and 20X7 there was an increase in both gross profit margin and operating profit margin. However in 20X8, when revenue grew by 6%, both gross profit margin and operating profit margin decreased. However, the fall in the operating profit margin was relatively a great deal larger than that of the gross profit margin, indicating that expenses are increasing.

Return on capital employed did not follow the increases in profitability in 20X7 but instead fell due to a significant decrease in the asset turnover in that year. Asset turnover and non-current asset turnover both stabilised a little in 20X8 but ROCE still decreased due to the falling profit levels.

WORKING CAPITAL

One of the main problems with the business appears to be control of its working capital. Both the current ratio and the quick ratio are excessively high showing that there are large amounts of capital being tied up in receivables, inventory and cash balances which could perhaps be used more profitably in other areas of the business.

The main problem areas appear to be receivables and payables. The receivables' collection period has increased from 38 to 52 days over the period whereas suppliers were being paid after just 25 days in 20X6 and still after only 30 days in 20X8. This means that cash is flowing out of the business much earlier than it is coming in.

Added to this the inventory holding period has also increased from 41 to 49 days over the three years meaning that even more cash is being tied up in these inventories.

6   (a)

	Flimwell	Hartfield	Groombridge
Gross profit margin	62.0%	56.8%	60.4%
Operating profit margin	12.0%	9.5%	13.5%
Return on net assets	11.8%	8.5%	12.7%
Net asset turnover	0.98	0.90	0.94
Inventory days	95 days	108 days	60 days
Payables' payment period	45 days	61 days	58 days
Sales per sq m	£225	£218	£240
Sales per employee	£19,286	£28,462	£18,462
Sales per hour worked	£17.70	£26.24	£16.96

Workings

		Flimwell	Hartfield	Groombridge
	Cost of sales	$51 + 210 - 56$ $= £205,000$	$45 + 165 - 50$ $= £160,000$	$30 + 192 - 32$ $= £190,000$
(i)	Gross profit margin	$\dfrac{335,000}{540,000} \times 100$	$\dfrac{210,000}{370,000} \times 100$	$\dfrac{290,000}{480,000} \times 100$
		62.0%	56.8%	60.4%
(ii)	Operating profit margin	$\dfrac{65,000}{540,000} \times 100$	$\dfrac{35,000}{370,000} \times 100$	$\dfrac{65,000}{480,000} \times 100$
		12.0%	9.5%	13.5%
(iii)	Return on net assets	$\dfrac{65,000}{550,000} \times 100$	$\dfrac{35,000}{410,000} \times 100$	$\dfrac{65,000}{510,000} \times 100$
		11.8%	8.5%	12.7%
(iv)	Net asset turnover	$\dfrac{540,000}{550,000}$	$\dfrac{370,000}{410,000}$	$\dfrac{480,000}{510,000}$
		0.98	0.90	0.94
(v)	Average inventory	$\dfrac{51 + 56}{2}$	$\dfrac{45 + 50}{2}$	$\dfrac{30 + 32}{2}$
		£53,500	£47,500	£31,000
	Inventory days	$\dfrac{53,500}{205,000} \times 365$	$\dfrac{47,500}{160,000} \times 365$	$\dfrac{31,000}{190,000} \times 365$
		95 days	108 days	60 days
(vi)	Payables' payment period	$\dfrac{25,800}{210,000} \times 365$	$\dfrac{27,500}{165,000} \times 365$	$\dfrac{30,500}{192,000} \times 365$
		45 days	61 days	58 days
(vii)	Sales per sq m	$\dfrac{540,000}{2,400}$	$\dfrac{370,000}{1,700}$	$\dfrac{480,000}{2,000}$
		£225	£218	£240
(viii)	Sales per employee	$\dfrac{540,000}{28}$	$\dfrac{370,000}{13}$	$\dfrac{480,000}{26}$
		£19,286	£28,462	£18,462
(ix)	Sales per hour worked	$\dfrac{540,000}{30,500}$	$\dfrac{370,000}{14,100}$	$\dfrac{480,000}{28,300}$
		£17.70	£26.24	£16.96

(b)   REPORT

To: Sales Director

From: Accounts assistant

Date: xx.xx.xx

Subject: Performance of stores

I have considered the performance figures for our three stores in Flimwell, Hartfield and Groombridge for the first six months of the year and have calculated a number of performance indicators (see part a). The key factors that have appeared from these figures are addressed below.

Flimwell has the highest gross profit margin but the highest operating profit margin and return on net assets are generated by Groombridge. Clearly therefore Groombridge has better control of its expenses than the other two stores and if the Groombridge practices can be emulated in the other two stores this could improve their profitability.

The Hartfield store has problems with profitability, having significantly lower gross profit margin, operating profit margin, return on net assets and net asset turnover figures than the other two stores. Possibly one of the reasons for the lack of profitability is in the high inventory levels at Hartfield. The inventory holding period in days is almost twice as high as that for Groombridge with inventories being held for about three and half months.

Hartfield, however, does have the highest productivity levels in terms of sales per employee and sales per hour worked as these are all very much higher than the other two stores. This might imply that the Hartfield store is understaffed which may also be part of the problem with profitability. As the gross profit margin of Hartfield is much lower than the other two stores it may be that Hartfield has to charge lower prices for the goods due to the understaffing in order to attract customers.

Groombridge appears to have the best control over its working capital with inventory only held for two months and suppliers paid after a similar period. If the inventory control and payables' control of Groombridge can be introduced into the other two stores this will help in their performance. Groombridge also has the highest sales per square metre therefore their store layout may be of interest to the other two stores.

If Flimwell's payables' payment period of 45 days was lengthened to that of Hartfield of 61 days the cash balance of Flimwell would increase by £9,205 (£210,000/365 × 16).

7

(a)   Gross profit margin $= \dfrac{\text{Gross profit}}{\text{Revenue}}$

       44% $= \dfrac{\text{Gross profit}}{£106,500}$

       44% × £106,500 $=$ Gross profit

       Gross profit $=$ £46,860

(b)   Gross profit margin $= \dfrac{\text{Gross profit}}{\text{Revenue}}$

       37.5% $= \dfrac{£105,000}{\text{Revenue}}$

       Revenue $= \dfrac{£105,000}{0.375}$

       Revenue $=$ £280,000

(c)   Gross profit $=$ £256,000 × 41%

                        $=$ £104,960

       Operating profit $=$ £256,000 × 13.5%

                        $=$ £34,560

       Expenses $=$ £104,960 – 34,560

                        $=$ £70,400

(d)   ROCE $= \dfrac{\text{Operating profit}}{\text{Capital employed}}$

       12.8% $= \dfrac{£50,000}{\text{Capital employed}}$

       Capital employed $= \dfrac{£50,000}{0.128}$

                        $=$ £390,625

(e)   ROCE $=$ Operating profit margin × Asset turnover

       15% $=$ 10% × Asset turnover

       $\dfrac{15\%}{10\%}$ $=$ Asset turnover

       Asset turnover $=$ 1.5

(f)   Average inventory $= \dfrac{118,000 + 104,000}{2}$

                        $=$ £111,000

       Inventory turnover $= \dfrac{\text{Cost of sales}}{\text{Average inventory}}$

                        $= \dfrac{£118,000 + 465,000 - 104,000}{£111,000}$

                        $=$ 4.3 times

(g) Receivables' collection period $= \dfrac{\text{Receivables}}{\text{Revenue}} \times 365$

64 days $= \dfrac{64{,}000}{\text{Revenue}} \times 365$

Revenue $= \dfrac{64{,}000}{64 \text{ days}} \times 365$

$= £365{,}000$

8

		Balanced scorecard perspective
Operating profit margin	19.9%	Financial or internal
Return on capital employed	24.7%	Financial
Inventory days	91 days	Customer
Asset turnover	1.24	Internal
Research costs as % of production costs	31.25%	Innovation and learning
Training costs as a % of labour cost	22.5%	Internal

Workings

Operating profit margin $= \dfrac{\text{Operating profit}}{\text{Revenue}} \times 100$

$= \dfrac{68+6}{372}$

$= 19.9\%$

– Financial perspective or possibly internal perspective as this is a measure of the control over the resources of the business

Note that operating profit is profit before interest therefore the interest deducted in the statement or profit or loss (income statement) must be added back – however if the profit after interest had been used this would be the net profit margin.

$$\text{Return on capital employed} = \frac{\text{Operating profit}}{\text{Capital employed}} \times 100$$

$$= \frac{68+6}{200+100} \times 100$$

$$= 24.7\%$$

- Financial perspective

$$\text{Inventory days} = \frac{\text{Average inventory}}{\text{Cost of sales}} \times 365$$

$$\text{Average inventory} = \frac{19+21}{2}$$

$$= 20$$

$$\text{Inventory days} = \frac{20}{80} \times 365$$

$$= 91 \text{ days}$$

- Customer perspective – the more inventory that is held the less likely it is that customer demand cannot be satisfied

$$\text{Asset turnover} = \frac{\text{Revenue}}{\text{Capital employed}}$$

$$= \frac{372}{300}$$

$$= 1.24$$

- Internal – intensity of asset use

$$\text{Research costs/production} = \frac{\text{Research costs}}{\text{Production costs}} \times 100$$

$$= \frac{25}{80} \times 100$$

$$= 31.25\%$$

- Innovation and learning perspective

Note. In this calculation we have used cost of sales of £80,000 as production costs however it would also have been acceptable to use production cost of £82,000 (28 + 40 + 14)

$$\text{Training costs/labour cost} = \frac{\text{Training costs}}{\text{Labour costs}} \times 100$$

$$= \frac{9}{40} \times 100$$

$$= 22.5\%$$

- Internal perspective

CHAPTER 8   Cost management

1

		Type of cost of quality
(a)	Products scrapped due to faulty raw materials	Internal failure
(b)	Training for quality control staff	Prevention
(c)	Costs of customer after sales service department	External failure
(d)	Lost contribution on defective products sold as seconds	Internal failure
(e)	Costs of inspection of raw materials	Appraisal
(f)	Maintenance of quality control equipment	Prevention
(g)	Cost of replacing faulty products returned by customers	External failure
(h)	Costs of production delays due to re-working defective products discovered in quality inspection	Internal failure
(i)	Claims from customers relating to defective products	External failure
(j)	Performance testing of finished goods	Appraisal

2

Cost of quality	Amount £	Category of cost
Repair of returned goods	£20,000	External failure
Advertising costs	£40,000	External failure
Lost customers	Unknown	External failure

Working

Repair of returned goods

$5,000,000/3,000 \times 60\% \times £20 = £20,000$

3

Cost of quality	Amount £	Category of cost	Explicit or implicit
Quality inspection	£60,000	Appraisal	Explicit
Lost contribution from defective units	£70,000	Internal failure	Implicit
Replacement of units	£37,500	External failure	Explicit
Lost customers	Unknown	External failure	Explicit

Workings

Lost contribution
 2,000 × (£80 – £45)   £70,000
Replacement of defective units
 1,000,000/1,000 × 75% × £50   £37,500

4

Cost per after sales service customer	£4.67
Sales returns as a % of sales	8%
Repair cost per returned units	£10.00
Complaints as a % of unit sales	6%

Workings

Cost per after sales service customer $= \dfrac{£280,000}{60,000} = £4.67$

Sales returns as a % of sales value $= \dfrac{£120,000}{£1,500,000} = 8\%$

Repair cost per returned unit $= \dfrac{£40,000}{4,000} = £10.00$

Complaints as a % of unit sales $= \dfrac{3,000}{50,000} = 6\%$

5   Total Quality Management (TQM) is a quality management system in an organisation that involves all areas of the organisation not just the production element. The philosophy behind quality management must be applied in all the activities of the business – design, production, marketing, administration, purchasing, sales and even the finance function.

TQM can be defined as a continuous improvement in quality, productivity and effectiveness.

Continuous improvement is the basic principle behind TQM. This can be described as the concept of "getting it right first time" and "getting it even more right next time". By getting it right first time the costs of internal failure and external failure will be reduced to the point where they should not occur at all. Costs of prevention are less than the costs of correction.

TQM seeks to ensure that the goods produced or the services supplied are of the highest quality.

In order for TQM to work in all areas of an organisation, training and motivation of staff is vital in order for each individual to have the attitude of constantly seeking improvement in what they do. All staff within the organisation must be taught that they have customers. These may be external customers of the business or internal customers in the form of colleagues in the business that use an individual's work. Each individual should endeavour to ensure that they get it right first time and therefore that their excellent work is passed on in the chain.

Another important concept behind TQM is that every employee is involved and anyone with an idea should be allowed to put this forward. This is often done by groups of employees being formed within the organisation known as quality circles.

These quality circles normally consist of about ten employees with a range of skills, roles and seniority who meet regularly to discuss problems of quality and quality control and to perhaps suggest ways of improving processes and quality. This means that there is input from all levels within the organisation and from different disciplines such as marketing, design, engineering, information technology and office administration as well as production.

6   **Development and launch stages**

During this period of the product's life there are large outgoings in terms of development expenditure, non-current assets necessary for production, the building up of inventory levels and advertising and promotion expenses. It is likely that even after the launch sales will be quite low and the product will be making a loss at this stage.

Growth stage

If the launch of the product is successful then during the growth stage there will be a fairly rapid increase in sales and a move to profitability as the costs of the earlier stages are recovered. This sales increase, however, is not likely to continue indefinitely.

Maturity stage

In the maturity stage of the product demand for the product will probably start to slow down and become more constant. In many cases this is the stage where the product is modified or improved in order to sustain demand and this may then see a small surge in sales.

Decline stage

At some point in a product's life, unless it is a consumable items such as chocolate bars, the product will reach the end of its sale life. The market will have bought enough of the product and sales will decline. This is the point where the business should consider no longer producing the product.

INDEX

Notes

Notes

REVIEW FORM

How have you used this Text?
(Tick one box only)

☐ Home study

☐ On a course_____

☐ Other _____

Why did you decide to purchase this Text? *(Tick one box only)*

☐ Have used BPP Texts in the past

☐ Recommendation by friend/colleague

☐ Recommendation by a college lecturer

☐ Saw advertising

☐ Other _____

During the past six months do you recall seeing/receiving either of the following?
(Tick as many boxes as are relevant)

☐ Our advertisement in Accounting Technician

☐ Our Publishing Catalogue

Which (if any) aspects of our advertising do you think are useful?
(Tick as many boxes as are relevant)

☐ Prices and publication dates of new editions

☐ Information on Text content

☐ Details of our free online offering

☐ None of the above

Your ratings, comments and suggestions would be appreciated on the following areas of this Text.

	Very useful	Useful	Not useful
Introductory section	☐	☐	☐
Quality of explanations	☐	☐	☐
How it works	☐	☐	☐
Chapter tasks	☐	☐	☐
Chapter overviews	☐	☐	☐
Test your learning	☐	☐	☐
Index	☐	☐	☐

	Excellent	Good	Adequate	Poor
Overall opinion of this Text	☐	☐	☐	☐

Do you intend to continue using BPP Products? ☐ Yes ☐ No

Please note any further comments and suggestions/errors on the reverse of this page. The author of this edition can be emailed at: ianblackmore@bpp.com

Please return to: Ian Blackmore, AAT Range Manager, BPP Learning Media Ltd, FREEPOST, London, W12 8AA.

REVIEW FORM (continued)

TELL US WHAT YOU THINK

Please note any further comments and suggestions/errors below